CONTEMPORARY
JUNGIAN
CLINICAL PRACTICE

CONTEMPORARY JUNGIAN CLINICAL PRACTICE

Edited by
Elphis Christopher
and
Hester McFarland Solomon

KARNAC
LONDON   NEW YORK

First published in 2003 by
H. Karnac (Books) Ltd.
6 Pembroke Buildings, London NW10 6RE

British Library Cataloguing in Publication Data

A C.I.P. for this book is available from the British Library

   ISBN 1 85575 975 6

Edited, designed, and produced by The Studio Publishing Services Ltd,
Exeter EX4 8JN

Printed in Great Britain

10 9 8 7 6 5 4 3 2

www.karnacbooks.com

CONTENTS

ACKNOWLEDGEMENTS

We wish to thank those patients whose permission was sought and graciously and generously given to include their personal material in their therapists' and analysts' reveries, thoughts and speculations about their mutual engagements. Without the patients' permission, this book would not have happened and the contribution to the reporting clinical work in the public and professional domain would have been absent.

We would also like to thank our authors. We are aware of what they faced and the careful judgements that they made in deciding to seek their patients' permission to publish material that was exchanged in the privacy of the consulting room. We also thank those authors who had a chapter in mind and were unable for various clinical and ethical reasons to bring their thoughts to the light of day in published form. We thank them too, both for the thoughtfulness of their approach to their clinical work and for the sacrifice made on behalf of the clinical work already done, in deciding not to carry on with the aim to publish.

We are pleased that our colleague Stanley Ruszczynski, a member of the Psychoanalytic Section of the BAP, and author and editor of volumes on psychoanalytic topics, agreed to contribute a foreword to this volume.

We are very appreciative of Karnac's openness to include Jungian titles in their list.

Finally we wish to express our appreciation of the secretarial support of Elizabeth Chan, who was most helpful and forbearing with our endeavours.

Elphis Christopher
Hester McFarland Solomon

PERMISSIONS

Chapter 10. Geraldine Godsil and the editors would like to thank Taylor & Francis Books Ltd for permission to reproduce two Woodcuts, Figure 6 page 259, Figure 7 page 267 from C. G. Jung's *Collected Works Volume 16, The Practise of Psychotherapy: Psychology of the Transference*, Second Edition, Routledge and Kegan Paul, 1966.

EDITORS' NOTE

Throughout this volume, references to Jung's *Collected Works* appear in the abbreviated form *C.W.* followed by the relevant volume number. For full bibliographical details see "Cited works of Jung" at the end of the book.

FOREWORD

This book is a timely and important contribution to the field of clinical analytic practice. At a time when, in many quarters, there are serious concerns about the ethics of publishing clinical material from patients, the editors of this book have been true to their professional training and ethos and have challenged the doubts and criticisms levelled at this long standing and professionally essential practice and produced a text made up mostly of detailed clinical work. They have done so having sought the consent of the patients whose material, disguised and made anonymous, is discussed. Great care has been exercised to take full professional and clinical account of the many issues that this raises and these are fully discussed in the editors' Introduction.

The final Section of the book offers further reflection on these and other professional issues crucial to good analytic practice. As well as matters related to ethics and to the process of seeking permission to publish clinical material, other issues also addressed include analytic dependency, supervision, racism, and questions that emerge at the end of a professional life when the clinician begins to contemplate retirement. These considerations form a reflective professional boundary within which the clinician is held and sustained. Training, continuing professional development and accountability as provided by ongoing supervision and publication, and adherence to ethical and professional codes are all ultimately in the service of enabling the clinician to undertake the task of analytic work with patients. And it is this detailed analytic work which lies at the heart of this book.

Developments in theoretical and clinical thinking and understanding and, as a result, developments in clinical training and further professional development, all contribute essentially to the broadening and efficacy of analytic psychotherapy for the benefit of the patient. These developments depend, to a large degree, on the professional presentation, sharing, and discussion of detailed clinical material from the consulting room, always made anonymous and treated with respect. This material is primarily "the clinicians story", told with integrity and honesty, of the experience they have had with the patient. The intensive training undertaken by all the authors of these papers makes them receptive to the patient and to their own affective reactions to the patient. This is the data from which analytic thinking takes place, which contributes to the patient's increasing understanding of him or herself and the ways in which they live in their relationships and in their world.

Analytic practice has been described as "the talking cure". Perhaps more accurately, though somewhat cautious in using the word "cure", we might say that it is a "talking treatment" and a "listening cure". In his "Recommendations to physicians practising psycho-analysis", Freud writes as part of his very first recommendation on analytic technique, that, "(The analyst) should simply listen...". This is said in the context of Freud describing the "fundamental rule of psychoanalysis", whereby the patient should "communicate everything that occurs to him without criticism or selection" whilst the analyst, in an equivalent way, listens, "giving equal notice to everything he experiences and in so doing maintaining an 'evenly-suspended attention' in the face of all that he hears" (Freud, 1912, pp. 111–112).

Jung significantly developed this clinical approach by recognizing and emphasizing the powerful impact such listening will inevitably have on the clinician and how this is central to analytic understanding. He writes, "In any effective psychological treatment the doctor is bound to influence the patient; but this influence can only take place if the patient has a reciprocal influence on the doctor." Jung then addresses the analytic clinician directly with his famous statement, "*You can exert no influence if you are not susceptible to influence*" (Jung, C.W., 16, para. 163; my italics). He continues:

> It is futile for the doctor to shield himself from the influence of the patient and to surround himself with a smoke screen of fatherly and professional authority. By doing so he only denies himself the use of a highly important organ of information. The patient influences him unconsciously none the less ... One of the best known symptoms of this kind is the countertransference... [*ibid.*]

Freud's recommendation to "simply listen", therefore, refers to the clinician listening not only to the patient but, as emphasized by Jung, to his or her own affective reaction to the patient. Such listening—what a simple word for such a complex and intense experience—now informs the fundamental analytic stance of most schools of depth psychology. At its heart, obvious but often insufficiently stressed, is the phrase, "...simply listen..." Listening to the patient in this way is the primary clinical task.

The authors of the chapters in this book have demonstrated with clarity how much, in their clinical work with patients, they have taken on this analytically far from simple task. Each chapter, eloquently and sometimes movingly, presents the patients' material, unencumbered by excessive theorizing or technical language. What we read are reports of patients' experiences as expressed in words, behaviour, and in the emotional atmospheres they created in the consulting room. The patient's voice is thus presented as primary, but, of course, the patient requires, at least in the more healthy and more mature part of their mind, that the clinician make use of his or her training, experience and theoretical and clinical knowledge to try to make sense of what they have been asked to hear and bear. The clinicians appropriate turning to theory is shown to be neither premature nor defensive, but in the service of making the links and connections between the fragmented strands of "the patient's story".

This task of listening is very far from simple because conscious and unconscious forces in both the patient and the clinician militate against this central aspect of the fundamental rule. The resistance against both the patient speaking his or her mind and the analyst listening—initially understood in the patient and called transference and then understood in the analyst and called countertransference—became one of the most important ways in which access was gained to an understanding of the patient's internal world.

Because of this unavoidable and, in fact, necessary resistance—necessary because it shields the patient from the unbearable or sabotaging or destructive aspects of their internal world and its objects—the ethical and supervisory framework in which clinical practice should take place is absolutely fundamental to analytic work. This book takes this very seriously and chapters are presented on the practice and ethics of supervision. It is suggested, in fact, that the analytic attitude, in essence, *is* an ethical attitude, and that both are necessary to meet the more primitive and dangerous states of mind that emerge and inevitably affect both participants in the analytic process, and which it is the task of clinical work to explore.

The history of psychoanalysis is littered with schisms, sometimes managed in a benign way but often leading to unbridgeable breaches. This is true of depth psychology around the world including the UK. One of the noteworthy aspects of this book is not only that the authors are free of theoretical dogma and rhetoric so as to be able to listen to and present their patients' material in an unadulterated way , but when they do, quite appropriately, turn to theoretical understanding to help them think about that which they have experienced with their patients, they demonstrate a capacity not to be restricted by an overdue and rigid adherence to a particular theoretical framework.

Clearly, the writers have all been trained in the Jungian tradition and demonstrate how they draw substantially on this way of thinking. What is very noticeable, however, is how much they are willing, in their struggle to understand their patients, to make use of other psychoanalytic frameworks.

Many of the authors refer overtly and clearly to this integrated approach. It is noted that Freudian, Kleinian, and Jungian thinking come from different perspectives and hence have different emphases. No one suggests that there are not differences and that in fact some of these differences may well be unbridgeable. Many authors, however, are interested in examining the common ground explored by different theoretical traditions and do so in the service of trying to think about their patients.

This exploring and making clinical use of the common ground of theory is done carefully and in relation to specific concepts, each treated with integrity. This integration of theoretical traditions is demonstrably different from a broad eclectic approach that in effect denudes and misrepresents the elements of the frameworks used. Real integration of theoretical concepts often results in a genuine marriage between ideas that then inform and help to develop analytic thinking towards further theoretical and clinical understanding.

It is worth noting that this capacity to bridge creatively between Jungian depth psychology and psychoanalysis is now not uncommon in Jungian literature, as exemplified by many of the chapters this book, but, by comparison, it is very rare in the writings of the various psychoanalytic schools, be that Contemporary Freudian, Kleinian, or Independent.

It is undoubtedly true that much of Jung's early contribution to what has now emerged in contemporary psychoanalytic thinking has been ignored, forgotten or denied. For example, it is fascinating for this psychoanalytical writer to note that from 1912 Jung used the term "participation mystique", borrowed from Levy-Bruhl, to describe an identification through projection of two people who momentarily, usually unconsciously, become indistinguishable in their subjective experience (Hester McFarland Solomon, 2002, personal communication). Jung defines "participation mystique" as:

> a peculiar kind of psychological connection with objects ...
> [consisting] in the fact that the subject cannot clearly distinguish
> himself from the object but is bound to it by a direct relationship
> which amounts to partial identity ... It is a transference relation-
> ship, in which the object ... obtains a sort of magical ... influence
> over the subject [(Jung, C.W., 6, para. 781, p. 1920]

Jung says that this describes a primitive defence that operates as a means of both control over the object and also as a means of communication.

It seems to me that this is remarkably similar to Klein's notion of projective identification (Klein, 1946, 1955), which she initially defined in a similar way, as a primitive form of defence based on projective and identificatory processes, and which Bion and Rosenfeld, amongst others, then developed to emphasize its communicative potential (Bion, 1959; Rosenfeld, 1971).

Such making of links and connections between different elements in the service of integration is crucial to both analytic theorizing and clinical practice. One chapter title in this book refers to the "difficulties inherent in having your own mind". It seems to me that this is indeed the crucial analytic task—to help the patient in this difficult process of exploring, integrating and developing a mind of their own. But, in fact, this is also the task of the training, continuing professional development, supervision and the ethical attitude of the clinician—for the clinician to develop their own analytic mind. This book is a demonstration of a very serious effort by a group of clinicians to do exactly that; it is also a text which others can use in their own efforts to do likewise.

References

Bion, W. R. (1959). Attacks on linking. In: *Second Thoughts* (Chapter 8). London: Heinemann [reprinted: London: Karnac Books, 1984].

Freud, S. (1912). Recommendations to physicians practising psycho-analysis. In: *S.E., XII*: 109–120. London: Hogarth Press.

Klein, M .(1946). Notes on some schizoid mechanisms. In: *Envy and Gratitude: The Writings of Melanie Klein, Volume III* (pp. 1–24). London: Hogarth Press, 1975.

Klein, M. (1955). On identification. In: *Envy and Gratitude: The Writings of Melanie Klein, Volume III* (pp. 141–175). London: Hogarth Press, 1975.

Rosenfeld, H. (1971). A clinical approach to the psycho-analytic theory of life and death instincts: an investigation into the aggressive aspects of narcissism. *International Journal of Psycho-Analysis, 52*: 169–178.

Stanley Ruszczynski

CONTRIBUTORS

Jennifer Benwell initially trained in fine art and has been an exhibiting artist for the past twenty years. She has worked for the Samaritans and graduated from the Westminster Pastoral Foundation. She is an Associate Member of the Jungian Analytic Section of the British Association of Psychotherapists (BAP). She has worked in a number of NHS Genitourinary Medicine Clinics as an external clinical supervisor since 1995 and is in private psychotherapy practice.

Dr Elphis Christopher is medically qualified and has worked in the field of family planning and sexual medicine for thirty five years. She is the author of a number of papers and a book, *Sexuality and Birth Control in Community Work* (1987). She has been a contributor to several books and co-edited (with Hester McFarland Solomon) *Jungian Thought in the Modern World*. She is the consultant for Family Planning and Reproductive Care, Haringey National Health Service Primary Healthcare Trust, a member of the Institute of Psychosexual Medicine, and Fellow of the British Association for Counselling and Psychotherapy. She is a Full Member of the Jungian Analytic Section of the British Association of Psychotherapy and a past member of the BAP's Jungian Analytic Training Committee. She is currently in private practice.

Eleanor Cowen qualified as a chartered clinical psychologist. She is an Associate Member of the Jungian Analytic Section of the British Association of Psychotherapists. She is currently a Member of the BAP's Jungian Analytic Training Committee. She works in private practice and in the National Health Service.

Arna Davis originally trained in nursing, specialising in psychiatric nursing in Finland. After moving to Britain, she qualified as a social worker becoming a deputy team leader in the Social Service Area Team. She is a Full Member of the Jungian Analytic Section of the BAP and has served as a BAP Council Member. She was a Clinical Service assessor for BAP for twelve years. She is on the Editorial Board of the BAP Journal and has published a number of analytic papers. She is interested in the visual arts and obtained a BA (Hon) in Fine Arts as a mature student.

Marissa Dillon Weston has a degree from Milan University and a Masters Degree from London University. She trained at the Institute of Group Analysis, qualifying as a group analyst in 1989. She is an Associate Member of the BAP's Jungian Analytic Section. She works in private practice with individuals and groups. She also works within the National Health Service where she runs staff groups.

Nathan Field is a former Full Member of the Jungian Analytic Section of the British Association of Psychotherapists, and former Chair of the London Centre for Psychotherapy. He maintains a private practice, which includes supervising, teaching and lecturing. He is the author of *Breakdown and Breakthrough: Psychotherapy in a New Dimension* (Routledge).

Susan Fisher initially trained as a social worker and worked for six years as a social worker in St Charles' Hospital. She is a Full Member of the Jungian Analytic Section of the British Association of Psychotherapists and past training therapist and supervisor with the BAP. She has been a past member of the BAP Council and Chaired the Jungian Analytic Training Committee for four years.

She is a former member of the BAP Jungian Analytic Postgraduate Committee, and has published several papers on analytic topics.

Geraldine Godsil read English at Cambridge and was previously Clinical Director of Counselling in Companies in Kensington, London. She is a Full Member of the British Association of Psychotherapists' Jungian Analytic Section, where she taught infant observation, clinical seminars and theoretical seminars for the analytic training and for the BAP's MSc in Human Development. She now lives in Yorkshire and works as an adult psychotherapist in the NHS in Wakefield. She has a private practice, and teaches and supervises on MA Courses in Leeds and Sheffield.

Margaret Hammond graduated in History from London University, and has a postgraduate diploma in Applied Social Studies. After a short period as a social worker in Africa, she returned to England and trained as a Marriage Guidance Counsellor (now Relate). She worked as a counsellor and later, a supervisor in Relate for many years, with a special interest in Group Work and Counsellor Training. She is a Full Member of the British Association of Psychotherapists' Jungian Analytic Section, and works in private practice and supervises individuals and groups.

Birgit Heuer is an Associate Member of the British Association of Psychotherapists' Jungian Analytic Section, having completed her previous training in body orientated psychotherapy. She has worked in full time private practice for over twenty years. She was also clinical supervisor at Kingston University Health Centre for a number of years. She has served on the BAP's Jungian Analytic Training Committee, and has written and lectured on the subject of the body and analysis.

Marilyn A. F. Mathew initially trained in the visual arts. She is a Full Member of the British Association of Psychotherapists' Jungian Analytic Section. She is a Member of the Jungian Course Team for the BAP's MSc in the Psychodynamics of Human Development, running Infant Observation Seminars. She is the Vice Chair of the BAP's Jungian Analytic Training Committee. She has a private practice and has published several analytic papers.

Helen Morgan studied physics and education at University before turning to mental health work. She worked in therapeutic communities with adolescents (the Cotswold Community) and adults (the Richmond Fellowship) for a number of years, finally becoming a trainer and then, Regional Director for the Richmond Fellowship. She is a Full Member, training therapist and supervisor for the BAP Jungian Analytic Section. She is in private practice and has published several analytic papers and contributed several chapters to books including *Jungian Thought in the Modern World*. A former Member of the Postgraduate Training Committee of the Jungian Analytic Section of the BAP, she is currently Chair of the BAP's Jungian Analytic Section.

Jean Pearson has a first degree in sociology and psychology and a postgraduate diploma in applied social studies. She worked as a social worker in the field of psychiatry for a number of years. She is a Full Member of the BAP Jungian Analytic Section. She was instrumental in setting up the first free psychotherapy clinic outside the NHS, working for many years as its first Director. She is in private practice and has published analytic papers and contributed a chapter to *Jungian Thought in the Modern World*.

Elizabeth Richardson is a Full Member, training therapist, supervisor and Chair of the Postgraduate Committee of the British Association of Psychotherapists' Jungian Analytic Section. She has a MA in analytic psychotherapy. Originally from a medical background, she has a particular interest in working with aspects of birth, separation and death, and is in full time private practice.

Joan Reggiori qualified first as a social worker working in the mental health field both in the community and in the Psychiatric Department of a London Teaching Hospital. She is a Full Member, training therapist and supervisor of the British Association of Psychotherapists' Jungian Analytic Section. She was past Chair of the Jungian Analytic Training Committee. She supervises analytic trainees in the Psychiatric Department at St. Bartholomew's Hospital. She is a Fellow of the Royal Society of Medicine. She has a private practice and has published many analytic papers.

Stanley Ruszczynski is a Full Member of the British Association of Psychotherapists Psychoanalytic Section. He has a private practice, and is a Principal Adult Psychotherapist at the Portman Clinic (Tavistock and Portman NHS Trust), London. He is a founder Member of the Society of Psychoanalytic Marital Psychotherapists and for a number of years was a Senior Member of staff in the Tavistock Marital Studies Institute, London, serving as Deputy Director, and both Clinical and Training Co-ordinator. He has edited and co-edited several analytic books and is the author of a number of book chapters and journal papers. He is currently Joint Editor of the Journal of the BAP.

Hester McFarland Solomon took her first degrees in literature and philosophy before turning to psychology and social psychology. She trained with the Jungian Analytic Section of the BAP, where she is now a training therapist, teacher and supervisor, and a Fellow of the Association. She is past Chair of BAP's Council, Ethics Committee, and Jungian Analytic Training Committee. She is in full time private practice, and has published a number of papers linking Jungian analytic and psychoanalytic theory and practice. She co-edited (with Elphis Christopher) *Jungian Thought in the Modern World* to which she contributed two chapters. She lectures and pursues a variety of professional activities in Britain and abroad. She is Vice President of the International Association for Analytical Psychology (IAAP).

PART I
CONTEMPORARY JUNGIAN
CLINICAL PRACTICE

Introduction

Elphis Christopher and Hester McFarland Solomon

Having co-edited a largely theoretical book on contemporary issues as addressed by practitioners steeped in Jungian thinking, *Jungian Thought in the Modern World* (Christopher & McFarland Solomon, 2000), it seemed appropriate to produce a book in which Jungian analysts and psychotherapists trained by the Jungian Section of the British Association of Psychotherapists (BAP) presented their clinical work. This would serve several purposes, not only to give moment to moment clinical accounts of work with individual patients in the consulting room, but also to illustrate the standard and depth expected of practitioners at different levels of clinical development from trainee to qualified and established members.

In the current climate of expectation of clinical accountability and of transparency for the claims of clinical competence and ongoing continuous professional development, we hoped that such a book would make a significant contribution in providing evidence of how professional Jungian members of the BAP are seeking to meet these concerns.

As this is a clinically based volume, it is appropriate to address related issues such as confidentiality, obtaining permission from the patient to publish their clinical material, disguising the patient's identity without distorting the value of the clinical account, and the various ethical issues attached to these questions. Given this clinical emphasis, the authors were expected to deal with the question of consent to publish with their patients and in some cases supervisor, analyst or other colleagues, in the most appropriate way, such that they would avoid any imposition or abuse of the therapeutic relationship, including embarrassment, giving offence, or other negative consequences that would be detrimental to the ongoing treatment, the therapeutic relationship or the eventual outcome. In addition to seeking consent, the contributors had to consider such issues as how to ensure anonymity, patient disguise, the possibility of creating composite patients by weaving together relevant material from more than one patient, or using oneself as a patient. In the event, the contributors gave clinical accounts of individual patients, not of composites.

There were a number of potential contributors who were obliged, at various stages in writing their clinical accounts, to withdraw their proposed chapter. This was due to concerns about confidentiality, as well as about the adverse effects of seeking consent to publish, either because the therapy was ongoing and perhaps at a critical point, such that it might have been jeopardized by the therapist's request, or because even though the treatment was finished, the therapist judged that such a request would have adverse effects on the former patient. Consent might have been obtained (as happened to one of us, Elphis Christopher), but a decision was taken not to publish because, on later reflection, the author considered that it would have a possible detrimental effect on the patient.

These considerations and concerns inevitably influence the kind of patients and the clinical problems that are written about and published. The effects of these such unavoidable restrictions on analytic theory building and the accumulation of clinical expertise through publication cannot be discounted. Moreover, by virtue of the very nature of clinical, depth psychological work, the question remains open whether it is ever possible to obtain truly informed consent, given the power imbalance inherent in the analytic and therapeutic relationship, the ongoing and ever-changing nature of the patient's transference and its impact on the analyst's countertransference, and the possible and unforeseen consequences on the patient of publishing their clinical material. Nevertheless, as several of our authors have observed, seeking the patient's permission to publish clinical material often provided a unique opportunity of reviewing the analytic work and of doing further valuable clinical work. At a more personal level, this experience enriched the therapists' self understanding through the struggle with the various dimensions touched on by seeking permission from the patient.

As co-editors, we experienced a certain heaviness and tension in producing this volume in comparison to the more theoretical book *Jungian Thought in the Modern World*. The feelings seemed to reflect the tension of the opposites inherent in maintaining the central underlying ethical principle of doing no harm (*nil nocere*) while at the same time responding to the professional need to contribute to clinical knowledge and experience by encouraging practitioners to write about their clinical work. It is, perhaps, inevitable that this should be so, given the conflictual interests between the desire of the therapist to publish and the possible ambivalence of the patient towards such a venture. Rather as in supervision, when the experience of focusing on the patient becomes an experience of a *"massa confusa"* (Jung, C.W., *16*, para. 387) from which a shape may eventually be discerned, we found ourselves, as the editors, both within the consulting room with the therapist and patient, engaged with the process of work, and also, at the same time, outside it attempting to arrive at an overview in order to assess that process. This was a parallel process to the very writing of clinical material itself, at the same time being engaged in the clinical encounter and yet distanced enough to be able to write about it in a coherent way, even if the writing was about tolerating states of incoherence.

Nevertheless, we remain convinced of the intrinsic value of the struggle to publish clinical accounts in the face of the above mentioned two apparently contradictory but equally valid ethical demands: firstly, to safeguard the patient's interests at all times and to protect their confidentiality; and secondly, to respond to the needs of the profession, which as with any other healthcare or psychologically based profession, can only develop through on-going clinical reflection.

The ethos of the training of the Jungian Analytic Section of the BAP is the expectation that the trainee psychotherapist will be qualified to work independently, in depth, with unconscious processes, by seeing the patient three or more times a week over several years. To this end, patients who are to be treated by trainees are assessed as to their suitability for this kind of treatment. It has become a truism that the types of psychological problems facing the would-be, as well as the qualified, therapist have more complex psychopathology than was perceived in the past, often exhibiting narcissistic, borderline or psychotic features. While adhering to the aim of training—that is that the therapist should be able to work independently—we would stress the importance of judging when the therapist needs consultation and further supervision on their work with patients. This capacity of the therapist to discern their need for further consultation has an ethical dimension with impact on clinical work.

In seeking intensive analytic psychotherapy, a potential patient will be motivated by a number of factors, such as a desire for self-knowledge, improvement in their interpersonal relationships and a greater capacity for self-expression. In assessing potential patients for their suitability for intensive analytic psychotherapy, the practitioner will bear in mind a number of factors. McDougall (1989) offers a useful depth psychological profile for treatment assessment that includes the potential patient's awareness of their psychic suffering, their search for self knowledge, the implicit if not explicit understanding that they have an unconscious mind with motivations that might be at variance with conscious thoughts and wishes, and the assessor's judgement that the potential patient has the psychological resources to bear the intensive analytic situation (tolerating the non-gratification of wishes and impulses).

We were impressed by our authors' facility as practitioners to access and foster their patients' capacities to activate their own self-healing. This follows Jung's teleological understanding of the psyche's resources for development and growth, while at the same time fully appreciating the antithetical forces for negativity and destruction that act as defences against the risks, suffering and sheer hard work involved in the analytic endeavour, including the unfolding and development of the analytic relationship. It is as if what is being assessed is the person's potential to recover the lost or damaged parts of the self in order to give the self a second chance to develop and grow.

While the theoretical approach is Jungian, this has not imposed a restraint in utilizing psychoanalytic texts where these were appropriate. Jung's unique contribution to psychological thinking and theory building was largely structured by his theory of the archetypes. These are immutable and powerful influences on the development of the psyche. Of particular relevance are the key concepts of the self, encompassing the conscious and unconscious totality of the psyche, with its need to fulfil itself, giving purpose and meaning to life; the ego, the "I" that faces the world but which is partly unconscious; the shadow, comprising those aspects or parts of ourselves which we do not like, and which we often unconsciously split off and project outside ourselves, and which has some equivalence to the Freudian repressed unconscious; the anima and animus (the contrasexual archetypes) and the Wise Old Man and the Great Mother, the internal conjoined or warring parental couple. Jung repeatedly stressed the importance of the teleological nature of the psyche that seeks to heal itself. Thus, neurosis is not seen as a condition that requires "curing", but rather as drawing attention to a difficulty or complex that needs addressing in order for change to occur. It enables the person to work on the process of individuation, to be more of the person that he or she really is, and be more ready to fulfil their potential. This is an ongoing task throughout life that is never completed. All an individual's potentials can never be fully realized. While the process of individuation goes on throughout life, it can get blocked and require therapeutic help. For this help to occur, the therapist has to be as much "in the therapy" as the patient.

Jung stressed the importance of therapy as an intersubjective, two-way process. His maxim "the doctor can have no influence unless he is influenced" (Jung, C.W., 16, para. 163) is reiterated in many of the chapters of this volume. Furthermore, the therapist takes on the suffering of the patient in a particular empathic and immediate way. There inevitably follows a shared unconscious identity, a "participation mystique", whereby the patient's unconscious processes can be better understood by the therapist. In psychoanalytic terms, this is referred to as projective identification whereby the patient projects parts of him/herself into the therapist and then identifies those parts as belonging to the therapist. The task of the therapist is to recognize that this is happening, often through vivid experience that requires rigorous self-examination in order to metabolize it. Through this activity, which is the essence of the analytic attitude, the analyst can achieve an understanding that it is a form of unconscious communication that needs to be acknowledged, worked on and transformed, in order to enable the patient to recognize it and accept him/herself in a healthier way. In psychoanalytic psychotherapy, James Fisher (2001) has described the therapists' imaginative identification with the patient to convey the therapist's capacity to receive the patient's projections without the undue loss of the therapist's self-reflective capacity.

Another form of communication is the clinical use of dreams. The manner in which our authors refer to the role of dreams in their clinical accounts led us to reflect on Jung's understanding of dreams as a direct communication from the unconscious to the dreamer. Jung demonstrated the importance of dreams in each stage of a person's life (Jung, 1963). In the context of the analytic treatment, the therapist bears witness to the meaning and value in the dreamers' quest to address and resolve the worries that had brought them into analysis and so to create more freedom to fulfil themselves.

Part II, "Qualifying Papers for Associate Membership" offers four representative papers written as the final requirement for qualification as a Jungian analytic psychotherapist member of the Jungian Section of the BAP and Jungian analyst member of the International Association of Analytical Psychology. Training patients had to be seen for a minimum of three weekly sessions for a minimum of either two years (in the case of the first training patient) or for a minimum of eighteen months (in the case of the second training patient).

These papers reflect the struggles of the trainee to act as an effective clinical therapist while at the same time enduring the anxieties inherent in their own training status, the fact that they themselves are patients in their own analyses, and where sustaining recurrent periods of questioning and self-doubt are inevitable but alarming when experienced.

The first chapter *"An oedipal struggle towards individuation"* by Eleanor Cowen explores the struggle of a young man to move beyond the seductive comforts found in the first relationship with his mother in order to be able to establish later intimate relationships. The patient's difficulties were reflected in the analytic relationship as described by the author.

"*The search for emotional truth in a perverse scenario dominated by the trickster*", Marissa Dillon Weston's account of the first two and a half years of intensive psychotherapy, considers the patient's and therapist's struggle to make a genuine contact and to recover emotional truth by working through a set of perverse defences. The archetypal theme of the "trickster" is used to illustrate destructive and creative processes in the individual, the family and the culture.

Birgit Heuer's chapter "*The deer behind the glass wall: on becoming human*" gives an account of working with a borderline patient who could only make limited use of interpretation. She describes a process of incarnation unfolding both intrapsychically and within the growing transference relationship, as explored through the developmental theories of Winnicott, Bion and Fordham, while Jung's and Hillman's ideas are used to illuminate the process of incarnation from a transpersonal perspective. By combining a reductive and a synthetic perspective, she seeks to convey the complexity of the clinical process.

Jennifer Benwell describes in her chapter, "*The processes of restoration in a deprived self*", the early stages of therapy with a patient who suffered from an impoverished sense of self, and how she gradually becomes more able to use the therapist as a source of nourishment. From initially feeling that she had control over her, the patient eventually experienced her as a benign environment rather than an impingement upon her internal world. The archetypal elements of her internal landscapes are shown to be mediated in the transference with a resultant lessening of her defences. There are the beginnings of a sense of an other from whom the patient can safely draw sustenance and with this an emergent sense of self.

The chapters included in **Part III** "In the Maelstrom and in the Doldrums" address intensive work over extended periods of time in the analytic consulting room. Here, the reader has an opportunity through clinical narratives to have a perspective on the experience of long term in depth clinical work. This includes both the maelstrom of the eruption of tumultuous unconscious contents and processes impacting on the therapeutic interchanges between analyst and patient and the doldrums of those periods of defensive and malignant stagnation when no movement seems possible and when the analysis may flounder. Here, Jung's use of the alchemical images illustrates the vicissitudes experienced, evoking the various intrapsychic and shared intersubjective states upon which the authors reflect in their clinical writing.

In "Unlocking the Uroborus", Marilyn Mathew describes the process of working with a young female artist suffering from a compulsive eating disorder. The concept of the Uroborus, the snake that eats its own tail in an eternal round, is explored as a powerful primitive defence employed by the patient against the terror of real relationship with an other. Sight is examined as a defence against seeing and the production of artwork is considered as an omnipotent creation of a world in one's own image. The tension produced by the emergence of the transcendent function finally allows an alternative to uroboric experience to develop within the locus of artwork.

In her chapter "The elusive elixir: aspects of the feminine", Margaret Hammond explores the growing internal differentiation of feminine imagery in a male patient. At the beginning of analysis, the feminine appeared as an all-embracing figure. Through events in the transference, which were illustrated in dreams by a number of archetypal scenes, a transformation took place which allowed for a growing capacity for separateness and relatedness. The evolution of the analytic container is discussed, as the infantile transference evolves to a position where the analysis acts as a container allowing the emergence of new patterns of relating.

Elizabeth Richardson considers, "In excretions and interpretations", a clinical situation in which the analytic work suggested that the inability of the mother to contain and to understand her infant's need to imagine may prevent the infant from moving on from a somatic to emotional experience. In later life, this can result in an inability to symbolize. The mother's uterus is likened to the alchemical, well sealed vessel described by Jung. The "fluid" psychological space between analyst and patient is contrasted with the amniotic fluid in the intrauterine space which the developing foetus swallows, digests and excretes into. Actual contamination of this fluid space by meconium passed by a distressed infant is compared with symbolic contamination of the analytic space by the poisonous projections of the abandoning mother the patient has internalized.

Nathan Field's chapter, *"Psychotherapy as a two-way process"*, offers a modified perspective on the practise of psychotherapy from that with which it began. Psychotherapy was originally assumed to be a one-way healing process following the medical model where the doctor makes the patient better. It was one of Jung's major insights to recognize psychotherapy as a two-way process, owing more to an alchemical than to a medical model. Nathan Field is mindful of the profound but subtle impact of the therapist's subjectivity, and considers that *both* parties can benefit from a successful therapeutic relationship.

In *"Life gives and life takes—therapy in the waiting room of birth and death"*, Arna Davis explores the external reality of birth and death that was part of the context that coloured and gave a sense of urgency to the analytic work with the two patients described. The common task for both patients was to re-unite with the core of the self that had been split and sealed off. Each had experienced a breakdown in the maternal container in infancy and had needed to provide "self holding", developing a primitive, defensive "self-care system", now useless and harmful. For the woman, the actual birth of her baby, and the thinking presence of a therapist, translating and separating signals both from the patient and from the baby, was a healing experience. Being in the stillness of the waiting space of death was a journey full of deep sadness, fighting, defiant anger and almost unbearable pain that could not be soothed away. The hero's journey of separation had started and in the final stage the patient felt free to die and the analyst understood that she no longer served a useful purpose.

Finally, in this section Geraldine Godsil's chapter, *"The difficulties inherent in having your own mind"*, uses Freudian, post Kleinian and Jungian ideas regarding the difficulties in linking and early triangulation to explore the changes in a young woman's internal world. The writer traces the shift over a number of years in the analysis from attacks on meaning to a growing link, with internal objects that generate thoughts. Having a mind of one's own depends on a connection with internal objects that have a *life* of their own and that are experienced as not under one's omnipotent control.

Part IV, "Reflections on Clinical Practice", comprises chapters that attempt to stand back from the immediacy of intensive one-to-one analytic work in order to reflect upon a number of contemporary clinical issues relevant to such work. These include issues concerning analytic dependency, racism, retirement and a number of ethical dimensions that are involved in writing about that most intimate of relationships, between the patient and the analyst, and the supervision of that relationship.

Joan Reggiori in her chapter, "*Analytic dependency*", points to the degree of dependence in every meaningful relationship, and thus by implication within the analytic relationship. In exploring the idea of the interdependent analytic relationship, she shows that an essential element is the emotional maturity of the analyst in contributing to change and healing in the patient.

Helen Morgan in "*Between fear and blindness: the white therapist and black patient*" explores the impact of differences in colour in the consulting room. Writing from the point of view of the white therapist, she discusses how easily defences such as denial, splitting, shadow, projection and avoidance—are forms of "colour blindness" on the part of both therapist and patient that can be used to skew and abuse the analytic relationship, with real consequences for the outcome of the therapeutic endeavour.

In "*Reflections on retirement: questions raised*" Susan Fisher reflects on the clinical and personal consequences following her decision to retire from active professional life. The process of ending an analytic practise activates such issues as the loss of professional identity, with connotations that are both positive and negative, where there is an ending as well as a beginning, a rebirth as well as a "small death", all aspects that she considers touch personally on the process of developing a meaningful spiritual life.

This section then proceeds to a selection of chapters devoted to some of the ethical and clinical issues pertaining to post qualification supervision of clinical work, including the internal supervision involved in writing clinically based papers and seeking patients' permission to publish their clinical material.

Jean Pearson in "*Some thoughts on supervision*" addresses aspects of the current debate on the impossibility of achieving an objective perspective when the intersubjectivity of patient and analyst as well as that of supervisory relationship between supervisor and reporting analyst is involved. She discusses the value of process recordings and illustrates this with clinical material.

In the "*Ethics of supervision: developmental and archetypal perspectives"*, Hester McFarland Solomon argues from both the developmental and the archetypal perspectives that ongoing post-qualifying provision of supervisory space creates the necessary triangulation requisite to fostering the ethical attitude in analytic practice. In this way the capacity to think, including the achievement of ethical thinking, may foster and protect genuine object relating in the consulting room. This can occur whether the supervisory provision is classical weekly one-to-one supervision, occasional consultation with a senior practitioner, or in peer supervision groups, and it will amplify and influence the clinician's ongoing processes of internal reflection.

Elphis Christopher in *"Reflections on the process of seeking to obtain permission to publish clinical material"* gives an overview of the inherent dilemmas facing practitioners wishing to publish clinical material. This is illustrated by the struggle internally and through the dramatic dynamic with the patient when she requested permission to publish the patient's clinical material.

The book ends with a speculative exploration *"Clinical paradigm as analytic third: reflections on a century of analysis and an emergent paradigm for the millennium"* by Birgit Heuer. She contrasts the traditional emphasis on a reductive, dyadic understanding of the analytic relationship with the teleological view posited by Jung with his central concept of the self in transformation and individuation. This latter she compares to recent theories of four dimensionality as found in quantum physics and links this new clinical paradigm to spiritual ideas regarding psychic change.

We are fully aware that any book whose title includes the word "contemporary" must be a work in progress. If our authors' reflections upon current clinical practice have moved analytic understanding forward to a certain degree, then we will have achieved our aim, for there are always new frontiers to be explored in this most human of endeavours—analytic practice.

References

Fisher, J. (2001). Poetry and Psychoanalysis: twin sciences of the emotions. Paper given to a BAP Conference entitled *Changing Times*, Oxford, September 2001.

Jung, C. G. (1963). *Memories, Dreams, Reflections*. London: Routledge & Kegan Paul.
McDougall, J. (1989). *Theatres of the Body*. London: Free Association Books.

PART II
QUALIFYING PAPERS FOR ASSOCIATE MEMBERSHIP

CHAPTER ONE

An oedipal struggle towards individuation

Eleanor Cowen

"... there appears before you on the psychological stage a man living regressively, seeking his childhood and his mother, fleeing from a cold cruel world which denies him understanding. Often a mother appears beside him who apparently shows not the slightest concern that her little son should become a man, but who, with tireless and self-immolating effort, neglects nothing that might hinder him from growing up and marrying. You behold the secret conspiracy between mother and son, and how each helps the other to betray life.

... There is in him a desire to touch reality, to embrace the earth and fructify the field of the world. But he makes no more than a series of fitful starts, for his initiative as well as his staying power are crippled by the secret memory that the world and happiness may be had as a gift—from the mother. ... It makes demands on the masculinity of a man, on his ardour, above all on his courage and resolution when it comes to throwing his whole being into the scales. For this he would need a faithless Eros, one capable of forgetting his mother and undergoing the pain of relinquishing the first love of his life"

Jung, C.W., *9(ii)*, para. 21–22

Introduction

The Oedipus myth begins with the infant boy abandoned by his parents. In the myth, the drama of the relationships between child, mother and father unfolds through a process determined by fate. Despite the efforts of its protagonists to escape these entanglements, they seem destined to experience those dangers and attractions foretold by the oracle. Although Freud originally saw the Oedipus myth as representing the child's actual, if unconscious, wishes towards the parents, Jung considered it rather as "a symbol of a complicated internal process of development whereby the young man struggled to free himself of his mother" (Astor, 1995, p. 2). The oedipal struggle could then be viewed as an inherent individuation process, through which each individual must pass in order to leave the orbit of his family of origin and venture alone into the world, in search of new relationships. Where this process is successful, the child comes to recognize his separateness from the parental couple with the loss of possession of the mother.

This paper describes the first two and a half years of three times a week analytical psychotherapy with Jack, a young man who has been caught in such a struggle for many years. The first part of the paper reflects the oedipal nature of his difficulties and preoccupations. Jack entered the therapy very much as the infant pushed out by the parents. His feelings as the "third" to the couple were soon constituted in the transference and the meaning of that position, as well as Jack's resistance to surrendering it, will be examined. Threaded through the work is a second strand of conflict: whether or not this patient can bear to know about these oedipal configurations and their meaning. The defences and illusions he adopts in order to avoid the pain and loss of separation from the mother and the recognition of the parents as a couple, separate from himself, are discussed. The paper ends with consideration of an unanswered question: has the therapy, to date, helped Jack achieve internal change and growth or has it become incorporated into his psychic defences in the service of emotional stasis?

Oedipal dynamics

Our first meeting

Jack sought psychotherapy in his late twenties because he had been unable to form relationships of any intimacy or to consummate other aspects of his vocational and recreational life. He described how, "If I have made a friend, progress does not mean deepening that relationship, it means finding another new friend". Similarly he embarked regularly on hobbies and "projects" which were never completed, and despite having qualified as an architect had not pursued a career in architecture. Instead he worked in accountancy, which reflected the solitary retreat Jack had found during his adolescence.

Our first meeting introduced me to some of Jack's difficulties in forming relationships. A thin, awkward man, he seemed uncomfortable to have me follow him into the consulting room where he was intensely watchful. I felt he both scrutinized me for clues as to what I expected of him and yet also adopted an air of wanting to appear unperturbed by the interview and my opinion. He denied any feelings of anxiety and spoke quickly and rather intellectually about his reasons for seeking help.

Jack began by saying that he has problems in forming relationships and getting close to people. This included intimate relationships where he had had only one sexual encounter and he added rather begrudgingly, "As you must have read about me". He thought he had been depressed for years but felt he had "really broken down" over the past six months, although his family "had not noticed". He felt deeply hurt by this. But, he said, "I wouldn't have wanted them to know anything about me anyway, I could never trust them. They would never be able to cope with knowing anything about me". He had once read a poem about himself to his mother and said, "She really couldn't deal with it".

I was told that none of the work done with previous therapists had touched him, and his scornful tone felt extremely attacking. He wanted to be understood, but said he never shows his feelings to anyone. He wanted me to remain interested in him, but noted that "if anyone does like me I despise them and think they are stupid". It was important for him to be "on top intellectually", which held a warning for me of his potential competitiveness for thinking and control. He told me of his "resistance to being seen in simple terms which would make me responsible for the mess in my life". Jack said he had chosen a Jungian approach for its spiritual aspects which he thought might help him overcome a fear of death he had experienced since childhood, especially when he was alone in bed at night.

Towards the end of that first meeting he asked if he could read me something he had written, saying, "I like to think of myself as a writer". He produced two long pages of prose written the previous weekend after he had met a girl he liked. He felt elated initially until he realized that she did not want him. "She could get to know me and find she really loves me", he said, "...but it will never happen". The writing was a portrayal of Jack as a Frankensteinian monster, terribly ugly and rejected by everyone, filled with pain and wanting to destroy the world for its rejection of him. For the first time I was able to feel an expression of real sadness as well as the attacking destructiveness of his rage at his isolation.

My experience, during and after that hour, was of feeling alternately drawn towards, and pushed away from, Jack. This seemed to reflect his desire to form relationships followed by retraction from any deepening of attachment. When I recognized the pain of his isolation, his feelings of rejection and fears that he could never be loved, my own maternal aspects were stirred and I found myself wanting to offer him comfort and relief. I felt that he wanted me to see the breakdown and depression his family had not recognized and that he hoped I would admire his poetry, intellect and complexity. But, having drawn nearer, I felt suddenly pushed away by his attacking scorn and dismissal of any capacity I might have to understand or offer him anything. He seemed to want to be loved and yet was somehow also terrified of this. The warning was that he would despise me if he thought I mattered too much.

With hindsight, I can identify the embryonic emergence of aspects of Jack's oedipal difficulties and defences expressed in that session: the link between his state of mind and his place in relation to his parents and, in particular, his mother; his feelings of hurt and rejection in finding he is not in the centre of their thoughts; the adopting of a defensive reversal, where it is they who become the ones who are too inadequate to cope; and his ultimate thought that it is he who chooses to be on the outside.

Early relating in the therapy

From the beginning I felt challenged by Jack in any efforts that might establish a relationship between us. This was reflected in the process of the analysis. He disliked the times I offered for sessions and the fees I proposed. He questioned whether he could come later in the evenings or over weekends but supposed I would want these spaces for myself without his intrusion. On Mondays, for the first session of the week, he arrived on time and with an abundance of material, far too much to deal with in the hour. Dreams and thoughts he had written down to bridge the weekend gap left me feeling stimulated by their rich potential. It was, however, almost impossible to halt Jack's outpourings for us to settle into any thinking together. Instead it felt as if he used the first weekly session to relieve himself of the emotional overload and let me know about his distress and loneliness. The second and third sessions of the week, on Wednesday and Thursday, then seemed to undo what had been shown, especially Jack's need of me and the therapy. He often arrived late, without apology or explanation, and was difficult to reach emotionally. He periodically complained about the lack of therapeutic progress that would help him find a "real" relationship. In fact, I found it very difficult in those early months to distinguish his inner from his outer worlds, to know what 'real' relating meant to Jack.

The therapeutic material was filled with fantasies of relationships, especially their sexual possibilities. Jack dismissed any suggestions of potential attachment to me. He hated the interpretations I made about his neediness or feelings of being left outside of my space at night and over weekends, and his attacks on my thinking left me wondering, for a long time, whether he might be right in suggesting it was me who needed him rather than the other way around. I felt sure he would not tolerate the first term, let alone the two-year period to remain a training patient. I wondered about his early relationship with his mother and whether they had had as much difficulty in establishing a fit.

Jack offered little history in terms of his actual early experiences. Instead, I drew on transference and countertransference experiences for clues which might help me to understand his difficulties in beginning relationships. In the transference, I felt his attacks as potentially lethal, despite an understanding that his contempt was of his own neediness and vulnerability in exposing this. My resultant anxiety and timidity left me wondering how Jack's mother responded to a furious, intolerant baby who nevertheless needed holding. I felt afraid of his ability to demolish my thinking which rendered me helpless in keeping the firmness I knew was required to challenge his sadistic and destructive defences, to help him feel safer with me. My capacity to understand his fears and communications depended on the containment and reflecting space of supervision where I could return to some analytic functioning. This raised a question in my mind about the absence of a father/supervisor as a helpful "third" to the new, nursing couple. I did learn that Jack's father had been at the theatre during the births of both him and his brother.

While I silently questioned Jack's attachment to me in the first months, I felt strong emotions towards him in the countertransference. The most powerful of these countertransference feelings coalesced around an image of him as a peeping, prying little boy. I feared he might invade every room and corner of my life if he could. He did show great curiosity about who lived with me and where these others were, especially when he came for his two early morning sessions. His fascination with my husband became apparent through dreams he brought in later months and while he acknowledged such fantasies he could not speak of these openly. I also felt that if I let him in to me he would consume all he could and I might never be rid of him. Although I did not feel ready to use these images with Jack, they did help me to begin to think of two emerging aspects: the baby within the nursing couple, consumed by passion and greed; and the boy outside of the parents' room, wanting to peep in, and imagining them engaged in similar passions.

These transference and countertransference feelings suggested the "couple" as the union which is both longed for and yet dangerous. I could not discern any real shape to, or image of, the couple, or link any actual experience of his parents as a couple or early events between the nursing couple, with these ideas. As Jack continued to resist any notion of dependency on me, or of us as a therapeutic couple, I tried to understand why this might be so threatening. I began to feel that some of these difficulties might stem from a terror of loss particularly since, through the first year of therapy, he revealed a history punctuated with the pain of lost relationships.

A history of loss

Jack's parents were a young, immigrant couple who left their extended families to seek a better life in Scotland. Their first child Tom was followed two years later by the loss of another child in a late miscarriage. Jack felt that his own life was created to fill the pain of the loss of the dead baby. He reported a conversation shortly after the beginning of therapy in which his mother said that, "from the first minute she held the dead child in her arms all she wanted to do was to fill them again". He added that as she spoke "her eyes were voracious". When he responded that he was a just a substitute for that child she became extremely angry, banged her fist on the table and shouted, "No!" Jack said he felt very afraid that she would stop loving him there and then and he ran from the house. His fear of losing his mother's love seemed unbearable.

Jack's first memory, at the age of two, was of his mother's pain when he felt a sadness which he thought emanated from her as they sat with her terminally ill father. He first began to fear death when he was five. Jack felt his own experience of isolation began when his family moved to England in his early adolescence, and the loss of friends and a sense of belonging. Descriptions of this period also conveyed a sense of destruction within the marital relationship, following which Jack's perceptions of an insensitive, cruel father and an unhappy, dependent mother, hardened. He also recalled his maternal grandmother's death a few years later and his horror at his mother's reaction when she ran into the garden in a downpour, "howling with pain", and flung herself on to the grass which she clutched in despair. Jack spoke of the "knowledge" of the inevitability of relationships not being forever and I thought this terror of pain and loss might have shaped his subsequent relationships.

He described himself as a late developer and socially isolated as an adolescent. When he left home to attend university he discovered ways of concealing his sense of inadequacy with social "tricks" and fantasies of intellectual superiority. He spent much time fantasizing about sexual intercourse and conquests where he was admired, potent and powerful. But at a distance from his family circle he also experienced debilitating bouts of fear and depression. He felt like "a sinking ship in relation to the parents' shore". After graduation he considered becoming a doctor but was dissuaded by his mother who said he was too self-centred and did not care enough about other people. Jack spoke of "bottled up feelings of pain and regret at the loss of time and relationships". This dual aspect, in which relationships are both longed for and yet avoided, seemed to characterize his adult life and reflected my own early experience of Jack. It was also mirrored in the way he described current relationships within his family.

An Oedipal drama

When Jack spoke of his parents, it was to describe his emotional experience of them. I felt he was showing me not his actual parents, but objects of his inner world, the figures of the oedipal drama that was played out in unconscious phantasy. I came to see this version of the mother and father as parental imagos, in the sense of imagos as "images ... generated subjectively... That is, the object is perceived according to the internal state and dynamics of the subject" (Samuels et al., 1986, p. 73). The force and power of the scenes he described had an archetypal quality with archetypal elements to the relationships between the figures.

... THE FATHER

Jack felt his father to be powerful and animalistic. He was described as a physical man, taller and stronger even in his older years than Jack would ever be. Recalling seeing his father naked for the first time, Jack thought that his father's penis was as large as a horse's. By comparison, he felt small and inadequate. He doubted he could ever match his father's size or power. This physicality translated into a perceived sexual potency which was both admired and feared. Jack thought that, during his childhood, he had heard his mother call out in the night that his father was hurting her, presumably in sexual intercourse. To this was added recollections of his own verbal humiliation by his father. The father–lover was cruel, animalistic and brutal, yet potent.

Early in our second year, Jack began a session by describing a scene from a film called "Trust" which conveyed his mixed feelings towards the father. He explained, "One person forces another to climb up against a wall and they have to fall backwards and trust the person to catch them. I wouldn't trust my mother, she would collapse. I would trust my father..." Unusually, he became tearful and was able to say, "I think the tears are related to my father and thinking about trusting him to catch me. But he can be so hateful!" and went on to describe how his father had recently publicly humiliated his brother. He continued, "My father has always conveyed a quality of disgust which I still feel for myself. I remember as a very small boy crawling on all fours over my parents' laps, first my mother and then on to my father". He paused to say he felt so humiliated in telling me this. "And I farted. I'm not sure whether my father actually hit me off his lap or just said something to make me feel like that but it was 'Wham! That is disgusting!' You know, as a boy I was anally retentive, I didn't go to the toilet for days, just held in my stools. I used to hate shitting. I thought, 'Why do I have to produce such disgusting things?' It's the same with all my body products".

From this, I understood that Jack felt puny next to the strong father who, he felt, saw him as shit and this was internalized. His fear of the humiliating father overcame his trust in the good, holding father. Klein (1945) suggests that this position may lead to a number of difficulties for the boy when he may find it hard to face his oedipal hatred and rivalry towards his father without a strong enough belief in the goodness of his own and his father's penis. For Jack, too, his sense of having disgusting insides reinforced his aggressive impulses, leaving him fearing that sexual intercourse could be destructive (Klein, 1945). At times he expressed alarming fears of his tongue or penis being bitten or cut off during sexual intercourse and at other times, his own sadistic phantasies towards women seemed to contain an identification with the cruel and humiliating father. Jack feared that he might be potent only when he was "fucking" a woman who submitted to him as he took what he wanted from her. I thought he was both afraid of his hatred of his father and of his love of him. He seemed to feel both repulsion at his father's attitudes and yet also identified with these.

In the transference, aspects of the father imago were projected onto the fantasied figure of my husband. In one dream Jack described meeting a very tall, grey-haired man with piercing eyes, outside the therapy door. I had left Jack there in order to make up the therapy "bed" which had been slept in during the holiday break. This husband–father figure nodded in acknowledgement of Jack, "obviously knowing who I was, or rather, what I was". In his associations to elements of the dream, Jack imagined my husband to be successful and secure in his possession of me. By contrast, he feared he would be looked down upon as "impertinent" by this older male figure for having any pretensions of being important when he was patently so small by comparison.

... THE MOTHER

Jack spoke more of his mother than his father and with a greater range of feeling and involvement. At times, he could acknowledge his love for her, especially in recollections of lounging across her body as a small child when her ample breasts held special appeal to him. He felt, then, that he possessed her and had total access to all he wanted from her. At other times, he despaired of getting close to her, despite his efforts to be the boy-lover who might offer her what he felt his father could not, through a shared love of poetry, literature and the arts. But Jack feared he would never be enough to make her happy. He could not fill the void he sensed within her as he described her "languishing on the couch in a freezing house ... her pain so deep, so impossible". When I reminded him of the "Trust" film, saying that he felt his mother was too depressed to hold him and would collapse, he became tearful. "What I most want", he said, "is to be held by a woman but it is what I most resist". He added later that holding by his mother was always affectionate but stifling. The loving and stifling mother images sat side by side as two poles of the maternal archetype, loving and devouring. I also linked this with his description of her voracious look in wanting to hold a baby and thought he was afraid of how greedy he could be for his mother's breasts and of being engulfed by the extent of both of their feelings.

At yet other times, when he felt secure and in possession of his mother, he seemed elevated into a position similar to the potency he felt his father represented. Jack could then become cruel and dismissive of the caring mother. Now, his shitty mess could be a way of taking control over her. He recalled, as a boy, summoning his mother to the toilet to wipe his bottom and it pleased him that she loved him so much that she would clean his mess, he said. In the transference I experienced this through Jack's demands of me, as if I should love him enough to tolerate the mess he could produce for me in his late arrivals or cancelled sessions, his crumpled cheques shoved in my direction and his amused avoidance of interpretations and serious therapeutic work.

... THE COUPLE

In Jack's internal drama, the couple presented the most taunting and the most tantalizing possibilities, symbolizing both that which is wished for, in the passionate intercourse in which all needs are met, and that which is feared, in the sadistic, humiliating father within the mother.

The following session reflected this dynamic. Jack began by telling me about a girl he had met at a party who reminded him of me. He described an intimate encounter between them and his mounting excitement at the prospect of a relationship developing. However, as soon as he realized how much he was looking forward to seeing her he thought, "What if it isn't reciprocated?" and said that immediately "something shut off" inside himself and he drew back from pursuing another meeting. He passed over any feelings of disappointment and hurt saying, rather brightly, that maybe that it was better not to be too involved and perhaps they could have a sexual relationship anyway. Suddenly, Jack became reluctant to continue saying, "You might know her. What if she has already told you about me and you already know that she was not interested in me?" I said that I thought he felt exposed and angry at having to talk about what had occurred between himself and this girl who might also be me. He replied, "I can't tell you. You are forcing me to tell you details which means you will see me as she did, without clothes. Perhaps she didn't like what she saw, like the hairs on my chest, some women don't. I don't. It makes me feel small talking like this". When I said that what he feared was this girl and me laughing at the small boy who is trying to be a man, he was able to say that this was what had made him close off to her. "I can feel it now! It's terrible to think of being laughed at. That's exactly what I'm terrified of, laughing women and men who have women, humiliating me".

... THE COUPLE AND THE "THIRD"

Implicit in images of the couple was always a third, sometimes observing, sometimes sneering, always critical. Feeling himself as the third, Jack's response to the feared humiliation by the couple was to adopt a defensive reversal, where he could be the omnipotent, vengeful one who chose to be on the outside. This helped him to avoid feelings of envy and exclusion.

Two stories were told to me which helped me to understand this dynamic. The first concerned his mother and brother. "When I was small she was very protective of my brother. Me and my father were on the outside. I thought of my mother and brother as aliens". I interpreted his feeling of alienation from his mother and the couple who have each other and that when he knew how much he wanted to be in his brother's place his revenge was to turn them into aliens. He agreed quietly to this interpretation. The second story recalled how, at about eleven years of age, Jack would leave his own bed where he felt afraid and lonely, and knock on his parents' bedroom door to be taken into their bed to lie between them. He remembered twisting his leg around his mother's and thinking that he could be special to her in a way which his father could not. After a while his father became fed up with this ritual and moved Jack to lie outside of him, so that father was next to mother. Lying beside his father, Jack deposited snot under the iron bedframe with a feeling of revenge and satisfaction.

His anxiety, that the couple or the man-within-the-woman are sadistic and humiliating of the third, presented an ongoing difficulty in the therapy. When Jack and I tried to work together in a creative way, the "third" within him frequently smashed up what we endeavoured to produce. At a distance from me, he could feel the pull to get close to me and looked forward to our sessions. I could imagine then his desire to relate to the mother in an exclusive and intimate pairing. But as soon as the time for our meeting approached, the imagined voice of the mocking "third" led to an emptying out of all feeling. He feared having to wait outside my house in case I would see him as "a lurking animal". From within the house he imagined the husband-within-me sneering at Jack's primitive need of the breast. His anxiety about getting close to me was heightened by a sexualized aspect where he was terrified of feeling stimulated or having intimate thoughts of me, in the session. Almost unthinkable images of being excited in my presence included fears of sweating excessively or ejaculating on the couch. At such moments his response was to enter his sessions with an emotional blankness and to mock my efforts at relating. He agreed with my interpretations that he hated all couples, even when he is part of that couple.

Jack's retreat, both from relating to me and to his own feelings, functioned to restore to him a sense of control but also returned him to depressed isolation and thoughts of death. For almost two years there seemed to be little change in Jack's position but he also voiced a reluctance to give up this safe and comfortable place. Despite the many interpretations I made and his acknowledgement of most of these, I felt despondent at the repetitiveness of old patterns and defences.

An intimate relationship

Towards the end of the two-year period, an incident occurred between Jack and his mother which challenged his position as her boy-lover. After a party where he had once again pursued an unattainable woman, Jack returned to his parents' house feeling alone and unhappy. His mother was awake and eager to engage him and she asked whether he had had "any luck". The question infuriated him. He stormed from the house and outside shouted to his mother, "Fuck you!" I interpreted his fury as coming from her challenge to his illusion of them, Jack and his mother, as the "fucking" couple, for implicit in her remark was the suggestion that he should find a sexual partner of his own. Jack replied that he felt trapped in his bond with his mother and that it was she who had helped promote his sense of security in not needing anybody else. He felt that other relationships now seemed impossible and he could not imagine a way of ever being free of his need of his mother.

Over the following weeks he spoke increasingly of being on the outside, socially and at work, and commented often on how cold it was outside. We were approaching the end of the two-year period of the Reduced Fee Scheme commitment and Jack voiced his fears that I would not want to keep him on. However, he did allow himself to imagine an end to the therapy and was surprised at how much this saddened him. His ability to think about leaving me and to express ambivalent feelings about his dependency on me seemed to mark a watershed for Jack. He changed jobs for a position which bridged his desire to move forward and the pull back to the familiar: he joined an architectural firm in their accountancy department. The appointment brought new responsibilities and doubled his income. He also changed accommodation to share a flat with two young women, one of whom was Debbie.

Jack's attraction to Debbie was awakened when she showed care and concern in ways which he identified with his mother, although the links between mother and girlfriend made him very anxious. Although he reported no interest in Debbie as a person, and was aware of this, he encouraged the development of a relationship and was especially agitated and aroused in anticipation of a sexual intercourse. He seemed to stand outside of any mutual relating and she was valued rather for her interest in, and acceptance of, him. He was eager to promote himself to her as a caring and intelligent young man, the boy-lover who had seduced mother away from father. At the same time he was terrified of lustful thoughts and feelings he had and consciously tried to keep these out of his awareness and away from Debbie. He felt he could not be responsible for what he might do if these erotic thoughts took hold. We linked this with his anxieties that he might have to be like his father, brutish and crude, if he was to be potent and sexually successful. He seemed both fascinated and disgusted at intrusive thoughts he had of the couple in the sexual act. He reported this from the position of the third, as if an outsider to the unfolding relationship and I too felt invited to watch in a rather detached and voyeuristic way.

Debbie was treated in other ways which repeated Jack's relationship with the maternal object. He expected her to clean up his mess, including the mess he created in intercourse. He seemed to use her to satisfy his needs but became critical when she revealed needs of her own. When Jack felt he took second place, he wondered whether he should look for a new, better girlfriend and drop this "weak nutter". At times he and I were the couple and I felt invited to collude in accepting his humiliating descriptions of Debbie. When she remained with him despite his cruelty I feared he would despise her rather than value her acceptance of him. I wondered whether, like the boy on the toilet demanding that his bottom be wiped, he demanded this as proof of Debbie's love for him. I reflected on how quickly my therapeutic tolerance could be despised. As I observed the ongoing parallels in Jack's attitudes towards his mother, myself and Debbie, I asked myself whether the therapy was achieving any internal change or merely functioning as a container which strengthened long-standing psychic defences. The questions raised by these fears led me back to theory to make more sense of the clinical material.

The oedipal struggle and individuation

The internal oedipal drama which Jack presented over the first two years of therapy consisted of a world with three primary players: mother, father and child. Despite a defensive position adopted by Jack which could convey that he was the one abandoned by the couple, I came to understand through the nuances of the transference and countertransference that he harboured secret phantasies of possessing the mother and having a deep, hidden relationship with her. The cruel, destructive father imago represented the threat to this couple.

In normal oedipal development, the child must face the realization of the reality that the parents are a couple who are separate from himself and have a sexual relationship. This gives rise to a great sense of loss as the child gives up the idea of having exclusive and permanent possession of the mother (Klein, 1926 in Britton, 1989). However, in what Britton (1989) calls "the tragic version of the Oedipus complex", acknowledgement of the three-person configuration is felt to be disastrous: "... the discovery of the oedipal triangle is felt to be the death of the couple ... the arrival of the notion of a third always murders the dyadic relationship" (ibid., p. 100). The oedipal reality may then be distorted: although the parental relationship is recognized, it is "denied and defended against" (ibid., p. 85) and turned away from in consciousness. Steiner (1985) suggests that the individual must "turn a blind eye" to what he knows. This is achieved through the adoption of a defensive organization of "oedipal illusions" (Britton, 1989). It then follows that maintaining the oedipal illusion means that curiosity cannot be allowed which might challenge the barely concealed truth.

Although Jack could feel threatened by the spectre of the couple, he nevertheless protected himself from experiencing his actual exclusion and what this meant, both in the therapy and the transference in particular, and in reality. Steiner and Britton both imply that there may be a collusion in the patient's outer world which supports the oedipal illusion; and it seems apparent from Jack's descriptions of his mother and her ongoing need of Jack, that some fantasy was permitted which supported his oedipal illusion of son and mother as the true couple. When he looked at his parents with his view of an animalistic, sexual father and a sensitive, asexual mother, Jack voiced his conviction that they could not possibly have a creative and sexual intercourse. Over the first period of therapy it seemed that Jack's struggle had been primarily to protect this oedipal illusion. This meant that he could not permit any "knowing" which would make him see that his apparent comfort rested on an illusion. It also accounted for my frustration in our apparent lack of therapeutic progress.

Britton (1989) warns that the oedipal illusion can find its counterpart in the transference in similar, secret fantasies which the patient imagines are shared by himself and the therapist but dare not be acknowledged. Although some images of me as mother–girlfriend were revealed in dreams and some fears expressed about my husband in relation to Jack and me as a couple, Jack has been unable as yet to talk about conscious fantasies and anxieties he may have. The hope for future analytic work is that as the work deepens and gathers further into the transference, the transference oedipal illusion will expose us to an immediate experience of what happens in phantasy between the couple and in the oedipal triangle, with all its intensity and apparent danger.

With the external oedipal reality denied, Jack remained trapped in the paranoid–schizoid position (Klein, 1945; Britton, 1985). In a recent paper which extends Britton's post-Kleinian understanding of oedipal development, Jungian analyst Colman (1996) suggests that within the paranoid–schizoid position, "archetypes appear in their projected form as fascinating, larger than life figures whose distinction from the figures who embody them is at best blurred" (*ibid.*, p. 52). He cites Jung's frequent references to the coming together, in the boy's psyche, of mother and anima and suggests that: "At the height of the Oedipus complex parental and contrasexual images are fused and, in a way, this 'creates' the complex, since the intense longing for union with the oedipally loved parent is due to the fascinating power of the contrasexual archetype with which they are identified" (*ibid.*, p. 40).

Jack's difficulties could then be seen in terms of his being in the thrall of the anima and unable to differentiate the anima from his actual mother. Astor (1995) defines the anima as "the imaginative and inspirational aspect of male psychology, which often takes the form of an alluring and potentially dangerous female figure" (p. 224). In our analytic work, Jack and I had seen how he remained captured by the feelings which were evoked when he climbed into bed with his parents and pushed his leg between his mother's, and the anxieties which this experience stirred. He remained fascinated and terrified in almost equal measure by conscious and unconscious thoughts of intimacy, revealed most clearly at the beginning of his relationship with Debbie when Jack expressed fears of being "trapped", "consumed" and castrated by her. This reflected his need to resolve the anima/mother confusion before he could negotiate an intimate, personal relationship (cf Astor, 1995). In mythological terms, the boy "needs to kill the dragon–mother in order to free the captured anima. If this separation between anima and mother cannot be achieved, the anima takes on dangerous, threatening qualities, luring the man to a destruction he feels powerless to resist" (Colman, 1996, p. 42).

Resolution of the oedipal struggle and the differentiation of mother and anima takes place through the emergence of a symbolic capacity which is vital for individuation (Colman, 1996). When the anima can be recognized as "imaginative and inspirational" (Astor, 1995) it becomes located in the individual's inner world rather than sought through a quest for realization in the external world. A symbolic capacity further frees the individual to move around in what Britton (1989) terms "triangular space", where "a third position then comes into existence from which object relationships can be observed. Given this, we can also envisage being observed. This provides us with the capacity for seeing ourselves in interaction with others and for entertaining another point of view whilst retaining our own, for reflecting on ourselves whilst being ourselves" (*ibid.*, p. 87). This would enable Jack to develop the capacity to be in a creative, rather than a persecuted, "third" position.

The working through of the oedipal struggle goes hand-in-hand with working through the depressive position (Klein, 1945; Britton, 1985). The experience of the coming together of internal and external realities, of internal oedipal phantasies and external limitations and frustrations, leads to the sense of loss which heralds the achievement of the depressive position. The work with Jack showed that significant change had come about when he could contemplate the loss of me as mother and face challenges to his oedipal illusions, but as the quotation by Jung at the beginning of this paper suggests, this oedipal struggle is ongoing. It is an internal drama of advance towards individuation and retreat back into the undifferentiated: the progressive longing to "touch reality" and venture into the world of adult relationships against the regressive desire towards continued "happiness ... as a gift ... from the mother". It implies a deep and enduring struggle, described in deeply symbolic terms, and one which must be fought in the psychological world.

Final thoughts

My final thoughts lie in the work done, and the work ahead with Jack.

In looking back I asked myself whether internal change has been achieved to date. This question remains unanswered although I feel I am beginning to understand more about the dynamics which have contributed to this powerful struggle between growth and stasis. In external terms, it could be argued that the therapy has fulfilled its main stated aim: for Jack to be able to develop relationships and an intimate one in particular. He continues in a settled, sexual relationship with Debbie after eight months despite his frequent doubts about her capacity to meet his many emotional needs. He has also remained with me beyond the initial two years, paying more for his sessions in a grown up way and withstanding the difficulties inherent in sustaining an analytic relationship. Other external changes have taken place over the past year which he attributes to the work we have done together. However, he continues to struggle against giving up his inner world as he knows it, dominated by the mother and the comfort she offers.

We will continue to work with the difficulties within Jack's family which have contributed to his oedipal conflicts and inhibited their resolution. He can still feel trapped by the "loving but stifling" mother who does not encourage his separation and who colludes with her sons to undermine the value of their father. Identification with the father would offer the normal route out of the Oedipus complex but Jack's continued battle with his own ambivalent feelings towards his father frustrates this path. His fears of his own masculine potency, with its homosexual overtones, remain a thread of our work not discussed in detail in this paper.

Future work will need to continue to focus on the transference relationship and the transference oedipal illusion of Jack and me as a couple, although I suspect we share anxieties about the emergence of this intense dynamic between us, with its archetypal intensity and dimensions. In the countertransference, I still draw back from the boy I think I may never be rid of if I let him inside of me, which may indicate his own fears of becoming incorporated into, or consumed by me. At this time I can only guess at his own terrifying fantasies of us as a couple: if he believes that he might steal me from my husband, might he also fear this leading not only to the breakdown of therapeutic boundaries but to the breakdown of his psychic defences too?

Like Oedipus, Jack's exhortations to search for the truth conflict with what he knows will bring a painful loss once seen. My hope remains that as the therapy progresses, he will be able to face the loss of the mother and all that she stands for at this time: "it is through mourning for this lost exclusive relationship that it can be realized that the oedipal triangle does not spell the death of a relationship, but only the death of an idea of a relationship" (Britton, 1989, p. 100).

References

Astor, J. (1995). *Michael Fordham: Innovations in Analytical Psychology*. London: Routledge.

Britton, R. (1985). The Oedipus complex and the depressive position. In:

R. Anderson (Ed.), *Clinical Lectures on Klein and Bion*. London: Tavistock/Routledge, 1992.

Britton, R. (1989). The missing link: parental sexuality in the Oedipus complex. In: R. Britton, M. Feldman & E. O'Shaughnessy (Eds.), *The Oedipus Complex Today: Clinical Implications*. London: Karnac Books.

Colman, W. (1996). Aspects of anima and animus in Oedipal development. *Journal of Analytical Psychology*, 41(1): 37–57.

Klein, M. (1945). The Oedipus complex in the light of early anxieties. In: *Love, Guilt and Reparation & Other Works*. London: Hogarth Press, 1975.

Samuels, A., Shorter, B., & Plaut, F. (1986). *A Critical Dictionary of Jungian Analysis*. London: Routledge.

Steiner, J. (1985). Turning a blind eye: The cover up for Oedipus. *International Review of Psycho-Analysis*, 12: 161–172.

CHAPTER TWO

The deer behind the glass wall: on becoming human

Birgit Heuer

Introduction

"I watch, as a baby-deer climbs onto a stage which is empty save for an antique bed. The deer moves towards the bed and sits down on it, folding its legs under daintily. I am looking on mesmerised; it is a fascinating sight".

Annie told me this dream in her very first session; later I was to learn that the deer had worn a golden crown, too. Annie's dream got an immediate countertransference-reaction from me: from the start, I persistently misspelt the deer as "dear" in my notes, as if a bit of Annie, in need of being dear to someone, had got projected into me almost instantly. The elements of this dream—as well as its initial effect on me—have, over time, increasingly informed my thinking about the structure and topography of Annie's inner world, even though she never produced any associations.

My patient's initial dream can usefully be understood as functioning both as a metaphor—an organizing principle of *limited* meaning—and as a symbol—carrying and generating *infinite* meaning. The former can be contained by description, whereas the latter is essentially beyond being thus captured. As a metaphor, the dream leads into thinking about Annie's early history and the corresponding transference/countertransference exchanges between us: the deer as Annie's infantile self. Conversely, the symbolic reading is concerned with existential purpose and impetus: the deer as Annie's soul. These distinctly different functions of the initial dream correspond to a reductive and a synthetic perspective respectively, and I am interested in employing these conjointly, rather than exclusively.

Whilst such metapsychological considerations form one important aspect of my paper, the main thrust of it is a clinical exploration. My clinical theme is incarnation, by which I mean the process of becoming human by developing a capacity for being and for inner and outer relatedness. Diagnostically speaking, Annie was a borderline psychotic, whose early development had been severely curtailed. Despite this, she functioned to some degree in everyday life and was quite adept at practical matters, but psychotic processes dominated her inner life and hampered her relationships. In an essential way, she was—although a grown woman and a gifted designer—not really there and not really available for contact. "A journey towards incarnation" is the term that perhaps best expresses Annie's struggle in therapy over the first twenty-four months. The work has centred around ego-development, a chief ingredient in becoming human. I will describe this in the main body of the paper and weave in various perspectives of clinical theory to underpin it: Bion, Meltzer, Bowlby, Jung and Winnicott, in the main. Each of these writers has a somewhat different idea of human development, and—accordingly—I shall use them to highlight different facets of my work with Annie. They also serve the added purpose of illustrating my metapsychological theme as described previously. In concluding, I shall then attempt to draw together and discuss clinical and metapsychological perspectives and see how they have illuminated two years of—both difficult and rewarding— work with Annie.

The first session

I opened the door to a petite woman who looked much younger than her fifty-one years. She smiled brightly at me as she entered, and I found myself smiling in return, liking her on sight. As she went upstairs, with graceful movements, I noticed she was dressed rather like a schoolgirl in a white blouse combined with a blue skirt and big boots. She looked round my consulting-room, taking it in, still smiling. I felt that there was something very appealing about her. As soon as she sat down, however, I became aware of difficulties: she was looking down at her hands, wringing them nervously, and seemed unable to speak when I addressed her. When she managed to speak later, it was not in comprehensible sentences but in clusters of words. I became confused, wondering if I made her nervous by looking at her when I spoke. It was quite impossible to make sense of what she was saying, in spite of my many questions. My heart sank, as I remembered the assessor referring to Annie as a "rather complicated woman". When I asked if she felt a bit nervous, never having been in therapy before, she denied this. It seemed there was either confusion or denial in her response to me. She became coherent though, when I asked about her dreams, which had been mentioned in the questionnaire. She related a series of baby dreams in which she had had babies, had forgotten about them and later discovered them in various neglected states. Then she told me the deer dream. When I tried out an exploratory interpretation, linking the baby-deer with a baby part of Annie, she replied: "But I'm not a baby!", taking my words at their most concrete level. By the end of the first session, I felt unable to make up my mind about Annie, and had to suggest another consultation. It took me a further session and a leap of faith to decide to take her on.

Why was this decision so difficult? Annie had been intensely appealing in a child-like way, partly through her manner of behaving at the beginning of the session and partly via the contents of her dream. By the time I made my notes, smiling as I realized that I had misspelt the deer as "dear", I thought that she had already found a way to my heart. On the other hand she seemed to use words to confuse and distance to an alarming degree. In the countertransference I felt pulled towards her and pushed away in equal measure. Quite possibly, Annie produced ambivalence in me via projective identification, thus communicating her own ambivalent transference feeling.

There were additional factors complicating the situation.

According to the assessor, Annie had a history of developing intense crushes on men in positions of authority. At present, she was in love with Tim, her parish priest and also a psychotherapist, who had seen Annie and her husband for some joint sessions and had then passed her on to the B.A.P. Annie was likely to feel rejected by him and perhaps was distancing me in turn. I knew from the questionnaire that the theme of rejection had been there from the beginning of Annie's life: her mother had left her in a foreign country at eleven months. I myself had lost my first training patient six months previously and was still feeling somewhat rejected and anxious; in addition the assessor had expressed doubts about Annie's suitability. The combination of this made me unsure and ambivalent before I had even seen her, and, I am sure, became part of my countertransference, mirroring the ambivalence Annie's mother may have felt towards her baby.

Thus my initial meeting with Annie was already complicated by the various factors each of us brought into it. These engendered a considerable amount of rejected and ambivalent feelings in both of us, which could not be worked on immediately and therefore had to be tolerated, thought about and contained by me.

A brief family history

Annie is the eldest of three siblings and was born during the Second World War. For unclear reasons, Annie's pregnant mother—though married in England—left her husband and journeyed across the Atlantic to stay with her sister. Annie's uncle delivered her. At two weeks, mother abandoned her baby and went travelling. She returned some ten days later and stayed to look after Annie until she was eleven months old. With the war still on, mother left for good, returning to England to rejoin her husband. Annie grew up with her cousins but was mostly looked after by a maid. The child greatly admired her uncle who later also left for the forces. A photograph, taken at twelve months, shows Annie, looking pitifully bereft, a small face with almost expressionless eyes, dressed in hand-me-downs that were too large for her.

Annie's parents sent for her when she was four years old and the war was over. Her father and mother, of course, then were strangers to her. She found she had a younger sister, Pam, too. Life on their farm is remembered as fairly harsh, father as remote and only available at certain set times, while mother seemed constantly displeased and angry with Annie. Annie thought that mother preferred Pam who was prettier and more girlish. Mother herself had come from a broken home, her parents having divorced when she was eleven and then sending her away to live with distant relatives. Annie's father came from a military family and had given up his forces career to become a farmer. It seemed to Annie that he related to boys more easily and she became something of a tomboy. She spent a lot of time communing with nature on her own or with the farm animals. At eleven, she was sent away again to boarding school.

Annie met her husband Peter while studying design. Soon after getting married and while both found work as designers, they became involved in a religious cult. The cult taught a form of Eastern philosophy and practices, and was organized according to a strict hierarchy. Annie fell in love with the leader of the cult, who did not return her feelings. Her crush ended in anger and disappointment but the pattern was soon repeated with another senior teacher. With the births of each of her three children, Annie had psychotic episodes, which made her initially unable to look after the babies.

Annie managed to extricate herself from the cult several years prior to starting therapy. She then looked for a congregation to join and finally found a Catholic church in North London with a charismatic priest, Tim, who was a trained psychotherapist. She fell in love with him almost instantly. Aware of following her usual pattern, she approached him for help. He recommended Annie seek on-going psychotherapy and referred her to the B.A.P.

A difficult start

Annie broke into a wide smile and seemed pleased when I told her that I would take her on. My hope that her problems with communication would ease once we had started was, however, disappointed. At the most basic level, it seemed hard for us to be in a room together. Annie continued to look down, wringing her hands session after session. If I spoke while looking at her, she got terribly flustered and was unable to answer. Hoping to help her I often looked down myself, only to end up with a tension headache. She spoke in half sentences or mumbled clusters of words which were difficult to follow, seemingly making no sense at all. I strained my brain trying to find some meaning, succeeding at times but with great effort. When Annie spoke coherently, she jumped from subject to subject in a disjointed fashion and left no pauses for me to comment, so that I ended up feeling stuffed with undigested information.

I went through a gamut of feelings: I feared having made a mistake in taking her on, perhaps she was unsuited for psychotherapy after all. I doubted my capability as a therapist and felt as if paralysed; my ability to "shift gears" according to the patient I am with seemed non-existent, and I could not even remember that I usually possessed it; I needed my other patients to remind me. In Annie's sessions there was a constant onslaught of a confusing and undifferentiated mass, which I was required to digest and make sense of. Was this an impossible task?

Over and over again, I found that I could not reach Annie with words because she either fell to pieces or misunderstood me, so that there was only confusion left which could not be cleared up. Clearly Annie could not use my words positively but felt invaded and attacked by them instead. Later on, she remembered being given salad for lunch as a child in America which she carefully sorted into its ingredients and only then was able to eat. Another memory concerned her teddy and doll, she brought back with her at four. Apparently they all showed signs of having been excessively fed by her through their ears. All this pointed towards a disturbed feeding relationship with mother which I had to relive with Annie in the countertransference, where I was being stuffed like the dolls, while she picked to pieces—as she had the salad—anything I offered her.

During sessions a countertransference image evolved in my mind of a thick glass wall, dividing the space between us in my consulting room right down the middle. Through it I could only see Annie, but was prevented from any contact with her. This image was so intense I felt, I could almost touch it. It struck me as classic schizoid imagery (Winnicott, 1971). Conversely, the "dear" aspect of the deer dream continued to be projected into me. Whenever

Annie mentioned the dream, I spelt it as "dear". She also smiled at me at beginnings and endings of sessions, eliciting a smile and feelings of warmth towards her in return. Perhaps her need to be dear to someone, to be loved, utilizing my need to be a good therapist to her, kept us going through this difficult time.

With hindsight, I think two defensive elements were operating: Annie used both projective identification (Ogden, 1979) and intrusive identification (Meltzer, 1986) to a high degree. According to Ogden, the essence of projective identification is the communication of inner experience; based on primitive states, it can be a creative act, whereas intrusive identification is a more destructive act, as it is evacuative rather than communicative. Annie communicated her need to feel loved; also the fact that, in relation to me, she felt stuck behind a glass wall. On the other hand, she evacuated her mental confusion and her sense of being rejected and unacceptably flawed.

Earlier, I suggested that Annie's initial dream could be seen as a metaphor that functions descriptively: I think as such it implies mother and baby relations which have left Annie with an inner baby part that has not yet reached human status, as it takes the form of an animal in her dream. Bion's (1962a,b) theory of thinking unfolds around the building up of the baby's psyche in relation to the mother's psychically alive responses: thus baby's pure sense impressions, beta-elements, gain psychic, alpha, quality. Baby learns alpha-functioning by way of incorporation and its ego capacity is built up in the process. In healthy development an alpha-screen will form, dividing conscious from unconscious thoughts. In less favourable circumstances a beta-screen is created, blocking the possibility for alpha-functioning. The effect is one of attacking and deadening psychic life. Alpha-functioning metabolizes, beta just accumulates or evacuates. This process of "growing a psyche" seemed to have gone disastrously wrong for Annie; she had very little ego-alpha-capacity and she could not utilize my words. The deer dream reflected this, as animals do not have a psychic life and can be said to operate mostly on beta elements. The dream then described a psychic structure overwhelmed with beta elements and in need of becoming psychically alive and humanized. It also explained the confusing, beta element onslaught I experienced in Annie's sessions.

The softening

Gradually things began to feel a bit easier. I sensed a softening within Annie and a tentative opening up between us. I noticed how Annie seemed to have taken care over dressing for her sessions and would find myself silently admiring details of her appearance: a pretty combination of colours, a striking necklace or scarf. Her shoes in particular often drew my eyes as they were placed beneath the couch and—being quite a small size—looked touchingly girlish. Sometimes I felt almost like a mother admiring her pretty little girl. She also began copying bits of my appearance: having her hair cut by a hairdresser in my area, and then wearing it as I do; wearing lipstick as I do. In the countertransference I perceived the glass wall becoming thinner or at times even permeable. Annie brought a series of dreams which were all concerned with the feminine and the theme of mother and child: there were concrete basins, filled with a milky fluid, conical playground shapes in a park, where Annie took a child to play, and daydreams of a figure eight. She dreamt of numerous little children and then of a feverish, sick baby with a young mother.

I felt that in bringing all these dreams, something in Annie's unconscious was more actively engaged than the rest of her. Perhaps the Great Mother archetype had constellated between us and brought about the softened atmosphere, various images of the breast and a human, albeit sick baby. Annie was handing me the underdeveloped, sick part of herself, while harbouring some doubt in my capability to cope with it, expressed in picturing me as a young mother. Almost none of this could be verbalized as communication continued to be strenuous and difficult, so it had to be a mostly silent process which nonetheless felt more alive to me. It was striking how nothing could be effected with words, there simply were no right words, no helpful words to be found.

Fordham's developmental theory became relevant to the work: Fordham (1980) thinks of the baby as possessing an original self, containing all the archetypal possibilities in a kind of storehouse, ready to be activated and modified through mother and baby's interaction. In the absence of a sufficient positive experience the baby's inner world becomes overwhelmed with archetypes in their unhumanized form with their negative pole over-emphasized. In this state, the archetypes are able to wreak havoc with ego development and the capacity for apprehending reality. Annie's deer dream, in its metaphoric aspect, is descriptive of this kind of internal structure and dynamics: the deer is clearly archetypal in character and belongs with the world of Fordham's original self. It is then descriptive of a mother and baby interaction that did not sufficiently enable Annie to transform the archetypal possibilities, resulting in a severely weakened ego. This would account for Annie's extreme nervousness, her getting flustered and falling to pieces to the point of inability to speak and think in my presence. Possibilities for de-integration became instances of dis-integration instead.

However, I think Fordham's theory also expresses a degree of hope for potential development, as the original self—the store-house—is thought to still contain the archetypal potential which may get constellated positively under favourable circumstances. This links with my hopeful feelings about the softened atmosphere: archetypal motivators were then responsible for drawing us together as a mother and baby pair via Annie's dreams, her way of appealing to me and my countertransference positive responses to her. We were drawn together almost despite Annie's conscious self, where she saw herself as completely self-sufficient: "I always felt that I came ready made!" she once told me.

The deepening

Annie visited her parents for a weekend, and on her return, I sensed that she was distressed but had no words to talk about her inner experience and metabolize it. Eventually, speaking in a distant tone of voice, she told me how her mother addressed her as "dearest Annie" in letters but was constantly angry and critical with her in person. Presents Annie had brought had been thrown back at her in rage. I felt shocked, hurt and angry on Annie's behalf; the sheer onslaught of her mother's rage was almost tangible to me. My attempts at returning these projected feelings to Annie were politely attacked and ridiculed: she could not see why I was "always on about feelings", they were fairly unimportant in the larger scheme of things, why was psychotherapy so biased towards feelings? I was made to feel as her vulnerable inner self *vis-à-vis* her mother, battered, worthless, my verbal offerings thrown back at me like her presents had been. This was on one hand communicative of her experience, but on the other evacuative, as she also wanted to rid herself of it and insisted it belonged with me. Feelings, and especially hurt and angry ones, were to be my domain, not hers. Annie's inimical mixture of projective identification and intrusive identification was operating here, in response to distressing events which she was unable to process, bearing out again, how her weak ego became overwhelmed with beta-elements, the majority of which could only be evacuated.

When my summer break arrived, Annie treated it in a manner that was to be characteristic of all breaks during the two-year period. She became quite detached, insisting that breaks made no difference whatsoever, treating them as practical matters only. After the break though, I was dismayed to discover that we were nearly back to square one: her communication had almost completely deteriorated, she spoke in mumblings and clusters of words, and I distinctly perceived the glass wall between us again. I was reminded of how Annie's mother would have been a total stranger whom she probably rejected, on the child's return after the war, as this was how I felt treated, too. Annie had removed herself beyond reach, though not in an overt way: she used words to detach, rather than to relate, as she often spoke paradoxically, denying and stating the same thing almost in one breath. Feeling confused and rejected a lot of the time, I had to work hard to comprehend what was happening. Bowlby (in Holmes, 1993) sees the need for attachment as a developmental factor in its own right. Successful attachment in infancy is reflected later in a person's capacity for a coherent and emotionally alive self narrative. Bowlby's extensive study of attachment behaviour resulted in categories of different attachment styles. Annie's reaction to my breaks fits with what Bowlby terms anxious-avoidant attachment: children show few overt signs of distress or anger on separation but ignore mother, when she returns, in what Bowlby calls defensive exclusion.

Once more, a parallel can be drawn to the metaphoric–descriptive aspect of Anne's deer dream: the deer is completely alone on the stage, Annie herself a distant observer. As deer usually move in herds, this expresses a degree of isolation equal to Bowlby's defensive exclusion; the dream is then descriptive of Annie's defensive detachment and the external life circumstances—her mother's abandonment of her—contributing to bringing this about as a permanent attitude.

A second visit to Annie's parents was accompanied by much moodiness and fears of an accident. Annie saw these as external to herself, almost like events that happened to her. I worked to return them to her as her feeling experience in anticipating the visit. Again I was attacked for "going on about feelings too much". Annie's experience came as raw beta elements and my attempt to transform them was rejected and could not be utilized. Help arrived in the form of two dreams, both featuring downtrodden, abused and unattractive girls of about eight years of age:

> In the first dream, Annie witnessed a scene, where a girl, fitting the above description, was cruelly beaten by her mother with a hairbrush for lagging behind the rest of the family on a coastal path near her home.

Annie professed herself very distressed watching this scene but saw it initially as external to herself, because she "looked nothing like the girl". She also stressed how popular she had been at boarding school.

> In the next dream, a similarly awkward, unhappy girl was left in Annie's care by a strange woman, who inhabited a holiday home where Annie was due to stay with her children. After getting the woman to leave the premises, Annie found the girl who had got entangled in her shoelaces when tying them, rather, as Annie remarked, "like me here, with my boots".

She was referring to her own awkwardness at the ends of sessions with doing up the laces of her winterboots. There! She had made a connection herself, having also previously identified the similarity of both girls. The dream images had come alive to her in relation to her experience in the sessions. I was seen as the sadistic mother, of course, so the negative pole of the mother archetype was operating in the transference. Annie told me that her only memory of bodily contact with her mother in childhood consisted of mother's daily brushing of Annie's hair which often hurt as mother was rather ungentle. I used this memory to point out a further connection between Annie and the girls in her dreams. Finally, in her next session, Annie came in saying that she had realized the girls were part of her, in that she *felt like* them, adding she found it hard to accept this. From being like external events, both Annie's moods and the image of the girls could be taken inside for the time being. Briefly, she was reunited with a hitherto split-off and projected part of herself. How often had she managed to make *me* feel awkward in the countertransference!

I felt that a process best described as deepening was taking place, Annie was starting emotionally to come to life in small ways, where there had been complete detachment before. It was also as if the deer of Annie's initial dream was metamorphozing and slowly becoming human. The symbolic aspect of the deer dream then became relevant. When it is taken to function as a symbol, the emphasis shifts from the developmental models used previously, and a different aspect of the overall situation comes into view.

Jung's synthetic approach is above all concerned with generating meaning. For Jung human development continues throughout life and is centrally motivated by the archetypal or deep structure of the psyche which is imbued with psychic impetus. Individuation is motivated by deep structure: there is a psychic urge for us to become progressively more differentiated and integrated. Jung's model is not causal but dialectic, using the interplay of opposites. In mythology, the deer/stag (Annie's deer had antlers) is opposed to the unicorn, and they are likened to the archetypal forces of soul and spirit respectively (Jung, C.W., 12, p. 518). Hillman (1975) movingly writes about the soul as the principle of life-in-becoming, of deepening of experience, of incarnating and becoming human in a psychically alive way. Life is the "valley of soul making".

The stag renews its antlers every year and is thus also connected with Christ (Jung, C.W., 8, p. 559) who psychologically can be seen as a symbol of renewal and incarnation: God becoming flesh and experiencing human life. Following the way of the soul and the way of Christ, Annie struggled to bring about her own second—psychic—birth by incarnating: psychically inhabiting herself. In conscious life, she valued spirituality above all and would, in any given situation, tend to draw out its spiritual and transpersonal aspects. Her dream deer, surrounded by numinous energy, crowned in gold, fascinating to behold, forcefully symbolized the soul and its urge for Annie to deepen, to descend into depth, to feel, to live. This was then a strong underlying motivational force which, at the time, I was only intuitively aware of. I believe this was appropriate, as it would not have done to put any of the above into words to Annie, words might have taken away from the process. The symbolic reading of the initial dream then is concerned with the interplay of opposites: deer/stag and unicorn; soul and spirit. The soul, as the force opposing the one consciously valued by Annie, is being constellated, not to produce abstract meaning, but to generate human life and depth of experience.

The psyche–soma split

Annie's two years of therapy were interwoven with a host of physical illnesses. A sprained ankle, lower back pain, colds, toothache, sciatica, a gallstone, indigestion and heart pain, though she hardly ever missed sessions through illness. Illnesses were noticeably concentrated around my holiday times and visits to Annie's parents but also occurred at other times. They did not seem to follow a clear psychosomatic pattern in terms of a set physiological reaction with specific events. At times, I felt almost as if something in Annie could only live and be expressed through illness, her whole body seemed continually ready to react psychosomatically.

In exploring ego development, Winnicott (1987) points out three developmental phases: integration, personalization and object-relating and matches them with maternal holding, handling and object-presenting. The first two phases concern the baby's sense of continuing in time and space, and a sense of being rooted and contained in the whole of its body, respectively. It seemed that Annie had not been enabled to negotiate the first stage well enough: she went through disintegrated states on the couch, where her sense of self vanished and she existed only through her eyes and outside herself, projected onto the visual pattern of my lace curtains. Winnicott's second stage, the integration of the psyche and soma and the capacity for bodily being, was also underdeveloped and tenuous in Annie: she had, for instance, found that she was unable to meditate, which is based on being still. I think Annie's frequent illnesses developed around the parameter of Winnicott's first and second stages. Perhaps her different illnesses were all one illness in essence, based on, and expressive of, her lack of integration and psychosomatic unity. Each time she fell ill, she was, in a sense—albeit negatively—more united with her body.

The fact that the baby-deer of Annie's initial dream had fully grown antlers, indicates faulty ego development along the lines of Winnicott's ideas: the ego-antlers—the mark of an adult animal—are incongruously rooted in and supported by an immature baby-animal body and infantile self. In its metaphoric aspect, the initial dream then implies Annie's lack of psyche–soma integration, while the symbolic aspect, the soul-induced deepening, would give meaning to this and see it as a struggle for incarnation: becoming real in her physical body and acquiring a capacity for bodily being.

I did not verbalize this second aspect to Annie; instead I talked to her about her baby-self which she brought into sessions through illness. Although often attacked, this gradually trickled into her awareness. I was also conscious of being the pre-relational environment mother, in the form of my continuous presence and response to her, but also in the form of my consulting room and particularly the couch. The importance of this was borne out by her regular attendance and prompt illnesses at breaks.

The delusion

Annie frequently mentioned Tim, the priest she had a crush on, often in admiring tones. At other times, she tried to overcome her feelings by distancing herself from them, or she was disgusted with herself when they were erotic. Her pattern of infatuations had started with a young, friendly obstetrician, when she had had her first baby. His white coat reminded her of her uncle, whom she admired as a young girl. Perhaps the uncle had occupied the void left by her mother's departure and—because of his close association with her birth—became a mother of sorts in Annie's mind. The way Annie talked about Tim gave further clues about the roots of her infatuations or "attachments", as she called them. She described how Tim had looked her fully—and she felt—lovingly in the eyes when they had first met: "The sun shone when he looked at me". There was no "as if" about this: she had experienced herself totally at one with him through the eye-contact. And he always "just knew" what was going on inside her. I thought Annie was looking for the baby's experience of being able to put a smile on mother's face, as well as its experience of successfully projecting into mother, so that she senses what is going on inside and responds. Annie's infatuations were structured around her infantile needs, which had not been sufficiently met by her mother. But this was at odds with her stance of detachment and would have created a conflict. Her baby needs were then defensively eroticized and experienced as sexual, as Masud Khan describes in "Grudge and the Hysteric" (Khan, 1983). Although Annie's feelings for Tim, who was married, appeared triangular and oedipal on the surface, they belonged in essence to the mother–baby dyad. Whenever possible, I drew Annie's attention to these deeper needs and longings, using in particular her baby dreams as a reference, and explaining that these particular needs were more bearable for her if experienced as sexual. Over time, I felt that she gradually took this on board.

The roots of Annie's infatuation were not only infantile, they were also archetypal. Her glowing descriptions of Tim could easily turn into their opposite: he was then seen as manipulative and sadistically controlling to an unbearable degree and she felt completely at his mercy. He embodied the negative, as well as the positive pole of the Great Mother archetype, and could change from one to the other rapidly. In either case, he appeared larger than life to her, and her weak ego-structure meant that she was rather in the grip of this. She often became flustered and overwhelmed in his presence and unable to speak—could not relate to him, which served to keep Tim archetypal rather than human. The link with the metaphoric–descriptive aspect of Annie's initial dream lies, once more, in the fact that her infantile self is depicted as animal/ archetypal and—implicitly—in need of humanizing, just as her feelings for Tim were archetypal and insufficiently humanized.

Annie's transference onto Tim persisted strongly for the first eighteen months and lessened only very gradually thereafter. In relation to me, it served to make her more detached and to keep awareness of her needs out of the therapy. I felt that Annie probably needed this defensive detachment to a degree to enable her to be in therapy at all. However, I was sometimes aware of seeing Tim as sinister and malignant in the countertransference and hoping that he would somehow fade out of her life. Although I refrained from any comments about Tim, Annie then accused me of being against her involvement with him. I thought that these were the workings of an intrusive identification. Annie dealt with the confusion about her contradictory feelings towards Tim partly by projecting the negative pole into me, and then insisted that it originated and stayed there. For a while, the archetypal force of Annie's experience was so overwhelming that it became delusional: she believed that I secretly made tapes of her sessions which I gave to Tim afterwards, so that he always knew what went on inside her and, in this way, was part of her therapy. She told me, she knew about the tapes because Tim's Sunday sermons were—mysteriously—always about the subject of her most recent sessions and my tapes were the only explanation for this. Far from feeling indignant at what would have been a violation of confidentiality on my part, Annie smiled a lot and seemed extraordinarily pleased. I thought that—archetypally motivated—Annie created the parents she needed, albeit magically and via a delusion. The force of the archetypal wish was such that I, countertransferentially, almost sensed Tim's benign but ghostly presence in my consulting room. I found the degree of Annie's delusional conviction and her proportional absence of ego-capacity quite frightening initially, fearing to be overwhelmed with her by an archetypal deluge. When—motivated by fear—I stated that, in fact, I did not secretly tape her sessions, this had no effect on Annie. Later I was able to talk to her about her need for a parental couple who concerned themselves with what went on inside her and I felt that Annie eventually took this in.

Both the metaphoric and the symbolic reading of Annie's initial dream can be applied to the delusion. The symbolic reading is to do with a deepening of experience, with Hillman's soul making, here expressed as an urge to create not only psychic but also real, live parents which lay at the root of the delusion. Its hidden intention then is incarnation. Earlier on, I have linked the metaphoric reading of the dream with developmental theory: Fordham's original self can be assumed to be operating in the delusion. Tim and I were brought together as a parental couple through the archetypal expectation of the original self; this was the more positive, hopeful component of the delusion. It can also be seen as an attempt at Winnicott's making real gone wrong, object seeking and presenting are unmatched, go haywire and the ego is weakened in the process.

More deepening

A change occurred around fifteen months, when transference feelings began to emerge haltingly but more directly. On being charged for some sessions she had missed due to illness, Annie had initially refused to pay my bill with a stubborn and angry air. The next day, she abruptly dumped a cheque on my desk and refused to discuss the matter further. I had felt a bit mean charging her, but had decided to stick with my usual policy and to hold her to our contract. I had been prepared to give her some time, though, to address her feelings and pay me when she was ready. A couple of sessions later, Annie made a cryptic reference to rigid systems and psychotherapy. When I related this to how she saw me, she communicated in clusters of words again: "Like chrome..." she muttered and, a bit later: "not alive". I had to piece together what she meant: for Annie, I was a chrome-like mother, hard, cold and unresponsive. Her anger with this mother was partly directed at herself, as she later self-accusingly mumbled that she was "critical" and "destroying all relationships". Annie's image of me as the chrome-like mother fitted with my countertransference experience of myself over the bill incident. The negative, totally unresponsive mother was now openly constellated between us.

After attending an eco-conference, Annie mentioned with some glee how she had challenged a panel of scientists when questioning them about the practical use of their findings. She had been "shaking them into life", she said. I linked this with her challenging a chrome-like me. She agreed there was a link. Haltingly, she added that I never talked about myself to her and was "only reflective, like chrome". She was not sure, if I was real. Totally coherent now, she told me I kept far too few personal things in my consulting room, but perhaps this was intentional. I replied that I felt she wanted to shake me up like the scientist, so that she could then perhaps experience me as warm and real. In the countertransference, I thought she was making me understand that she needed a slightly different and more flexible kind of response from me. With regard to the symbolic aspect of Annie's initial dream, a deepening of relating was taking place between us, as her sessions became alive with angry feeling and challenge which in turn got me to respond more actively.

When Annie learned that her father—at ninety-four—had cancer, she reacted with her characteristic detachment, claiming to be completely unaffected. Subsequent visits brought psychosomatic responses: heart-pain and indigestion. Once more, Annie's feeling experience could not be processed and became physical instead. In the following weeks, she began to relate a sense of depression which often quite overwhelmed her. She saw this as random at first, and attributed it to "getting out of bed on the wrong foot". She also sought ways of getting rid of it through activity. As all this was explored in sessions, Annie gradually came into contact with a deep sense of pain within, although she could not bear to stay in touch with it for very long. I felt that this pain—clothed in depression—signified the emergence of the deepest, most split-off part of Annie's inner self, (Guntrip, 1968). I worked to find ways of making it bearable for her to keep a connection with it. Finally one day, in a softened atmosphere, I was able to say that the pain, at a deeper level, lived within her all the time, but it was hard to be aware of this. She nodded and called it her "soggy pool". Later she alternated between acknowledging its existence and cutting herself off from it while attacking me for "going on too much about feelings".

The process of deepening, symbolized by the soul-deer of Annie's dream continued. Here Annie struggled with the deepening of inner experience, depression leading to feelings of pain which then became real for her. As a consequence, the glass wall image had almost gone from my mind and my countertransference experience. It was as if she had broken through it with her earlier angry challenge and further melted it by connecting with her pain. Further cycles of anger and pain were to follow. Annie's first grandchild, a boy, was born with Annie present at the birth. This had me quite worried, as I was mindful of Annie's psychotic episodes with giving birth to each of her children. However, Annie managed by using a spiritualized detachment. The birth became a spiritual rather than an emotional experience, the latter being projected into me and surfacing as my anxious concern about her. Then Annie wanted to experiment with different uses of the couch. She put a big cushion behind her back and snuggled into it, telling me it was like leaning into a pregnant belly. I felt that I was the pre-relational environment mother again, and the couch an extension of my body. A dream about an empty supermarket heralded more angry challenge: was I real? Did she bore me? She would like to see me chop a cabbage (prepare nourishment for her). I clearly had become the empty breast, providing no sustenance, of the super-market dream. I felt that I was being pulled and tugged at by Annie's angry efforts to get the breast to feed her. Again I talked to her about feeling that I was remote and about wanting to make me respond and feel real to her. I had thought for a while about how I could be more flexible. Now I experimented with becoming more active and giving her my spontaneous ideas—though not in a confessional way—rather than thought-out interpretations. Annie took to this, becoming more verbal and lively herself. My remarks were less attacked and nullified, and her sessions began to feel more alive. She was mostly coherent too, and now only used scrambled communication in extreme situations or after holidays. Annie's initial dream—in its symbolic aspect—can be understood as underlying and structuring this process.

Detachment prevailed as Annie learned of her father's death. She could not mourn him, wearing his hat and his trousers for sessions instead. Her depression resurfaced after visiting her mother and sister to help with settling mother's affairs. Without consulting Annie, they had decided that mother would move abroad to where Pam lived who could then look after her. Annie stated that she felt relieved about her mother's move, while I felt it repeated mother's initial abandonment of her. Towards the end of the two-year period, Annie had another dream:

> Her daughter's baby-son was screaming with pain because he had dislocated his arm. Annie knew how to rectify this and worked to put the arm back in but did not succeed. Then the baby became smaller and—to Annie's horror—turned into an inhuman thing that was fading away.

We spoke about the use of arms in reaching out and making contact. I said that perhaps there was a part of Annie that had dislocated its arm in an effort to hang on to mother at eleven months and was still screaming in pain. Annie was then able to tell me that she felt a dead and empty space inside her, where the relationship with mother should be.

I thought that this final dream summed up Annie's pathology and clearly depicted her struggle with incarnating. This was organized around her conflict between being human and in pain, or employing splitting defences which also killed off her humanity and made her into the inhuman thing of her dream. Accordingly, Annie had gone through cycles of being in touch with anger and pain, interspersed with cycles of detachment and spiritual aloofness. Annie's initial dream, in its metaphorical aspect, was descriptive of the developmental roots of this conflict, while the symbolic aspect was motivating, structuring and giving meaning to the way this conflict was increasingly played out between Annie and me through the medium of transference and countertransference. In linking the first and the last dream of the two-year period, it could be said that the deer—on the one hand divine, life-giving soul, on the other inhuman, undeveloped infant—had metamorphosed into a human infant in pain. The dichotomy between human and inhuman remains of necessity, though, as the struggle to incarnate continues.

Conclusion

In this paper, I have given an account of my work with a borderline patient, who could only make limited use of interpretation. To begin with, Annie used words—mine as well as hers—to distance and confuse, and she communicated mainly through projective identi-fication or intrusive identification. I have outlined what I describe as a process of incarnation, involving both my patient and the use she made of me and the growing transference-relationship. This process had different aspects, including ego-development, psyche–soma integration and relatedness to the world within and without. I have drawn on different developmental theories to bring these aspects into view and provide some explanation for clinical phenomena.

In addition, Annie's initial dream has been employed to give an underlying structure to this chapter. This dream had puzzled me greatly to begin with, but, by the end of the two years, it had become truly meaningful. It has been my special interest, to approach the dream from a reductive and a synthetic point of view, as both perspectives have informed my work with Annie. From a reductive perspective, the dream implicitly pinpoints the lack of development, the lack of a "humanizing other"—be it the container or the environment mother—and the unintegrated, unrelated inner structure this resulted in. It left Annie insufficiently human, in need of becoming human. Her conscious values, at the beginning of therapy, were all superhuman ones, centring around a rigidly detached spirituality. The synthetic aspect of the deer dream—the deer symbolizing soul—provided an all important counterbalance to Annie's spiritualization of life. If soul dialectically opposes and compliments spirit, then the deer-soul was the living symbol, the archetypal force behind and within Annie's process of incarnation, that had lain dormant in the archetypal storehouse and, with Annie's starting therapy, had gained a "workshop", a place to go and fashion life. The symbolic aspect of the dream thus both motivated and facilitated her process of becoming human, which was at the heart of our work. As a metaphor, Annie's dream yielded much useful explanation and meaning in a descriptive and therefore limited way, while as a symbol it pointed towards the miraculously unlimited creative potential of the human psyche. This I see as Annie's gift to me and I am grateful for it.

References

Bion, W. R. (1962a). A theory of thinking. *International Journal of Psycho-Analysis*, 43: 306–310.

Bion, W. R. (1962b). *Learning from Experience*. London: Heinemann.

Fordham, M. (1980). The emergence of child analysis. *Journal of Analytical Psychology*, 25: 311–324.

Guntrip, H. (1968). *Schizoid Phenomena, Object Relations and the Self*. London: Hogarth.

Hillman, J. (1975). *Re-Visioning Psychology*. New York: Harper & Row.

Holmes, J. (1993). *John Bowlby & Attachment Theory*. London: Routledge.

Khan, M. M. R. (1983). *Hidden Selves. Between Theory and Practice in Psychoanalysis*. New York: International University Press.

Meltzer, D. (1986). *Studies in Extended Metapsychology: Clinical Applications of Bion's Ideas*. Perthshire, Scotland: Clunie Press.

Ogden, T. H. (1979). On projective identification. *International Journal of Psycho-Analysis*, 60: 357–373.

Winnicott, D. W. (1971). *Therapeutic Consultations in Child Psychiatry.* London: Hogarth.

Winnicott, D. W. (1987). *Through Paediatrics to Psychoanalysis.* London: Hogarth.

CHAPTER THREE

The search for emotional truth in a perverse scenario dominated by the trickster[1]

Marisa Dillon Weston

From feelings in the countertransference to the narrative of a life

What struck me most from the very beginning of my work with S. were the intense, uncomfortable feelings he seemed to trigger in me. This reaction started even before I met him. He rang me to arrange an appointment. He was friendly and chatty and went into all sorts of details about practical issues. I felt overwhelmed by the flood of speech coming my way, which seemed to have no self-containment. I also felt that there was something inappropriately seductive in his friendliness and this irritated me. I had to make quite an effort not to be curt and openly hostile. As I put the phone down I felt drained and confused. Why did I feel so emotionally entangled? Thinking of my first reaction later on, I thought that the trickster psychology was already at work.

When I met him in person, at the first session, he seemed pleasant, easygoing, suave in an effeminate fashion. He was dressed casually, but with great care and he spoke softly, choosing his words and gazing at me in a way which felt both flattering and possessive. The words "ensnaring glance" came to my mind and my discomfort grew. For the first time I asked myself a question which I would repeat endlessly in the months ahead and which rose from my perception of the defensiveness under the seductiveness. I asked myself "Where is he hiding? Where is he?" And yet somehow I realized that before I could even begin to answer these questions I would need to become familiar with what Jung calls "island fortresses from which the neurotic tries to ward off the octopus". According to Jung, (C.W., 16, para. 374) "the patient needs an island and would be lost without it. It serves as a refuge for his consciousness and as the last stronghold against the threatening embrace of the unconscious". Were my feelings a guide to S.'s unconscious as well as a reaction to his defences? Was my frustration at being deprived of real contact with him linked to his frustration? These were my thoughts as I was listening to his empty talk. Then suddenly his manner of speech changed, he looked at me in a different, freer sort of way and he said "Why is it that you therapists are so cold?" I was stunned. Suddenly the layers of defensiveness had been cast off and I was exposed to a genuine feeling, straight from his unconscious. Before I had been able to collect myself, he had retreated again to his "island fortress", denying his moment of truth. With this moment of truth I thought that he had expressed his longing for warmth together with his conviction that no warmth would be forthcoming and yet, if the question had been formulated, the negative expectation could not be total. "Why is it that you therapists are so cold?" was perhaps a rhetorical question, but it invited a reaction, it opened up the possibility of genuine contact and it expressed a whole range of feelings waiting to be deciphered. So I referred back to that question and I said "You seem to be wondering what kind of a presence I might be for you. Will I be a cold, remote presence, or will I be emotionally available to you?" Quickly he cut me off, almost in mid-sentence. Having glanced at his watch he said "We have got to come to a close now" and immediately after, he added "I know that I am not supposed to say that". I felt angry and confused. What was he playing at? It seemed as if he had to try and outwit me at all costs, in order to be ahead of me and forever elusive.

With these thoughts and feelings I listened to his story. As I listened I felt that the reaction he had triggered in me had already begun to tell me in a different, but no less effective way, that his had been a history of abandonments and losses and humiliation. Perhaps playing tricks was the only strategy he knew which allowed him to survive.

Personal History

S. was born and brought up in Kenya of Asian parents. His father ran some sort of financial business and the family had money and status. S. was the second of two boys, his brother A. being seven years his senior. S.'s family lived with father's brother and his family, which consisted of his wife and five daughters.

At birth S. needed special medical attention and so he was kept in hospital for a longer period than usual while his mother went back home. This was the first traumatic separation S. was to experience in the course of his life. At the time of his birth, his father was away in London and he only saw his son when he was six weeks old, but in spite of this, the two of them became strongly attached, indeed inseparable. When S. was six months old, he developed a problem with his kidneys and his doctor suggested that he should be taken to London for treatment. He was taken by his mother.

The separation from his father was traumatic. S. did not want to let go of father when the time came to say good-bye and in the end father was allowed on to the plane to help calm the little boy down. In other words S. was tricked into believing that his father would accompany him. He was tricked into giving up his fight not to be separated from his father and so he was defeated. The little boy psyche must have registered this deep blow, and experienced the confusion of the cruel deception. In London, the doctors found nothing seriously wrong and mother and son could easily have gone back, but mother stayed in London for six months, visiting relatives and friends. This development revealed another trick: S.'s health had been only a pretext to justify a separation between the parents. Nothing was what it seemed. When finally they returned. S. would have nothing to do with his father. In his own words he had become "mother's boy".

In order to be mother's boy, S. had to be nice, obedient and properly trained. S. personally remembered very little of his childhood, but he knew that it had been difficult for him to become toilet trained and he often wetted himself. Whenever this happened mother would become extremely angry and hit him. His older brother A. used to intervene vigorously on his behalf and shield him against mother's attacks. S. tried to pacify his angry mother by cancelling out his messy sides. Not only did he become toilet trained, but he cultivated an interest for feminine pursuits, he loved shopping with his mother, he loved women's clothes and jewellery and he learnt to dance, dressed as a girl and performed in front of family and friends. A. was always tough and combative, whereas from a very early age S. became the delicate, sensitive and weak one, who let mother control him. The scene was already set for him to become homosexual. In describing the mother of the homosexual to be, Stoller (1978, p. 129) writes that she is "a woman who hates males". The son of such a mother learns "by the system of reward and punishment she has set up, that behaviour she considers masculine will be punished but that soft, graceful, passive, 'sweet' behaviour will please her". So the boy tries to "suppress evidence of masculinity" and he learns to hide anger. "The disguise is in the effeminacy, where, in his mimicry, he subtly adds anger to his gentle, unmasculine appearance" (Stoller, 1978, p. 129).

When S. was nine, his father, who had lent a great deal of money to the Kenyan government, was told that he would not be repaid for many years to come. As a consequence, his business collapsed and he decided to move to London with his family and to try and start a business there. S. lost his familiar environment, half of his family, his school, his friends, the Asian community, his status and his identity. The family went to live in a middle class, mostly white area. S. and his brother were the only two non-white children in the school and S. remembers being teased endlessly because he was Asian and because he was effeminate. In his smiling, impersonal manner S. told me how tough his first months in England had been and how his brother always defended him until their paths parted. A., the tough one, was sent to a state school whereas S., deemed unsuitable for that environment, was sent to private schools. He was academically gifted. He passed eight "O" levels and had started his "A" levels when he became infatuated with Richard, a boy in his class, and then he lost all interest in his work. Richard was white, tall, blond, and athletic.

His father was a rich and respectable English establishment figure and they had an upper class type of family life, which must have seemed like a fairy tale to the little boy from an ethnic minority whose family life was crumbling.

At this time S.'s father had lost any hope of starting a business and he was going through a deep depression. For seven years he led the life of a recluse, not even bothering to get dressed, listening obsessively to Asian popular music, cut off from the world and from his family, a ghost of a man.

As I pictured S.'s father in his seven years of depression and penury, themes from the Bible and from classical literature echoed through my mind as well as memories from my visit to Asia and from what I knew of the history of that country. I felt that what happened to S.'s father expressed not only something of the man's individual and family history, but also a deeper and wider fatalism which belonged to his culture. Within such fatalism, disasters happened, years of abundance were followed by years of famine and man's will was powerless. It was all in the hands of the "gods" or of the colonizing forces, or of the higher caste. The only way to deal with it, as an individual, was to be resigned. I realized that the burden on my patient's shoulders went beyond what his personal history had impressed on his unconscious. Beyond that was the unconscious belonging to his culture which is in itself a complicated conglomerate of many cultures with different languages and histories and religions and all this lay upon the background of the collective unconscious.

As his father yielded to the power of the archetypes and withdrew from the reality of those around him, S. tried to drown any consciousness of his second loss of his father in a fused state with an idealized self represented by Richard, a hero figure, with which he hoped to be able to identify. Engrossed with Richard, he scraped through his "A" levels, stayed on at school for another year and took the exams again, but with the same results. He decided that he could not apply for university and found employment as a clerk. S. continued living at home with his parents until he was twenty-six. By then he had a job as office manager with a small company selling baseball caps.

At twenty-six S. left the job in London when his brother offered him work in Morocco where he had a business. S. felt that this was his chance to leave home, although he did not realize that he was exchanging one type of dependency for another. A. was another hero figure although he was, in his excesses, almost the caricature of the hero. S. was totally dependent on his brother who treated him with generous condescension giving him no proper salary, but all the money and privileges he wanted. His brother led a princely life and was well known; he was extravagant, profligate and a great womanizer. S. was very much A.'s little brother. When A.'s business began to collapse, as super-heroes' dreams inevitably do because they are not tempered by the mediating influence of humanity, S. was caught in the middle. He lost his work and his savings.

At twenty-eight S. was back in London without a job. He visited his parents who had gone to live in Asia and then came back to London where he lived with his brother and was able to go back to his old firm in a less prestigious position. At the same time he was given, by his brother, a flat in central London where he could live rent free. It was not clear to S. to whom this flat belonged, but A. promised it to him. His brother's promise seemed rather unsubstantial if not a downright trick and S.'s life was once again rootless and devoid of any secure attachments. This is the time when I first met him.

Beautiful images as aesthetic disguises for primitive sexuality

S. told me the story of his life in an impersonal, unemotional kind of way as if all the feelings attached to these events had been cast off and all that was left was an empty shell. The shell however had been polished to its utmost sheen and it was being used to reflect and project a sequence of beautiful images, with which he had carefully woven the texture of his "false self" (Winnicott, 1985, pp. 140–152).

"I am extremely lucky", S. would regularly say, "I have a nice flat in Knightsbridge, a job, a boss who loves me, lots of friends, an interesting, cosmopolitan life and now I even have psychotherapy three times a week". Psychotherapy had become a social asset, to be paraded in front of others as a sign of privilege. In the countertransference I felt consistently cheated and infantilized, caught in the web of his make-believe strategy, wanting at times to break through the illusion and get hold of the horrors behind the screen and at the same time instinctively aware of his fragility and of the need to respect the defences surrounding what Steiner calls "psychic retreats". In Steiner's view (1993, p. I): "Perhaps the most difficult type of retreat is that in which a false type of contact is offered and the analyst is invited to engage in ways which seem superficial, dishonest, or perverse".

Style and beauty seemed to be major reference points for S. Experiences had to be aesthetically pleasing and he made every effort to ensure that they were. When he went out to eat it was not just to any restaurant, it was to a nice or an extremely nice one; on business trips, he carefully selected where he would be staying, always choosing on the basis of beauty and class rather than convenience. He often told me about the way he had arranged his flat, what colours he had chosen, what objects were around and it was clear to me that he tried to create an aesthetically pleasing environment.

I wondered to what degree this concern for a polished frame was a defence against something which he perceived to be ugly. primitive and violent in his psyche and to what degree it was a sign of his creativity. His concern for beauty seemed to me in strong contrast with the rawness of his sexual fantasies and behaviour which often consisted of brutal encounters and mutual, perverse abuse. In her book on *Creativity and Perversion*, Chasseguet-Smirgel (1985) gives a psycho-analytic view of this contrast when she writes about a pre-genital, anal level of sexuality, typical of the man who was seduced by his mother into believing that he was an adequate sexual partner for her and could take the place of his father. According to this writer, the boy in this position, instead of choosing "the long path which leads the subject to the Oedipus Complex and genitality", will choose "the short path" (p. 29) which perpetuates fusion with mother, ensures instant gratification, but leaves him feeling stuck at a pregenital level of sexuality and therefore unfulfilled. Unable to idealize Father and the genital sexuality he represents, such a man idealizes instincts and part-objects from the anal stage to convince himself and others of their superiority. She adds that "This accounts for the pervert's obvious affinities for art and beauty; the pervert is often an aesthete". She distinguishes between aestheticism and creation "Idealisation tends more towards aestheticism than creation, and when creation nevertheless develops, it often bears the stamp of aestheticism" (p. 92). Chasseguet-Smirgel understands the tendency to idealize the environment as an attempt at turning everything which surrounds the ego into a mirror. "This mirror must be refined, and in exquisite taste in order to disguise anality, covering it with a thousand glittering jewels" (p. 95).

Jewels were important in S.'s imagination. He told me early on in the therapy that he would like to buy his mother some good jewels, with real pearls and real diamonds. Whenever he talked about women he knew, he would include in his description what kind of Jewels they wore or failed to wear. He said that he was of a particular sect that love "all that glitters" and they have a reputation for being rather materialistic and *nouveau riche*. In the sessions with me S. was trying to turn therapy into an aesthetic experience, where we would gracefully play-act our roles and create a pleasing fantasy world.

However, his eye for shapes and colour could also be used towards creativity.

I realized this when he told me about his "painting". When he was living with his brother he suddenly started painting. He just bought brushes and paint found himself covering one large canvas after another in abstract patterns of colour. Unexpectedly he gained some recognition. Local gallery owners sold some of his work and commissioned him. He accepted the commissions, but lost the inspiration and soon stopped painting. I felt that there had been a creative urge in his spontaneous turning to painting, but this had been spoilt when the paintings had to be on show and had to please others. In a way this was a sign of genuineness. He had not wanted to paint for others, for effect, so to speak. However he had allowed others to spoil something which was his and could express something important for him.

What his painting indicated to me was an ability to symbolize and symbols are at the centre of psychic development and particularly so within a Jungian perspective. In his essay "The transcendent function", Jung (1916) wrote about the formation of symbols and their value in acting as a bridge between conscious and unconscious. In S.'s case, I had felt from the beginning of our work together particularly bereft of symbols as, for the first six months or so, he never brought a dream and very rarely a day-dream.

S. found it difficult to talk about his painting. He said he had enjoyed it at the time but it had led him nowhere, another proof of his inertia, another failure. His pictures were "just blobs on canvas". I felt that those pictures had been an expression of a genuine core of the self, the "blobs" being fragments of his personal unconscious on the backcloth of the collective unconscious. It seemed to me that those "blobs" were clusters of painful feelings and brought with them an awareness of emptiness, fragmentation and possible annihilation. That is why S. tried so hard to bury them behind the beautiful, well-formed images with which he presented himself to the world. He constantly needed to see a reflection of those well-formed images in other people's eyes to try and avoid knowing their illusory nature. At the same time, he was searching for some confirmation that others existed and would confirm his own existence by becoming the "mirroring mother" (Kohut, 1977) who had to a great extent been lacking in his early life.

S. seemed to need a constant audience. This led to a hectic social life; if he was alone, he was on the phone. In the sessions with me he tried to get me to perform the role of an approving audience. He referred to me by my name over and over again, he used expressions like "do you agree?", "as we have said", "don't you think?", all the time. He also had a way, whenever he made a statement, of looking at me tentatively as if to check whether I approved. There was something controlling in his attitude towards me, but I also sensed that he needed to keep my presence alive and to make me respond to him as a way to keep himself alive. I thought he could not be alone. It was almost as if being alone threatened his psychic survival. In his paper "The capacity to be alone", Winnicott (1958) looks at such capacity as "one of the most important signs of maturity in emotional development" and sees it as stemming from the experience of "being alone, as an infant and small child, in the presence of mother". He continues, "In the course of time the individual introjects the ego-supportive mother and in this way becomes able to be alone without frequent references to mother or mother symbol" (pp. 30, 32). In his anxious references to me. S. was showing me that he had never been sufficiently sure that someone was truly available, in the sense that "an attachment figure is both accessible and responsive" (Bowlby, 1973). In object-relations theory terms, S. had internalized unreliable objects on whose presence he could not count and whose response to his needs, was dictated by "misattunements" (Stern, 1985), "a lack of fit" (Balint, 1979) and "deprivation in the area of the sustaining matrix of empathy" (Kohut, 1977, p. 188). This resulted in an early "narcissistic injury" in Kohut's terms, which lay hidden in S.'s unconscious together with the feelings of terror and anger derived from it.

On the surface were the beautiful images and the soothing empty words behind which he hid his depleted, hungry and murderous self.

Perverse defences

In spite of S.'s continuous effort to turn his life and his therapy into an aesthetic experience I often felt as if, in his transference to me, he was throwing shit on to me, and yet he was trying to seduce me at the same time with the honeyed forms of his delivery. In the countertransference, I often felt driven by frustration to feeling nasty and aggressive, wanting to shake him out of all his tricks. Not only was I being shitted upon, but he seemed to gain a sense of triumph from it. These elements, put together with what I learnt from listening to him about the way in which he related to people, made me think that he had assembled a powerful perverse mechanism as part of his defences.

I often had the impression when I was with S. that I did not exist for him as a separate person. Often, when I said something, he would say something back which was like a repetitive echo. On one occasion he put words to my feeling when he said "I never think of you as a person, you are just my therapist". Everything was related back to himself, separateness was denied. Other people were just instruments in his hands. This attitude was particularly evident in the case of his boss, John. On the surface S. liked John and was grateful to him and yet he also resented him and tried to extract favours from him. In his relationship with Maria who was his tenant, one minute he would be declaring his deepest love for her and the next minute he would be feeling used by her. With me, he put off paying me until the last possible moment and then only if I reminded him. Others and their needs did not seem to exist for him, others were only potential robbers of what he needed and wanted. When, later in the therapy, he started remembering his dreams, the "robber" often appeared in them, leaving him in a state of terror.

However S. seemed to apply the same "de-humanisation" (Cooper, 1991) process to himself as he did to others. He did not seem to have a sense of himself as a separate person or as a whole person. "Dehumanisation is the ultimate strategy against the fears of human qualities—it protects against the vulnerability of loving, against the possibility of human unpredictability, and against the sense of powerlessness and passivity in comparison to other humans". In Cooper's (1991) words the core trauma is "the experience of terrifying passivity in relation to the preoedipal mother perceived as dangerously malignant, malicious and all-powerful, arousing sensations of awe and the uncanny" (p. 23). According to Cooper the perverse defence makes use of three key unconscious fantasies: the first denies the power of the mother, the second denies the pain inflicted by the mother, the third turns the pain of being controlled into pleasure. S. resorted to these defences all the time both in his life and in the therapy. He denied my separateness and therefore my existence, he deadened himself so he would not feel, and he set up situations where he engineered his own powerlessness and then derived pleasure from it.

This last scenario emerged very clearly in his sexual encounters. He was attracted to strong men who dominated him, devalued him and usually disposed of him in a brutal way. In telling me about these encounters he stressed the violence inflicted on him. but he remained emotionally detached from it. I felt and said that he might be attempting to reproduce the sado–masochistic interaction in the consulting room, by trying to turn me into a silent accomplice as a horrified spectator or a perverse voyeur.

Although he labelled himself homosexual, in the past he had had sexual relationships with women and he still does occasionally although he does not desire women. In his own words "they just don't make my heart go boom, boom". They seemed to desire him and he "just went along". He continuously thought about men and became totally absorbed with them or parts of them. He seemed particularly fascinated with men's hands. He wanted to be in their hands, totally passive and at their mercy. In his fantasies as well as in his real sexual encounters with men he was always the passive one. This behaviour, which put him in the role of the victim, seemed to be re-creating the scenario of his early childhood, but with one major difference. As a child he was totally powerless in the hands of his powerful mother. Now he stage-managed his humiliation and derived sexual pleasure from it. In a perverse way he was in control.

As the therapy progressed S. started to bring dreams. Two dreams he had at the beginning of the second year reflected the perverse defences and early humiliating experiences.

In the first dream S. woke up one morning expecting mother to be there for him, waiting on him. hand and foot, and ready to cook his breakfast. But mother was not there. When later she came back S. insulted her and reduced her to tears by shouting at her that she was not fit to be a mother.

In this dream S. demands from mother to he treated like a child, to be "spoon-fed" and reduced to a state of total dependency and yet at the same time he takes on a controlling position and uses it to take his revenge on her.

In the second dream S. was walking across Leicester Square trying to get home where two women friends were waiting for him. He had invited them to stay out of politeness but now he was feeling imposed upon. He stopped to go to a men's loo where he saw three Asian men having a pee. They were strong, "macho" men, dressed in black leather and he realized that there was some sexual interaction taking place between them and reassured them that they did not need to stop, in fact he encouraged them to continue so he could watch. The men did as they were told and S. went up to them and started rubbing their thighs and their crotches, deriving excitement from it. While this was taking place the two women friends he had invited were in a room just outside the toilet, no longer flattered by S.'s compliant niceness, but almost forced into the role of spectators of his more brutal side. In the second part of the dream, S. was back in Leicester Square. In front of a pub he saw two unknown women, one of whom suddenly collapsed on to the pavement saying she was going to faint. As well as her friend there were several people watching, including two policemen and nobody offered to help, in fact the two policemen were just "smirking", apparently drawing pleasure from the woman's helplessness. S. himself stood there without lifting a finger. He thought to himself "If she faints, she'll pee, let's watch her pee". This in fact happened, the woman fainted and then peed and then S. realized that she was a "hooker" and he thought "She's just a hooker, that's why she has no value in the eyes of the police".

In this dream S. is the onlooker, a voyeur, watching men and women pee and collapse and engage in mechanical sexual interactions. Both in this and other dreams he seems particularly fascinated with the act of peeing, and I wonder whether this amounts to a "revisiting" the original place/experience of his shame when mother humiliated him for peeing in his pants.

In both dreams S. gets his control by cheating. In the first dream he cheats mother by using her own sense of duty against her. In the second dream, he is the manipulative *voyeur*, who exercises control and extracts pleasure in secret, mainly through looking. Writing about a case of voyeurism, Hume (1996) writes that the intention of the voyeur may be "to harm and triumph over another. For example, looking can become sexually exciting if the voyeur believes he is acting forcibly upon an unwilling woman". Hume refers to Strachey, according to whom "the person looking makes an onslaught with his eye upon the world in order to devour it, and to render the object paralysed and defenceless" (p. 162). In his dream S. watches men and women in a state of uncontainment and collapse, without a will of their own, sneered at or hiding from the public eye, "the dregs of society". S. is able to identify with them and control them at the same time and he draws sexual pleasure from this double role.

The perversion in the consulting room: tricking me into beating him

With me there had been several incidents where I felt skillfully set up to beat him with a stick so to speak: having tricked me into putting him in the victim position he seemed to gain some sort of elation from my bewilderment. There was one particular occasion when he was talking to me about his job and he started talking in a jocular way about the baseball caps he was in charge of selling. He was very funny and I laughed. I thought I was laughing "with" him, but he took it as if I was laughing "at" him and he was deeply hurt although he said nothing at the time. When he later talked about this event, I thought of Freud's (1955) paper, "A child is being beaten: a contribution to the study of the origin of sexual perversions", in which Freud stresses how "beating fantasies" play an important part in perverse psychopathology. This concept has been developed in more recent studies of perversions which stress how "Most males with beating fantasies are likely to maintain an identification with a castrated mother" and a more hidden "identification with, and a vengeful fury toward, the phallic mother" (Rosen, 1979, p. 44).

In the language of the "core complex" theories (Glasser, M. in Rosen, 1979, p. 278) this is the area where subjugation and control, pleasure and pain, mix in a rigid pattern which promises an escape from the engulfing mother while creating an addictive bond with her which both protects her and prevents her from ever leaving. So the pain one receives or inflicts in perverse behaviours defends against the pain of separation and loss but does so at a cost, because:

> in our real psychic economy, it nothing is ever permanently lost, then nothing can ever truly be gained. For the price the sadomasochist pays by denying castration, loss, and death is to remain forever frozen into a lifeless stereotype which he is doomed to repeat". This way being requires the suppression of real emotionality. [Bach, 1991, p. 87]

In the grip of the archetypes

Within a Jungian perspective. S.'s psychopathology could be described by referring to the archetypes by which he seemed possessed, in particular that of the victim and that of the "trickster" which allowed him to turn from "victim" to "dragon" and back again in an orgy of adaptability and rapidity which left him dizzy with excitement and unawareness.

The trickster is extremely difficult to define because of "his powers as a shape-shifter" (Jung, C.W., 9(i), paras. 456–488). The trickster was associated by Jung with the alchemical figure ot

Mercurius with "his dual nature, half animal, halt divine, (*ibid.*). Jung sees in the trickster a "collective shadow figure" with a very primitive level of consciousness which, however, is in motion and is capable of achieving higher awareness and can even turn into a "saviour-like figure". He is both human and subhuman and superhuman, a bestial and divine being, whose chief and most alarming characteristics is unconsciousness" (*ibid.*). "He is so unconscious of himself that his body is not a unit, and his two hands fight each other" (*ibid.*). "Even his sex is optional despite its phallic qualities..." (*ibid.*). According to Jung, there are many versions of the trickster belonging to different periods and different cultures.

The trickster which seemed to be dominating S.'s unconscious was certainly a "shape shifter". S. could turn into many different shapes according to the people he was with. This behaviour seemed to be always dictated by a wish to manipulate so he could extract some gain for himself. He would do everything he could to be liked and trusted and then when the moment seemed right, he would become demanding and reveal his all consuming greed. At that point, if the person involved reacted with disdain, he would quickly retreat and take on the loving disguise once again. He was as much taken in by the deception as others were. When he proffered love, he thought it was real and when others were hurt by his sudden *volte face*, he could not understand why. He was telling himself beautiful lies about himself in the same way in which he told others. It was only in the course of his therapy that he began to see through the lies and acknowledge that he did not know who he was.

I commented that he seemed to feel that he had no rights. Everything had to be obtained through calculated operations which made it impossible for him ever to relax or be off guard. How exhausting for him never to be able to be spontaneous! He seemed to have learnt that lesson particularly from mother who appeared extremely calculating, telling S. "Never say no to anything, you never know what it might bring"; or "Play your cards well in life and you'll be rewarded".

However, beyond mother was the family and the culture. It is a culture where the individual wishes are often sacrificed to the family wishes as the practice of arranged marriages proves and where the servant/master psychology has been particularly strong especially *vis-à-vis* the colonial masters. When S. became more aware and began to fight towards autonomy and individuation he came up against, in those around him, this culture of servility and trickery and lip service being paid at all cost to appearances. Often his individual struggle seemed doomed to fail because the culture around him appeared so heavily biased against any form of emotional truth.

The trickster is a perfect presence in a sado–masochistic psychopathology, helping with role changes between victim and persecutor and with secretiveness. In his paper, "The archetypal themes in Uccello's painting", Gee (1995) sees the relationship of the dragon and the innocent maiden as a "good portrait of the nature of sadomasochism" because:

> the maid with her helplessness and the dragon with its sadistic power have all they need for an exciting and everlasting trap.
>
> The more innocent the maid tries to be, the greater is the danger of the dragon. When such a strong specialisation occurs then we see a relationship that can never come to an end. because no child can separate without having first integrated their capacity to be angry as part of their strength and therefore enabling aggression. [p. 40]

A number of people were seen as dragons by S., among them Maria, his tenant, who, spending more and more time with her boyfriend, was less available to him. S. felt she had discarded him. In his view, his parents too conspired against him, his father by never making himself available to him and his mother for being so self-centred, expecting letters and telephone calls and presents from him. but giving very little in exchange. His brother too made use of him, asking him for help when he was down and forgetting him when his own life took off.

The anger S. found so difficult to acknowledge, seemed to explode at times in the consulting room. I was stunned by the vitriolic viciousness behind some of his most unguarded comments. Of Maria who had just got engaged he said, "She got what she wanted, she swung her bottom and hooked her fish". Of girls in general: "These girls know what they want and everybody else can go and fuck themselves". Of his mother: "She's no great beauty and has no finesse, just like the fake pearls she wears". Of his parents: "They live in a cocoon of suburban nothingness". Of me: "You are just a middle aged woman, living in a suburb". Of Maria's fiancé: "He thinks he can rule the roost because he went to Harrow, but he's just a fucking, boring cold fish".

Towards emotional contact

These remarks betrayed an intense hostility which seemed to stem from envy. The hostility was hidden behind the contempt. He could not own his aggression for fear of retaliation which would lead to punishment and rejection. Yet, when his hostility surfaced, I felt that he became much more real and it seemed possible for us to make genuine contact. So I drew his attention to the anger expressed and to the authenticity which came with it. I said that he might be afraid of punishment coming from me if he allowed me to see his resentment and his envy and yet those feelings are present in every human being and it is all right to experience them. If we do not acknowledge them they tend to dominate us, but if we can become aware of them and accept them. they become freeing and help us towards creativity because where there is destructiveness there is creativity. Perhaps as a child he had been given the message that he could not be "bad", he had to he good and pleasant rather than being free to be himself, warts and all. He listened very intently and yet he seemed at the same time to he following an internal thread as if what I was saying had stirred something powerful inside himself, but he did not know what it was and he was battling to get hold of it. Then he was quiet for a few seconds, totally quiet and still, but immensely focused as if in his search he had come upon something. Then he spoke. He said there was a photograph of himself as a baby. He was in his pram, in the middle of the courtyard of their African house, he was clutching a toy tiger in his hands and he looked very serious. As he grew up he had looked at this photograph and had felt both enormously sad and angry. He had thought "How could they leave me all alone with a tiger?" He said that to this day he cannot look at that picture without feeling overwhelmed by a sense of abandonment, fury and terror.

I felt that I was hearing his real voice as never before and it moved me deeply. I thought and said that it brought to me the anguish of the child who makes no impact on those around him so that his emerging self gets no responsiveness and he finds himself alone with his fears, the tiger, threatening him with the disintegration of his very fragile, incipient self. I said I thought that the tiger also represented his "dragon" mother in whose hands he felt powerless, unprotected as he was by father. He looked at me with a mixture of total astonishment and gratitude. Something which could appear irrelevant, but was of fundamental importance to him, had been understood and valued by me. We had visited together the "place" of his abandonment; that photo was like a symbol for all his experiences of abandonment and deceptions. They had left him alone with a terrifying tiger, but tried to trick him into believing that it was only a toy.

It was the end of the session and I wondered how he would feel walking away from me with that experience of deep closeness. Would it frighten him by re-awakening deeply embedded fears of abandonment and annihilation? Would he be able to bear those fears or would he return time and time again to the relative safety of sado–masochistic interactions?

As we moved towards the Christmas break at the start of his second year in therapy, S. seemed better able to tolerate difficult feelings by expressing them rather than trying to dispose of them. When he resorted to "acting out" behaviour, he seemed to tire of it quickly as if the old buzz had waned and he seemed able to bring his sadness to me rather than blow it away.

But however, at about the same time, S. experienced a series of difficult losses. Maria, his tenant, moved out of his flat; his brother disappeared for many weeks: John, his boss, announced that within six months he would close the company, leaving S. jobless; Gianni, an Italian man with whom S. had developed an intense friendship, went back to his country and, to top it all, I would be leaving him too, during the break. S. talked about his emptiness and desolation, he said that his life was bleak and monochromatic, with no colour and no joy. He felt like a wounded animal, left alone in an uncaring world. He dreamt of a puppy drowning in the bath and soon the puppy took on a human face with a look of helplessness on it and S. recognized himself in that image.

I felt and said that his increased ability to bear depressed feelings without turning compulsively to manic action allowed him to have a more genuine type of contact with himself and with me. I was, however, extremely concerned. I feared that he might enter into a severe depression or even have a breakdown. I said that it might be difficult for him to trust that I was there for him when I was about to leave him.

During the break I thought of the helpless puppy in S.'s dream and how he represented the anguish S. was experiencing now that he had established an intimacy with me and with himself. Would he be able to tolerate that anguish or would he run away?

From painful intimacy to the trickster's master twist and to a new beginning

When therapy resumed after Christmas, S. seemed very detached. He had missed me. he said, but only for a day or two. He had spent most of his time with an Asian girl who was in London on business. Shareen was the daughter of one of his father's friends and she was "wonderful". As he recited Shareen's praises I felt and said that he was blaming me for not having been there for him, but he laughed in dismissal. The next session he missed. He said he had failed to hear his alarm clock. In the third session he commented on feeling cut off from everybody and from himself. After a few minutes of silence, during which I experienced an acute sense of depersonalization, he told me that the night before he had had sex with Shareen, not for the first time. He did not desire her, he just went through the motions as if in a trance. She knew that he was gay, but she did not mind.

I was totally confused. What was going on? He seemed to have reverted to servicing women. I felt that this regression was linked to the break and to my "abandonment". All this made some sense and yet I still felt I was in the dark and that an essential part of the picture was missing. Eventually I was told that during the break he had asked Shareen to marry him, as a joke but she had taken him seriously and he had found himself unable to take back the offer, so now they were engaged. I felt stunned and overcome by a sense of dismay I could hardly contain. He seemed to have staged an act which corresponded to a complete mockery of the concept of a couple, an act which saw everybody in it as both victim and torturer in a vicious circle of sado–masochistic enactment. My dismay deepened when he described the complicities surrounding this act of trickery, his brother's collusion and his parents' joy.

This was the masterpiece of the trickster's creations. In the countertransference I felt that this had been an act of revenge against me as a symbol of his abandoning mother. Shareen too was a symbol of such a mother and in deciding to give in to her demands he seemed to be performing the ultimate act of subjugation, but he knew that his performance amounted to a gigantic tease within which words of love covered feelings of hatred. I felt that he had acted behind my back, savouring my surprise and my defeat. I had been at his side encouraging him to separate from the castrating mother inside him, like a caring, strong father might have done, but when I left him, in his rage he had gone back to his engulfing mother.

I said some of this to him. I also said that unless he could acknowledge his anger, he was in danger of giving up his therapy. I felt this danger very strongly. It was impossible that he could pursue at the same time a perverse plot of such magnitude and a search for genuineness. This comment shook him out of the unreality of the perverse behaviour allowing him to re-establish contact with the healthy part of himself. Slowly he realized he did not want to live the lie of a loveless marriage and he began to disentangle himself from the deception. One day he found "his voice" with his mother. After listening to her ecstatic comments about the impending marriage, he told her there would be no marriage as he was gay and it had all been a mistake. His mother tried to sweep this stark truth under the carpet, but over and over again, in the period that followed, he repeated his truth to her and asked her to stop turning him into a product of her imagination. In his work with me, he became more challenging, better able to acknowledge both his angry feelings and his loving ones. A new phase was beginning.

I wondered whether his sado–masochistic masterpiece had been not only a road to revenge, but also a road to freedom and authenticity. After all, he had taken the mockery so far that it had to blow up and crumble, giving him the opportunity to rise from the ashes.

> If, at the end of the trickster myth, the saviour is hinted at, this comforting premonition or hope means that some calamity or other has happened and been consciously understood. Only out of disaster can the longing for the saviour arise..." [Jung, 1939, para. 487]

Note

1. Reading-in paper for associate membership of the British Association of Psychotherapists awarded Lady Balogh Prize, 1998.

References

Bach, S. (1991). In: G. Fogel & W. Myers (Eds.), *Perversions and Near Perversions in Clinical Practice*. New Haven and London: Yale University Press.

Balint, M. (1979). *The Basic Fault*. London and New York: Tavistock Publications.

Bowlby, J. (1973). *Separation: Anxiety and Anger*. Harmondsworth: Penguin Books.

Chasseguet-Smirgel, J. (1985). *Creativity and Perversion*. London: Free Association Books.

Cooper, A. (1991). The unconscious core of perversion. In: G. Fogel & W. Myers (Eds.), *Perversions and Near Perversions in Clinical Practice*. New Haven and London: Yale University Press.

Freud, S. (1955). A child is being beaten: A contribution to the study of sexual perversions. *S.E., 17*: 175–204.

Gee, H. (1995). The archetypal themes in Uccello's painting: St George and the Dragon. *Harvest, 1*(1): 38–46.

Glasser, M. (1979). Some aspects of the role of aggression in the perversions. In: I. Rosen (Ed.), *Sexual Deviation*. Oxford: Oxford University Press.

Hume, F. (1996). A case of voyeurism. In: E. Welldon & C. Van Velsen (Eds.), *A Practical Guide to Forensic Psychotherapy*. London and Bristol, Pennsylvania: Jessica Kingsley Publishers.

Jung, C. G. (1939). Archetypes and the collective unconscious. *C.W., 9*. London: Routledge and Kegan Paul.

Kohut, H. (1977). *The Restoration of the Self*. Madison, Connecticut: International Universities Press.

Rosen, I. (1979). The general psychoanalytical theory of perversion: a critical and clinical review. In: I. Rosen (Ed.), *Sexual Deviation*. Oxford: Oxford University Press.

Steiner, J. (1993). *Psychic Retreats*. London and New York: Routledge and Kegan Paul.

Stern, D. (1985). *The Interpersonal World of the Infant*. New York: Basic Books.

Stoller, R. (1978). The gender disorders. In: I. Rosen (Ed.), *Sexual Deviation*. Oxford, New York, Toronto: Oxford University Press.

Winnicott, D. W. (1958). The capacity to be alone. In: Winnicott, D. W. (1985) *The Maturational Process and the Facilitating Environment*. London: The Hogarth Press.

Winnicott, D. W. (1985). *The Maturational Processes and The Facilitating Environment*. London: The Hogarth Press.

CHAPTER FOUR

The processes of restoration in a deprived self

Jennifer Benwell

Introduction

This paper will examine how the limitations and needs of my patient shaped the form of her therapy. I will describe the development of the therapeutic relationship with Jane as it unfolded over the first three years, and how the tenor and dynamics of our relationship helped me to understand her early mothering experience and informed the therapy. Jane suffered from early failures of containment in the maternal dyad, and had no positive male figure available to help negotiate these early developmental stages. I will show that the repercussions of this have coloured her internal world, have affected her perceptions of her external world, and how she is now able to relate to it and myself as a result of intensive analytical psychotherapy.

My belief is that there was no "good fit" between the infant Jane and her mother. Jane may have been an innately introverted personality with whom her mother found it hard to relate. For her mother's part in this twosome, I think she was unable to detoxify Jane's aggressive impulses and I suspect also projected her own negative and aggressive impulses into her infant. Jane was therefore the repository for substantial negative projections and re-introjections. Her father was psychologically fragile, prone to anger and a kind of tyranny fuelled by obsession. It is in this way that the negative aspects of both the mother and father archetypes were constellated. Jung describes the terrible aspects of the great mother as,

> Anything secret, hidden, dark; the abyss, the world of the dead. Anything that devours, seduces, and poisons, that is terrifying and inescapable like fate. [Jung, C.W., 9i, para. 158]

As a result Jane used the primary defences of splitting and projection to protect herself from disintegration. I believe that these failures impaired the formation of Jane's ego.

During the early part of the therapy she sought to keep me under control, I was needed only as a listening ear, a background, an environmental mother. I was not wanted as, and not allowed to be, a separate person. I believe this was the only way Jane could tolerate the relationship, otherwise I would become for her either idealized with the resultant problem of envy and the concomitant slump in her self esteem allied with a wish to attack, or a bad, noxious, penetrating and death dealing figure. It also allowed me to experience, through projective identification, her sense of not being allowed to exist. Within the framework of the therapy it was as if I allowed her omnipotent control over me. Importantly, I also contained the aggressive impulses and was neither destroyed nor retaliatory. Jane needed me to create an environment in which her self could de-integrate (Fordham, 1985). As I fulfilled this role the relationship deepened, and she was able to express her anger and disappointment with the world, bringing in her material, archetypal images of destruction and magical transformation, the opposing forces in her internal world. As I continued to survive these forces, functioning as a mediator, she became more able to "use me" as an external object, to gain something from me. At the same time she could integrate some of the power that had previously been perceived as purely destructive, paving a possible way to some healing of the original split in her internal world.

Theoretical frameworks

Failures at an early stage of development are recognized and written about extensively in analytical psychology and psycho-analysis. It is recognized that when an infant's psyche is in a perilous situation early defences are erected and that these in themselves can impair development by preventing the infant from taking the necessary psychological life giving steps. In the setting of the consulting room this can appear as resistance to the analytic process.

I shall outline some of the historical antecedents to these analytic insights. Freud observed that the interpretation of his patients' unconscious libidinal wishes did not necessarily result in a lessening of their resistance to change. Patients' defences and their resistance to the analytic process, that of interpretation and working through, were fundamental areas of investigation for Freud. His work on resistance culminated in his monograph "Inhibitions, Symptoms, and Anxiety" (Freud, 1926) in which he delineated a number of modes of resistance.

Klein's object relations theory moved away from drive theory and towards the importance of relating, the dynamics between internal and external objects.

The dual concepts of the paranoid–schizoid and depressive position, clearly delineates two developmental positions; respec-tively they are a pre-oedipal stage where the unconscious world of the infant is dominated by terrifying levels of anxiety with the necessity to split the world in two, the good and the bad breast/care-giver, and the later stage of development where the good and the bad can be tolerated as belonging together, guilt can be felt for the attacks on the good breast and reparation can take place. I will describe how Jane often feels stuck in a two dimensional world, both internally and externally through projection, where she feels the powerless victim, terrorized and subjected to sadistic attacks. This corresponds clearly to Jung's concept of archetypal polariza-tion. Failure at this stage of development has major ramifications. The negotiation of the oedipal phase is intrinsically bound up with the negotiation of the depressive position. If the infant is failed or fails in this crucial step, "the individual cannot progress fully towards developing a capacity for symbol formation and rational thought" Britton (1998, p. 32). In analytical psychology there is the related concept of the transcendent function that facilitates progression;

a movement out of the suspension between opposites, a living birth that leads to a new level of being, a new situation. [Jung, *C.W., 8*, para. 189]

It is the means by which the individual's psyche survives the earlier two dimensional nightmare world which has latterly been termed by Kalsched as the self care system (Kalsched, 1996). "Self care" in this sense means that there is no reliable "other", no means of transformation available. F.'s inability to progress could be seen as her "self care system".

Each new life opportunity is mistakenly seen as a dangerous threat of re-traumatisation and is therefore attacked. [Kalsched, 1996, p. 5]

There has been much written about patients who regress to these primitive levels of functioning and the clinical approach and techniques that might be adopted. Balint (1968) who describes this level as the "area of the basic fault" has focused on the therapeutic aspects of regression. Guntrip (1968) describes it as a period in analysis which is an opportunity for "regression and regrowth". It is these theorists who have resonated with my experience of my patient. The emphasis being a recognition that a striving for genuine relatedness is taking place. Lambert writes;

at first these patients appear totally resistant to all normal analytic and interpretative processes. The paradox, however, is that they are not resistant at all in the deepest sense. They are really at a stage where the actual relationship with the environment is crucial, where the situation is presymbolic and where the true self and ego are not developed enough to understand and make use of interpretations, or to experience symbolism. As a result any conformity with or acceptance of the normal analytic and interpretative situation by them would actually represent a collusion of the false self with environmental expectations. [Lambert, 1981, p. 63]

I had initially to enter into my patient's world rather than encourage a compliance with mine. In understanding the "diabolical" nature of Jane's internal world, I have found Kalsched's thoughts about the nature of trauma and its impact on the psyche very helpful.

The mediational capacities that later become the ego are, at the beginning of life, totally vested in the maternal self -object who serves as a kind of external metabolising organ for the infant's experience ... The infant psyche gradually differentiates and he or she begins to contain his or her affects, i.e., to develop an ego capable of experiencing strong emotion and tolerating conflict among emotions. Until this occurs, the infant's inner self and object-representations are split, archaic and typical (archetypal). Archetypal inner objects are numinous, overwhelming, and mythological. [Kalsched, 1996, p. 18]

Kalsched's insights have been useful in understanding Jane's behaviour.

The work of Winnicott and Colman have corresponded closely to the needs of this patient and given me helpful insights into the dynamics of the transference and countertransference. Winnicott in his paper, "The use of an object and relating through identifications" writes,

This interpreting by the analyst, if it is to have effect, must be related to the patient's ability *to place the analyst outside the area of subjective phenomena...*

...in our work it is necessary for us to be concerned with the development and establishment of the capacity to use objects and to recognize a patient's inability to use objects, where this is a fact. [Winnicott, 1971, p. 87]

Colman in his paper, "Envy, self-esteem and the fear of separateness", states,

Envy is the *outcome of* a defective mother/infant fit in which the infant's need for illusory omnipotence is not met, resulting in a lack of sufficient internal recourses to manage existence as a separate individual (i.e. feelings of worthlessness and helplessness). [Colman, 1991, p. 356]

History

Jane was thirty-three years old when she first came to see me. She has a sister eighteen months older than herself. The family were comparatively settled until she was ten years old when they moved to a rural area, ostensibly due to father's need for peace and quiet at the onset of epilepsy. This involved the sisters changing schools, moving to mother's old school and closer to the maternal grandparents home. By the time she was fourteen father had had his first "breakdown". During her "A" level years she moved to live with her grandparents. During this time she was exposed to the fury of her grandfather and the frightening dynamics between the grandparental couple. When she was eighteen she went to university to study a foreign language which involved two periods of study abroad. At this time her parents separated and father suffered his second breakdown, needing hospitalization for hypo-mania. After she had finished her degree, she travelled abroad for a year to teach, and whilst away had one year of Jungian analysis. Her parents were divorced and a year later her mother remarried. On her return to this country she spent one year as an office administrator and then left for a further two years teaching abroad. When she was twenty-eight years old, she had an extended period of unemployment, during which she lived with her sister. Her mother meanwhile moved abroad with her new husband. Subsequently, Jane made the move to a new city, living in a flat-share where she shares a room with one other person. She has had various clerical jobs, and continues to improve her computer skills by taking short courses. There has been no mention of sexual relationships or of any close friends from her past.

Jane painted a picture of a conflictual family environment. Her father was obsessional in nature prior to his breakdown, insisting the home be kept in his "order". This caused continual arguments between himself and Jane's sister. He was also close to alcoholism for much of her life, after his retirement burning himself severely from setting his clothes alight with cigarettes. As children he would set both his daughters mathematical puzzles that he knew well they would be unable to answer and then taunt them for their stupidity. Jane was very aware that he would have preferred male children, and she recounted watching painfully as he showed uncharacteristic fondness towards his nephews. Nevertheless on occasion she found favour with him for her academic achievements. This set her apart from her mother and sister who she felt had a special bond and whose continued closeness was a source of great envy and jealousy for her. She seemed to feel both parents failed in the work place, father having been driven out by illness and mother as a low achiever, but most importantly to Jane, both "allowed" themselves to be victimized.

Mother was presented, on the one hand as shy and bullied, but on the other, in relation to Jane, as rejecting and critical. Jane has been told by her mother that her first response when handed her baby daughter was to say "you bitch!". She has also been told that the nurses could not stand her crying and so put her in a side room in order that they should not be disturbed. Mother's family predominates in influence. Grandfather ruled the family, a sixteen stone man who was violent towards his whole family, in particular the female members. Grandmother is presented as a silent, cowed and uncomplaining figure who continued to be beaten by her husband when she was an elderly woman. Mother had two brothers and is reported to have been very conscious of being unwanted as the girl. Within the family culture it seemed that females were a disappointment and men were ungovernably violent or "mad". There is only conflict between masculine and feminine, with no positive coniunctio between them. Within this framework I believe it was hard for Jane to identify with either sex. Her fear would have been that her femininity would result in rejection by inner and outer masculine figures and her masculinity connote destruction.

Clinical work

On our first meeting she sat before me, uncomfortable on the edge of the armchair. Her first thoughts were about our appointment times, unsure that there would be a fit between work and therapy. She spoke of her anxieties around starting a new job the next day, the headaches it was giving her, the nerves. She said she was "paranoid" about making mistakes and having them discovered later. She anticipated not being "up to it", but not knowing what "it" was, what would be expected. There was also some annoyance at having to suit her employers, fitting in with their timetable. There was a sense that she felt there had been bad management on their behalf. She brought in the figure of her old boss who was confident and skilled, therefore able to help, but unavailable and critical.

Throughout, Jane's anxiety was palpable, she sat taut and upright, rubbing her forehead as if trying to smooth out the furrows of worry. She would occasionally dart a look or nervous smile at me. In this first session I felt myself respond to this anxious child by containing her. I gave her the certainty of another session that week when she seemed close to saying it would be impossible for us to meet again, as our timetables would never "mesh". By the end of this session I was talking through with her the journey to work the next day. It felt like sending a child off to her first day at school. I became mother to Jane's little girl. My interpretations of her anxiety about her job as a communication of her anxiety and ambivalence about starting therapy were unheard or refuted.

Jane described her problem as her feeling that she had got stuck, that she was not where she should be given her age, qualifications and abilities. She felt she made a start, got her degree, got her first "proper job", but that was so disastrous that she had never been brave enough to try again, taking refuge in jobs far below her level of competency. Over the three subsequent years of therapy she returned repeatedly to this bad experience as if to prove to me that it is a dangerous world out there. I came to think this represented the failure of the deintegration/reintegration processes in Jane's early life.

Although I quickly became aware of the necessity of adopting the role of containing mother in that first session, I was not prepared for how long that role was going to be required. An early dynamic that sprung up between us was of me trying to hurry her up, wanting her to talk about feelings and family, to get on with what I felt was the "real" stuff of therapy, for the therapy to grow up. I heard her speak of her annoyance with those who always wanted to hurry her up and her determination to stick to her own pace. Jane needed to use me as a listener only, an object into which to pour her day's troubles. I duly held back and held on to my impatience and discomfort. I felt unwanted, my contributions were not used, I was not welcomed as a separate individual. I wondered then whether mother had felt the same, that what she had to give of herself was not of use to the young Jane or that Jane's innate timidity was such that she could not take what mother had to give. Or was it that Jane was not wanted by mother except as a narcissistically gratifying object? I in turn was only wanting Jane to gratify my narcissistic needs as a therapist.

Winnicott describes how:

The development of the capacity to use an object is another example of the maturational process as something that depends on a facilitating environment. [Winnicott, 1971, p. 89]

This environment is one in which the destructive impulses are received and survived by the mother and therefore she proves herself to be outside of the infant's omnipotent control and as an object to be used. I think Jane experienced a retaliatory object and so objects outside of omnipotent control became not useful but annihilatory. So in these early months of the therapy I think I had to be related to by Jane, first and foremost, as her own safe creation.

Jane would bring me material illustrating her sense of lack of control over her internal and external environment, describing how her living space was always being invaded. She was acutely sensitive to other people in the flat where she lived, particularly foreigners on whom she projected her aggression, talking about them getting inside her head, unable to shake them out, taking her over. She told me her whole body became taut and she was filled with anger, but felt incapable of confronting workmates or flatmates, instead putting up with the situation, never murmuring a word of protest or dissent. I think this echoed experiences in her infant life when her mother, who was not felt to be in the baby Jane's possession, but rather a foreign body, failed to process Jane's rage. As a result the foreignness of her mother had been reintrojected in an even more toxic form, filling her whole body. In the transference, if I were not controlled she felt I would try to control her by invading her mind with my foreign thoughts, felt as attacks, and so she would be wiped out.

When describing the process of the object's survival of destructive impulses Winnicott suggests that for babies:

'... who have not been seen through the phase well ... aggression is something that cannot be encompassed, or something that can be retained only in the form of a liability to be an object of attack. [Winnicott, 1971, p. 93]

Her material, especially in the first few months, was restricted to the details of the day's happenings at the office where she worked, and at the flat. As the work progressed she trusted me with more of her past and her feelings about the members of her family, and our sessions became increasingly important to her. Her response to the first breaks were destructive, firstly quitting her job, impoverishing herself financially to the extent she could not come to her sessions for a two week period following my two week break. There was then a relatively short period of unemployment, then part time basic data processing work, though the pay was hardly sufficient for her to live on. There was one brief attempt at getting better paid work, but this foundered on the rocks of the Easter break, and my second abandonment of her. I think that over these first months of her therapy she began to feel she had found a dependable environment, that I was controllable to a certain extent and that provided some safety.

However, my breaks were experienced as breaches of that safe container. She was unable to accept any interpretations of my importance to her but did bring material about other relationships where she felt dependant but unimportant. As the transference deepened over the summer months, we became more aware of her anger and how constricted she was by her need to comply, keep quiet, in order to escape the anticipated retaliatory attack. Through the process of projective identification I felt increasingly constricted in the sessions, less and less able to be spontaneous, operating within the narrow framework imposed by Jane. My hardest work was to tolerate what I experienced as claustrophobia.

I think that the more Jane perceived me as some one who could provide her with the nurturing, the "good management" or mediation, she so needed, the more aware she became of her feelings of deprivation. "I'm really starving now" became a familiar lament at the beginning of each session. Alongside of this was the reality of her mother's lack of contact over these months. She had returned to this country visiting other members of the family, staying with Jane's sister, but had made no contact with Jane herself. As the summer break came nearer, her circumstances became more extreme. She was not earning enough money and was threatened with eviction from her flat. She felt very much on the edge of survival. She was feeling cut off from any other help, with the prospect of being cut off from me for a month. This brought with it a lessening of both her resistance to acknowledging my importance to her and her ability to repress her anger with me. She became able to accept some of my interpretations. I now believe that her envy was aroused too, but I was unaware of it until later in the work.

As her anger about her deprivation came increasingly into the sessions after the first summer break, she expressed her wish to be invisible, for fear of the "nasty" destructive parts being exposed, the shame they evoked, and in her mind the inevitable banishment. It is as if for Jane, once they are in focus the rest of her will not be seen. In an unconscious attempt to rid herself of these malevolent forces, she projected them into the external world. Hidden and menacing violence was all pervasive. As the summer disappeared and evenings grew dark she spoke of her terror of what lay hidden in the blackness. The world became a more and more dangerous place.

Jane was living in a diabolized world, but longing for the idealized one. She was full of ideas for courses that she was going to take that would change her life. She struggled to find the right combination of courses as though there was one right answer. I interpreted this as her trying to find the combination to a safe, inside of which was the treasure of mother's love and approval, which would pour forth once she had the right job. She could agree to this but the search went on and so too, I believe, her conviction that she could get all she needed from me, but that I was withholding. Winnicott again has been helpful in my understanding of this. As I could not be used as an external object at this point, F could not "use the breast for getting fat" (Winnicott, 1971, p. 91). She could only feed on herself or projected aspects of herself.

Jane's need and fear of penetration was expressed in many guises. She talked about her great fears of penetration, her fear of damaging the inside of her own body, simply through touch. An image emerged of an internal body that was terribly fragile with membranes or boundaries, that could easily be rent, without her knowledge, leaving her unprotected from damage to deeper parts of herself. Around this time she became very hard of hearing, having developed blocked ears. This turned out to be an accumulation of wax, a very physical representation of a psychic defence with which she defends herself against my interpretations, which she fears will be harmful penetrations.

During this period there were also pictures of male figures that she wished to enter her life. In particular were the soft toys that she bought for herself and to whom she assigned mischievous "Fuck

You" personalities. She also talked about the character in the film "The Mask" who was possessed by the god Loki. In Teutonic mythology Loki is known as a night god and the god of mischief. This "trickster" figure is one close to Jane's heart. However, in his vindictiveness, he presaged the downfall of the gods and the burning of the entire world. In Jane's attempts to banish the destructive "mad" side of this spirit, which was I believe associated with father's hypo-mania, she has lost the enlivening potent aspects, that would enable her development.

After these images of the destructive male figure, a life threatening female was brought into play. In the early summer months of the second year of our work, one of Jane's acquaintances had an abortion. This appeared in several sessions and although Jane's feelings about it were not directly available, the material came in conjunction with a long elaboration of a meeting she had with another girl from her block of flats, in the basement. This seemed to signify the abortion experience. The girl walked into the room and asked if she could use Jane's washing machine, in other words break into Jane's washing routine. She experienced the girl's bodily movement of leaning towards her as a threatening impingement. She felt a heart pounding panic and felt she must protect herself from this vicious intrusion which I believe she experienced at some level as a life threatening event. This lead me to think that in her internal world there was a female figure that reached in and cut off the life supply, and provided further insight into the nature of her defences. This could be seen as an example of what Fordham terms defences of the self (Fordham, 1985).

Meanwhile life in the external world echoed all these themes. Jane hated the new consulting room to which I moved, feeling wrenched from the familiar, complaining that I had ruined everything. I was also abandoning her for the second long summer break. Her place at the flat was threatened. On the day of our last session before the break she received a phone call telling her that her paternal grandmother had died and on her return from the break, she told me that her father had suffered a stroke, a response she felt to his mother's death. In her fantasy children cannot live without their parents. When I raised the parallel with the therapeutic contract of two years and said that she may well feel that her time was up with me too, that I was about to get rid of her, Jane agreed through her tears that this had been a fear. She thought I might get rid of her because I had seen the nasty bits of her or because she was not getting better quick enough, or because I might think she was all right. Some of the anxiety abated after my assurances that we would be continuing the therapy. I think her realization that I was committed to seeing her irrespective of the two-year Reduced Fee Scheme contract changed the dynamics of our relationship. Albeit reluctantly she was now able to speak of her feelings about me, although the spectre of the terrible mother remained in the wings.

Jane still often started her sessions talking about how starving she felt, and how big her appetite was. Jane talked of wanting me to reconfigure her brain, give her a new brain, a happiness pill, a typing pill, a confidence pill, or an endless supply of magic potions. It was clear that the dynamic in her mind was not one in which I helped build something she already had, the nurturing of a potential, but it was an addition or a transformation and one which she informed me would not be permanent. Jane remained in the grip of the illusion of, and determined to preserve, the eternally bountiful good external object. There was no mutually satisfying relationship, only an other who had everything and refused to hand it over. The consequence is that you have to have permanent possession of the other and never be separate from them. Warren Colman's paper on envy has shed light on this dynamic for me.

> Envy arises from this sense of lack through the compensatory fantasy of an all providing other who possesses the qualities required to fill the gap. If the gap is felt to be intolerable, destructive spoiling ensues as an attempt to obliterate it. [Colman, 1991, p. 356]

At this point Jane dreamt about me. She found a plastic rubbish bag in her kitchen, looked inside and found my legs. They had been sawn off a flesh and blood body as there was blood dripping down them, but the actual legs were plastic. This meant many things to her. I was unreal, and so could not give her what she needed outside in the real world, I was plastic, so my feelings for her were synthetic. However the aspect that seemed most important to her was that I had cheated her. These were just one of several sets of legs, and I was simultaneously, as she stood in her kitchen with a part of me, enjoying myself with friends at a party. Again, Jane's envy of me weaves itself into the material, this time with clear reference to the attacks she would like to make, or has made in phantasy. I think that in this early work with Jane it was important to interpret her sense of worthlessness and distance from the good object, against which the envious attacks were a defence. There would otherwise have been a danger of reinforcing her sense of lack and despair and perhaps increasing her defences.

Jane also brought her infantile body into the sessions with more regularity. She would often start the session by giving me a rundown of her physical symptoms. The body she brought was often one from which fluids are either blocked or running out, vomit, shit, blood, wax or wind. Her fingers were in her mouth throughout our sessions, in part I believe to stop the vomit, as angry words, pouring out. As we talked more about her body and our relationship she began using more preverbal communications. She would make noises, fingers in mouth, shaking her head, noises that followed the rhythm of speech. We also seemed to build up a repertoire of facial expressions, particularly scowls and stares. I would mimic these expressions, as one might with a baby, in a "protoconversation". When I was unsure of their meaning, I would ask, what are you saying with that look?

In January of our third year, Jane's father died from a heart attack. In the wake of this Jane discovered many new things about her father. There had been an improvement in his health, prior to the stroke, and he had become an active member of his community. He appeared to have managed to belong in a way that Jane had never experienced, and although this prompted feelings of jealousy it forced a reappraisal. In her loss she was able to feel his worth and to benefit from a psychological and material inheritance. She re-defined her internal father in a positive way which went on to facilitate some mediation of her animus. With her new wealth, an inheritance from her father, she made plans to leave work, acquire some more skills and hoped to get a better job. Jane showed a determination and ability to follow her ideas through. She asked for things, specifically a loan whilst she waited for probate to be granted, and displayed a new assertiveness undeterred by the obstacles she met. This was a welcome development and relieved some of my frustration.

Jane left her job, did a diploma course, extending her administrative and computer skills. This external course of development was paralleled internally. There was a noticeable relaxation of her previously constricting boundaries. She was able to explore new physical and psychological territories. A tool with which we explored her internal world was the Internet.

On the first day of the course she had gone to the Reichstaag website, the first of many visits. Jane had always felt an affinity for Germany, its history and culture. I think, for her, the German state embodies the archetype of the father, in both its negative and positive aspects. For example in its characteristic orderliness it was a welcome antidote to her own father's "disorder". In other ways, particularly in this website, it represented the organizational centre of legitimized violence and authority, two concepts which are integrally bound together for Jane. It supported her feeling that it is only possible to have authority via the annihilation or submission of others. Jane continued to struggle daily with her omnipotent murderous feelings and her wish and fear that these feelings might find expression. I think by talking about these ideas, their total destructiveness was depotentiated. She experienced the reality that thinking is not doing, she was still accepted by me, and felt strengthened in her self. Some of the power of these figures could be integrated and utilized instead of warded off.

She was also able to draw upon a power greater than the purely personal in another way, one that had shown itself before in the form of the god Loki. During the course she bought herself several bits of equipment and her favourite was a lap top computer which soon acquired a male identity, Leo the lap top. There was an enjoyment and wonder at Leo akin to a child's awe and delight as its world seemed invested with magic. This corresponded with her feeling that there was a magical power out there, and Leo would wave the magic wand. A further important dimension to Leo's abilities was his transportation of Jane to the darkest most murderous regions of the web and back again, at lightening speed, with no consequences in reality. This could be seen to connote the spirit of Hermes, the messenger from the gods to the mortals, a spirit that can travel from one region to another, akin to the trickster. This was the first substantial sight of a positive male figure in her imaginary life. It was important that we, the male and the female figures, "worked together", she was able to come and tell me about her travels to the darker areas of her inner world, and have them understood and contained by me. By her tapping into this spirit and bringing her experiences to me, Jane's safe exploration was enabled.

As part of her course she had to do a sales presentation. She chose to do a presentation on a soft toy company whose website she had discovered. She told me how much she liked the idea of working there, and spent some time enumerating the benefits of this company, all of which were about child care. I think this indicated that there had been some broadening of the mother archetype. She was able to experience the loving mother who could produce babies, and not only the terrible mother aspects. I think this symbolized Jane forming a stronger relationship to her own fertility. It may be that she had previously been so threatened by her murderousness that she could not allow into consciousness her creativity for fear that she would in turn murder her own creations. With the fear lessened, she could now think about the possibility of making babies. She grew extremely interested in the field of animation and after a great deal of independent experimentation and study, managed to animate her drawings of animals for this presentation, mirroring as it were her wish to bring life to a baby. The wish for a boyfriend now also entered the sessions regularly.

Over this period of work Jane accelerated her soft toy purchases, and she would communicate with growls, and use childlike expressions. I think that it was only in this mode that she felt able to regularly bring both her loving and terrible aspects, in the form of the child to the loving mother, and to play. As if in an attempt to retain a sense of equilibrium during this unfolding and bringing to consciousness she also had to physically hide. She did this by pulling her jacket or jumper over her face, and sticking one and sometimes both hands in her mouth, biting her fingernails. She was protecting herself from my apprehension and penetration, my knowing of her and the anticipated rejection. I also understand this covering and plugging, as protecting me in two ways, firstly by vigilantly keeping the full force of the anger from spilling out, and secondly by disabling her mouth and "claws" from greedily damaging the breast. This often left her with only her eyes with which to take me in or attack me. I think these difficulties of being with me in the room indicated that alongside the negative archetypes of the terrible mother and father there is a negative coniunctio, the dynamic of the couple is to kill or be killed, to come alive is to invite death. However I think this too has been mediated in the transference. By my allowing this child with its dependency and its violence, I was the enabling mother, the allower of life, just like the company on the website. She could then become an animator herself, a life giving maternal figure who could tolerate conflict, who could accept the good and bad.

An important symbol was brought into the work at the end of the summer term, just before the break. She bought herself a hand made millennium toy animal, from a German company by mail order. When it arrived she was very unsure that she liked it, it had a strange face, lopsided ears, asymmetrical features, but most of all the circular millennium medallion around its neck had rough edges. Gradually she got used to it, except for the medallion. She was very torn as to whether to keep it or not, she had the option of returning it and getting a replacement. She wanted to keep her toy, as she had come to like its individual characteristics but not its rough edges. The medallion can be seen as a symbol of the Self. Her question was could we both tolerate the rough bits of her. I interpreted her need to be wanted for all the parts of her, good and bad. On my return from the break, a few sessions into the work, she brought the toy to the session. It was now a prized possession.

These developments paved the way for a shift in Jane's internal world and a corresponding shift in my countertransference and therefore the therapeutic relationship. She became braver, being able to explore parts of London she had never been to, and travelled abroad to France three times. Just as Germany represents some aspects of the masculine for Jane, I believe that France has associations with the feminine. I think this journeying in France was an attempt to integrate some aspect of her mother's sexuality as represented by France. I was able to be more real and separate, feeling less controlled by her. She has tolerated my feeding back some of my countertransference feelings of frustration in ways that did not seem possible before. I have interpreted the envious attacks on myself and the therapy, but have also simply acknowledged my frustration. My sense was that the time was right for me to start "failing" her, by not being ideal, failing her in the same way her mother did, but when she was able to tolerate it. Rather than an increase of her defences in response to my interventions, there was a lessening, particularly of the "little girl" persona. I think that these are signs of her strengthening ego and sense of worth and separateness.

Summary

In this paper I have shown how in the therapy with my patient I had to attune myself to her needs, in at first being an environmental "good" mother. She began to feel her dependency on me and in time expressed her anger about my unavailability. At first her anger was brought in archetypal images, first a mad and destructive father and then an aborting terrible mother figure. As she explored these murderous emotions in the safety of the therapeutic frame they became less toxic and more humanized, and her defences of splitting and projection lessened. The beginnings of a sense of herself, emerged and there was some strengthening of her ego's capacity to deal with conflicting emotions. These are just the beginnings of a process. As she has had the terrible mother mediated in the transference she has been able to make progress in allowing in the female and is making some important steps in integrating a masculine energy, enabling her to make her way in the outside world.

I wish to thank my patient for her bravery and generosity in sharing her self with me and agreeing to the publication of this material.

References

Balint, M. (1968). *The Basic Fault Therapeutic Aspects of Regression.* London: Tavistock [reprinted London: Routledge, 1989].
Britton, R. (1998). *Belief and Imagination—Explorations in Psychoanalysis.* London: Routledge.
Colman, W. (1991). Envy, self-esteem and fear of separateness. *British Journal of Psychotherapy,* 7: 356–367.
Fordham, M. (1985). *Explorations into the Self.* London: Academic Press [reprinted London: Karnac Books, 1994].
Freud, S. (1926). *Inhibitions, Symptoms, and Anxiety. S.E., 20.*
Guntrip, H. (1968). *Schizoid Phenomena, Object Relations and the Self.* London: Hogarth Press [reprinted London: Karnac Books, 1992].

Kalsched, D. E. (1996). *The Inner World of Trauma, Archetypal Defences of the Personal Spirit*. London: Routledge.

Lambert, K. (1981). *Analysis, Repair and Individuation*. London: Academic Press [reprinted London: Karnac Books, 1994].

Winnicott, D. W. (1971). *Playing and Reality*. London: Tavistock Publications.

PART III
IN THE MAELSTROM AND
IN THE DOLDRUMS:
INTENSIVE WORK IN THE
ANALYTIC CONSULTING ROOM

CHAPTER FIVE

Unlocking the Uroborus

Marilyn Mathew

"...the Uroborus, the snake biting its tail, is the symbol of
the psychic state of the beginning, of the original situation ...
the "Great Round" ... it is also a symbol of a state in which
chaos, the unconscious, and the psyche as a whole were
undifferentiated..."

(Neumann, 1955)

Introduction

Analytical psychotherapy is full of unexpected surprises. It
may be that we uncover a new depth of darkness or
intensity of passion, a numbing terror or a sudden
blossoming. The newness can feel astonishing, horrifying and/or
miraculous for both the one who lies on the couch and one who sits
alongside. As a consequence, the limits of what we "know" and the
boundaries of our understanding are continually extended.

The process of analysis harnesses the remarkable power of the
psyche to encounter, engage, unlock, survive, transform and heal.
While we, as therapists, may rely on technique, theory and clinical

experience in our work, the essential tool is our self, and in particular the willingness to explore the relation of self with other. Each analytic relationship is unique; each will bring a unique contribution to our understanding of the personal, cultural and objective psyche, and each will challenge the position we ourselves hold in relation to an "other" both subjectively and objectively.

Symptoms, I believe, contain the seeds of repair and individuation. I also hold the rather optimistic view that even the very worst that can happen to us contains a shred of potential meaning and purpose— although at the time it might seem completely hopeless. Experiencing, imaging and naming the elements of psychic pain can unlock the rings that defend against intolerable suffering and encourage the possibility of healing. But first the pain has to be experienced—or perhaps, sometimes more accurately—"re-experienced for the first time".

The self is ingenious. It devises cunning self-care systems (Kalsched, 1996) that protect a developing personality from unbearable pain whilst hopefully finding ways of expressing that all is not well.

Maintaining part of the self in a uroboric state of "eating one's own tail" is one of the most powerful and primitive defences. While much of the personality may appear to function rather well, a vital core has curled in on itself, winding itself into a rigid self-containing circle. It is a state of core complex (Glasser, 1979) where, at heart, any relationship involving dependency, trust and intimacy is shut down; there is only the continuous mouth and the tail, forming a "thumb-sucking" illusion of feeding oneself whilst excluding profound intercourse with an "other"—and real nourishment. To let go of one's tail and risk attachment to another, to risk a "real" feed or intercourse, evokes the impossible dilemma of schizoid compromise (Guntrip, 1969): a dreadful encounter with devouring hunger or intolerable abandonment to avoid the bliss of union. Remaining in the safe and rigid state of uroboric identification, being isolated with only one's self (distinctly different from being alone with one's self), jams individuation. The result is both numbing and unbearably lonely. However, even though a meaningful relationship with another human being may feel unthinkably dangerous, the psyche will prod with nightmare, symptom or psychic pain until we listen to its voice within (Perry, 1991).

One solution to the pain of uroboric identification is to create and control an "other". Some people may produce "others" in the form of children, whose birth might, sometimes catastrophically, crack the defensive ring. Or, if creating one's own flesh and blood feels impossible, creativity might find another outlet. Producing a company of "others", as self-objects in the form of artwork was the way Amanda had coped with her difficulties before she arrived in my consulting room.

Amanda's background, history and life before therapy

Amanda came into therapy with me because she was fed up with the way that her life was dominated by compulsive overeating. Food had become a monstrous goddess, completely dominating her waking thoughts. Unless she was sleeping, in company or working —engrossed in making art—the demonic urge to consume vast chunks of food overturned her rational intelligent mind. Whole loaves of bread, slabs of cheese, bowls of rice, kilos of fruit would be secretly consumed to the point of vomiting. Good wholesome nourishment became bloating, sinful and poisonous the minute it was swallowed. If there was food in the home it had to be eaten. Every last scrap had to be wolfed down mindlessly and then often got rid of in a purging ritual. In order to try and contain the desire to ravage, all Amanda's kitchen cupboards were bare—perhaps an apt metaphor for her internal nurturing resources.

Home was thousands of miles away where her family remained in close contact with each other ... but not with her, or she with them. Amanda told me about a normal, happy childhood, enjoying the rough and tumble with her older siblings, the warmth and care of decent parents, the freedom to roam and help out on the farm. The only hint of disturbance from the early days was that she knew she had been an excessively clingy baby (and, interestingly, the idea of becoming a mother herself is utterly abhorrent). Perhaps more worrying to my mind was Amanda's insistence that her early years were completely rosy—angry words simply did not exist.

There was one skeleton in the cupboard: Amanda's elder half-sister was illegitimate and her mother had been exiled because she insisted on carrying on with the pregnancy. It seemed to me that it was a courageous woman who would stick to her guns in the face of 1950s small-town disapproval. In the event, Amanda's mother sacrificed the relationship with her own parents for a single life with her baby. This stoic determination seems to have been a quality admired by the man she eventually came to marry, but as far as Amanda's mother was concerned, discussing this bitter chapter of her past was considered a totally shameful taboo.

Trouble erupted for Amanda with puberty. As the sexual hormones surged through her developing body, so began the secret stuffing of her face. She crept into the kitchen and raided the pantry. She had always been a well-built child, but now she ballooned and her school clothes split. No one said a word. Amanda cloaked her emerging female body with fat and shamefully withdrew from any chance of having a boyfriend, comforting herself with yet more "goodies". Could it be that Amanda had made an unconscious decision to avoid becoming an attractive young woman in case the disastrous consequences of her own emerging sexual appetite led her to the same fate as her mother—of eternal exile—or was there a more primitive root?

The desperate urge for nourishment and comfort had become a perverted form of self-abuse. However, while her gorging was carried out in secret, the evidence of the lost control declared itself to the world in folds of flesh. There was no escape. Amanda is tall and it is clear from her capable hands and feet that she was never meant to be anything but statuesque. But in our present culture, big women are viewed with disdain, if not derision. It is hard to be a well-built female unless you are sporty. To have one's infantile rage displayed for all to see in excessive flesh is ultimately humiliating.

Avoiding the mirror of the world and her own reflection, Amanda diverted her gaze and creative drive, pouring herself into her newly discovered talent for drawing. The aesthetic world of art and ideas was miles away from her sensible farming family and before long Amanda left the farm and made the miles literal by enrolling in art school in a distant city. She readily assumed the unorthodox art student appearance, values and behaviour, which totally confused and bewildered her family; they felt she was attacking all that they considered worthy. The good girl who had always done her best to please had turned into an alien monster. It was incomprehensible to them, and she in turn felt utterly rejected.

The flight from home, the subsequent flights into the crazy world of drugs and the intoxication of foreign travel could, in one way, be seen as a positive adventuring into the world, but it seemed to me to be more about a very desperate and concrete way of avoiding an internal emotional experience.

Amanda told me about her mother's sudden life threatening illness just before she left on one of her long travels. She might have well been telling me about the weather for the lack of passion. The absence of feeling in her voice brought out an intense sadness and loneliness in me. Somehow those feelings had been cauterized in Amanda but could be unconsciously projected into her therapist. What had happened to this mother–daughter couple? Had fire turned to ice? Was it Amanda's own passionate, needy and furious self that she persistently fled so violently, I wondered? Would I be able to hold her from fleeing when the going got tough in therapy?

When she came to London from the Orient, Amanda was walking on air. During the months of travelling she had starved herself into an acceptable shape for the first time in her life. A heady omnipotence gave her the illusion of almost being an angel. The magic and colour of the eastern culture, the drugs, the odd sexual encounter and the thrill of the mystical adventure had enabled her to stick to one small meal a day. The weight had fallen away and she had ended up feeling out of this world.

Soon after her arrival in this country, Amanda met a man and a relationship developed. At first all was well, but before long the oriental magic wore off. The ravenous urges returned and Amanda feared she would overwhelm her boyfriend if she let him know about her boiling messy insides. She swallowed her feelings along with more and more food. The fat snuck back on and the boyfriend backed off, sensing perhaps that there was more going on in Amanda than met the eye—and more than he could deal with. Amanda realized she needed some serious help.

The phases of therapy

Amanda threw herself wholeheartedly into therapy. She was living on the breadline, yet managed to scrape enough money together to pay me a substantial percentage of her very small budget. *I* was not to starve financially even if she feared unconsciously that she might suck all my insides out.

Stuffing

In the first phase Amanda stuffed every session so full that there was barely room for me to utter a syllable. My silent witness was clearly what she needed, but I also felt an intense counter-transference anxiety that there might never be any place for me in her therapy. Almost howling with the pain she had kept under wraps for so long, words streamed out in anguish. But there was an area of turmoil inside for which language was inadequate and seemed to be seeking an alternative outlet.

Amanda began to draw her inner world out on paper. Out stormed a series of illustrations of an enormous stupid monster mother/baby and the battle with her counterpart—a fully developed, intelligent but helpless and tiny woman prisoner. Their horror story was set in a bleak and blackened theatre pit from which there seemed no escape. It felt like an eternal tale caught in an eternal round and I wondered what would happen if the cycle could break.

Amanda worked hard in her therapy, both inside and outside the consulting room, almost as if the "food for thought" might replace the compulsion to stuff the mouth.

As each shame-filled picture appeared we would examine it carefully together, investigating all the details to try and understand the meaning of its contents and how they might relate to her internal world or the transference relationship with me. This was somewhat contentious as she insisted there was no relationship—I was only a professional.

The illustrations she showed me were exquisitely drawn images of torture. The feelings in the pictures could have been expressed by a splattering of red paint or attacking the paper with scissors, but Amanda had gently and painstakingly caressed the paper with her pencil. The way that scenes of mutilation and horror could be executed with such tender marks was thoroughly disturbing. It felt important for us to get into the revealing images and track their progress, but I was aware at the same time of how important it was for her that I could bear to simply hold her beautiful but grotesque artwork in my hands.

As the series of drawings developed, an important new character arrived on the scene in the form of a third observing female figure. Amanda began to take a slightly more objective stance in relation to the helpless victim and monster mother/baby. However, the onlooker in the pictures was passive and not helping her achieve her desired aim: to get rid of the dastardly duo. I knew that this desire to simply eject the badness was not going to be the answer, but was also somewhat bothered by the ineffective passivity of the character I assumed to partly represent myself.

The monster–victim couple seemed to explain why a uroboric state was so attractive to Amanda. To put oneself into the hands of another might mean being imprisoned and devoured; to need someone might lead to gobbling them up. Separation might feel like death. Was therapy as well as her internal world the bleak pit? Was I the passive observer? Was I in the picture at all?

Very gradually the over-eating subsided, but not without substituting a new cast iron structure. Food was bought one meal at a time, and still the kitchen cupboards had to be bare. Gradually the stream of secret pictures brought into the consulting room to show me trickled away and Amanda began to use the couch.

Drawing out the body

In the subsequent phase of her therapy Amanda began to slowly relax and there was a little more space in the sessions. However, if I made any reference to our relationship, I was quickly made to feel thoroughly insignificant—a complete nobody. Meanwhile Amanda was working on two other art projects.

One project involved making a series of life-sized drawings concentrating on the skin of her own naked body. These powerful monochromatic images portrayed her body, as seen through her own eyes (and therefore headless), floating in velvety black space. Accompanying the artwork was an academic exercise: an investigation of the relationship of her body with her unconscious and her art. This required working with an analyst and gave Amanda an acceptable reason for being in therapy—it was all for art's sake.

The other ongoing project involved creating books full of hundreds of drawings, beginning with images of single hands in various poses. Sometimes two hands would mirror each other on opposite pages (only touching each other when they became invisible, when the book was closed).

Amanda's work went on exhibition and she asked if I would go and see it. These paintings were too large to bring into the consulting room, but surely photographs would do? Then I recalled the way her family had not understood her work, not been able to travel the miles, and none of them would see this show either. So after some thought I decided I would visit the gallery. Only by seeing the exhibition did I discover that Amanda's pictures had been hung in the premier position and she had won a top prize, an achievement she had not mentioned to me. Her considerable talent as an artist was striking and I felt immensely proud as I gazed at the wall of huge images and leafed through the books of finished drawings.

Back in the consulting room Amanda showed no apparent pleasure or gratitude that I had made a special journey to see her work and she seemed excruciatingly uncomfortable when I commented on her talent. It dawned on me that therapy was a place for only the bad stuff and bringing in something good was disturbing the status quo. Would it have been more helpful if I had not been to see the exhibition, I wondered? Boundaries are such a vital aspect of our work. How and why we hold them tight or let them stretch is something we consider carefully in the patient's best interest.

Amanda continued drawing in her books and as the pages filled up, so the range of images expanded. Now there were illustrations of other parts of her body, companies of demons like little imps, flashes of humour, self-portraits of her face in many moods and pairs of twin-like women. Sometimes the women held hands and sometimes gently explored each other. Superficially it could be thought that I was now part of a couple with Amanda, but in fact, on examination they were clearly both mirror images of herself.

Then, out of the blue, something shocking happened. Amanda's best friend from home, who was also living in England, sent her a letter saying that she did not want to see her any more—ever. It was not that Amanda had "done" anything in particular; her friend simply felt that she couldn't cope with her any longer. Understandably, Amanda was devastated. How could anyone be so cruel? What was so awful about her that made people back off? She could not understand ... she had been so careful to keep her misery and torment to herself.

It would have been a hardhearted person who would not have been moved by her distress, and outraged by her friend's callous action, but I did have some idea in countertransference about how it felt to not really be related to. As far as Amanda was concerned, in her therapy there was only the professional relationship of a dispassionate couple. I was a nice, caring but ultimately uninvolved therapist who meant nothing personally to her at all (and I think she believed or hoped or feared that she meant nothing to me).

As time went on, it became very clear that Amanda viewed me as a "spider-woman" who would trap her in a web and devour her if she related to me. All she wanted to do was to escape and leave all her bad stuff (and me) behind.

The therapist as scapegoat

Thus we entered the scapegoat phase. It was a mark of progress that Amanda was having feelings about me—even if they were wholly negative. The attacking and rubbishing was relentless. Amanda would look brooding, sour and resentful as she dutifully but reluctantly arrived on my doorstep, never a second late. "Everything out there in the world is fine", Amanda would say, "So why am I still coming here? The only reason I'm finding problems is because I'm coming here. If I stopped everything would be just fine. It's all your fault". The solution was simple—get rid of therapy and all the problems would vanish.

Therapy held a mirror that was warped by projection. Amanda was as irrational and unreasonable as a bolshy toddler, and, like the mother, I was to totally to blame for the depth of her pain.

Holding the negative transference without retaliation was vitally important for Amanda, so that the family taboo on the open expression of anger could be redressed. The survival of the therapy in the face of her cold hatred was essential. However, it did not mean that I did not feel indignant and hurt that Amanda was trashing our work together.

Each session we would go over and over the fact that the pain resided in her, it could not be found if it was not there, and while she could blame therapy because that was the place where it was addressed, it was not where it originated. If she sacked me and fled, I insisted, the pain would probably not stay in my consulting room, split off. This observation evoked even more loathing. Amanda ranted and raved about wanting to stop her therapy. There must be some reason, I suggested, why she was so persistent and faithful in attending her sessions. If she really meant that she wanted to leave, I pointed out, all she had to do was walk out the door. Amanda was livid.

The venomous and guilty glance as Amanda arrived each time began to grate away at me and I wondered about my counter-transference desire to dismiss her. I think Amanda was trying to break away before the fierce phantasized attachment could be consciously acknowledged. Would she—could she—ever experience a "we"?

As the long summer break was approaching I suggested that perhaps her wish to flee might have something to do with my abandoning her. That met a blank wall, so I suggested that we see how the break went and think about it again when we met in the autumn.

During the break Amanda travelled through a foreign country with a new friend and had a fantastic adventure. When she came home, back to her own kitchen, however, she regressed to her past eating pattern. For a week she turned into a scavenging insatiable wolf. The experience absolutely terrified her and she knew she had to keep on coming to see me. That did not mean that she liked it. Indeed she resented it bitterly.

In spite of her stated reluctance, Amanda kept on coming, never late, and always anxious to tie her commitments in with mine. I was someone she *could* throw her angry words at, I told her, and unlike mummy and daddy, I would fight her threat to flee prematurely. I understood that her hatred of therapy/me was because she was terrified that she might become so attached that she would be stuck to me forever or that I would never let her go—or help her leave. Amanda smouldered in silence, but steadily the attacks started to fade.

The meeting point

One day, as Amanda was leaving, our eyes met and we shared a smile. To my surprise and delight she was able to talk about the connection in the next session, why it had taken so long to meet my gaze and see herself reflected in my eyes. It had impact and meaning. Perhaps she and I were tentatively on the verge of *coniunctio* after all.

Soon afterwards, Amanda came in beaming, full of good news. She had been thoroughly enjoying her new job and had been sent on a course. It had completely captivated her imagination; she had excelled and was firing on all cylinders. I realized that for the first time Amanda had spontaneously brought something positive to tell me.

The rediscovery of her self-esteem was accompanied by a series of large drawings of her upper body with various birds inspired by Egyptian images. They were funny, elegant, serious and tender in turn, were grounded instead of floating in black space and all had heads now firmly attached. Amanda's whole demeanour in the room and on paper had altered and she began playing with ideas with me.

Amanda had recently been stimulated by an art exhibition about the anatomical body, fascinated by casts of brains, insides of skulls, pickled foetuses and dissections of pregnant women. In one session she described the excitement of imagining travelling around inside her brain/mind. It sounded like a magical mystery tour, full of ideas, thoughts and inspiration. What was it that bothered me, I wondered? Gradually, I realized that although there were pathways through Amanda's body that were fine, that there was one pathway that I suspected was not.

Heart, lungs, circulation, skin, genitals and reproductive systems all related to Amanda's sense of an embodied "I" (Redfearn, 1985). The digestive tract, however, was another matter. What would it be like, I asked her in the next session, to take a tour of her digestive system as she had with her brain. Amanda froze in panic; she said she was terrified about investigating that path. She might find herself going backwards, and losing the solid ground she had gained.

As if holding tightly onto my hand, Amanda began the process of active imagination, investigating her scary digestive tract. The lips were fine, mouth and teeth no big deal ... but going down the throat towards the stomach was to descend into eternal hell. The plunge into her underworld seemed to be inextricably linked with a journey through the digestive system she wished to negate, one she had tried to plug with food. I encouraged Amanda not to flee, but just to look. It felt to me that we were standing together on the fiery brink of hell, gazing into a great dark boiling pit. I said I was not going to abandon her; she did not have to go there, but that in a sense (remembering her initial drawings) she was looking at where she had already been. It was a pivotal moment. However, I was aware that our analytic session was drawing to a close, and I wondered whether Amanda would be able to tolerate holding on to the position her active imagination had brought her to, of gazing into the terrifying pit. In the event, Amanda was able to think about the terrifying feelings both in subsequent sessions with me and develop her investigations through drawings.

The therapy continued. The next two long breaks went well and Amanda's external world began to flourish. A relationship with a man steadily blossomed, she visited her far away family and there were honest, open and affectionate exchanges with both mother and father. She arranged for a selection of family snaps which included herself to be taken and talked about the past—without avoiding the pain and without blame. Her weight now stabilized at her goal without dieting and she got a marvellous new job. Amanda began once more to talk about leaving—but this time without the desperation of fleeing or the need to rubbish. She said how tempting it might be to stay, but now it seemed that she felt confident enough to fly (not flee) the nest.

Discussion

Thinking about Amanda and the issue of uroboric identification has stimulated thought about the defensive and expressive elements of creativity as well as the origins of self and other in *coniunctio*.

Birth—the beginning?

We seem to hold the notion that life begins with birth—and in many ways it does. Emerging from our mother's body is a life or death journey, which sends adrenalin soaring and heart rate dipping. Birth is undeniably momentous. Our entry into the wide world brings air to dormant lungs, a re-routing of blood circulation, the shock of bright light and rainbows of colour, sharp smell, clear sound, cold air, rough texture, and the urgent search for a nipple. The umbilical cord, our previous central lifeline, is cut. The muscular wall of the uterus gives way to nappies, clothes, blankets, enfolding arms and a cradle. The constant umbilical drip feed is replaced with a new experience, of hunger, along with the effort of getting together with the breast, sucking, digesting and defecating.

Birth is such a big event that perhaps we lose sight of the impact of the vital months *in utero*. Human beings do not suddenly switch on their minds or psyche at birth. Freud wrote:

> There is much more continuity between intra-uterine life and earliest infancy than the impressive caesura of the act of birth would have us believe. [Freud, 1960]

The unfolding of the primary original self through deintegration as described by Michael Fordham (Fordham, 1957) probably does not begin at birth. I would imagine consciousness might begin to flicker like scintilla, the seeds of light in darkness (Jung, *C.W.*, 8, para. 430), in the waters of the womb.

Babies *in utero* can suck their tongues, thumbs, and hands. They can lick and swallow, stretch, kick and turn. They make practice breathing movements, touch, feel, drink, hiccup, wee, sleep and dream. A foetus is not simply reactive. As any mother knows, her unborn child explores and stretches the boundaries of its known universe. Twins *in utero* develop patterns of relating that carry on postpartum (Piontelli, 1992).

Touch as an act of separation and individuation

In late pregnancy, as a foetus has a particularly highly developed sense of touch around the mouth and hands, maybe an idea of self and other is already being laid down by the difference in sensation between touching oneself (mouth, cheeks, legs, arms, hands) and touching an other (amniotic membrane and uterine wall, umbilical cord, placenta).

Didier Anzieu writes:

> ... tactile experience has the peculiarity in comparison with all other sensory experiences of being at once endogenous and exogenous,

active and passive. I touch my nose with my finger: my finger gives me the active sensation of touching something, and my nose gives me the passive sensation of being touched by something. This double sensation, passive and active, is peculiar to the skin. [Anzieu, 1990]

Norah Moore recollected her conundrum concerning the role of touch in establishing self and other when she was small:

I remember how, when I was a baby, I used to suck my finger forming a self-containing circle with myself, but wondered if my mouth was touching my finger, or my finger touching my mouth. I would touch two fingers together and asked again, which was touching which? Which one was the sensation in? I touched my mother's finger: now who was touching who? Could she feel through her finger too, or was the feeling all in my finger? If I looked in her eyes, could she look out of her eyes too? Then I remember her saying, "I see you, I can feel you touching me", and then all was clear. I was feeling her and she could feel me, and she acknowledged that I was separate from her. [Moore, 1983, p. 240]

Drawing as defence and creation

Images bridge archetypes and consciousness, making numinous pre-verbal meaning. As Norah Moore indicated above, hands that touch, eyes that see and an "other" who affirms, all help us develop a sense of self. "I see" also means "I understand"; an archetype begins to assemble an image.

Amanda wrote in her thesis:

...hands are the primary anatomical structure for touching and feeling, and as babies the first other part of our bodies we become aware of...

...Skin (is) an elusive substance of no definable colour or shape, at once shimmering or dull, concealing and revealing, malleable and defining our changeable outer limits. It is the organ of touch that is touchable and untouchable, feeling and felt. Skin is at the interface of the visible and the invisible, which is one place I could posit my art ... isolated nudity as the bare evidence of existence.

In the womb, the unlocking of a primordial uroboric state of undifferentiated unity may have already begun, moving from the symbol of a snake biting its tail to the numinous duality of Archetypal Feminine, symbolized by the vessel, and Archetypal Masculine symbolized by the snake (Neumann, 1955). Perhaps for a daughter like Amanda, growing in the darkened belly of her mother, the Maternal Uroborus, symbol of not only containment and creativity but also suffocation and annihilation, has particularly strong meaning and archetypal image.

If, at puberty, Amanda's sense of self felt unable to deal with her emerging sexuality, she may have turned for support to the stimulation of an earlier erotogenic zone—her mouth (Kohut, 1977). However, if that zone in itself brought up a reminder of a crucial failure of empathy in the feeding relationship with her mother, the only way of dealing with this might have been by attempting to re-create her own uroboric world based on the uterine memory of there being "no-body".

Observing newborn infants can be helpful here. Tiny babies make repetitive circular movements with their arms and hands. Maybe their exploration meets an "other" or maybe simply feels the air. Does the movement have its origins in an exploration of the internal surface of the encircling womb? The following extract from an infant observation illustrates this:

> When she was newborn, Victoria used to fall asleep with her right hand up behind her right ear. Maybe this was the way she had come to hold herself *in utero*?

> Perhaps it was the long silky hair by her ear that contributed to her interest in touch and textures; the regular sounds of heartbeat and later sucking that led to repetitive rhythmic movements and play; and the round walls of the womb that linked with the circular movement which she would repeat, looping from her head to the breast with closed eyes. From two days old Victoria's right hand would stretch out and around, the index finger of that hand finding her mouth...

> When she was nearly two years old Victoria would push her buggy in circles linking the kitchen with the living room and hall. I wondered if there was some connection with the way she made loops to the breast. If Daddy sat down I saw Victoria push her buggy round and round him as though she was weaving a spell, a

hag track, a fairy ring around him, an enchantment to have breast and Daddy within her power?

I imagined with all this circling that Victoria was somehow making a cyclic connection with the boundaries of her world, perhaps in an attempt to define her self. [Mathew, 1992, pp. 111–112]

I wonder whether, for Amanda, the rhythmic stroking of pencil on paper in the production of art might be related to an omnipotent desire to re-create a sense of security and wholeness? Perhaps by drawing her own body, hands and skin over and over again Amanda was working away at producing more than art. Her drawings were minutely observed areas of her skin almost like landscapes, perhaps denying the existence of the external human "other" while at the same time creating a world in her own image. The symbol of the mandala is a circular defining and defensive ring of magical omnipotence representative of the self (Jung, *C.W.*, 12, paras. 122—331). Perhaps that archetypal image also has its origins in early psychosomatic experience *in utero*.

Sight can be used as a means of defence. We see the external world through our own eyes but we may choose to edit, blur or distort what is there, turn our gaze off or direct it inwards. When observing infants, we find that some babies show a clear preference for employing a particular sense. While making rhythmic sounds, focusing on muscularity or picking at textures may appeal to some babies, others rely very much on their sense of sight to "stick themselves" visually to objects, lights, or through windows, creating a second skin (Bick, 1987) "out there" in which to lose or get out of themselves, or to create an alternative vision. Perhaps all defensive manoeuvres are, at root, acts of creation, and vice versa.

The almost unbearable tension between the opposition of regression with individuation quickens the creative activity of the transcendent function described by Jung:

The shuttling to and fro of arguments and affects represents the transcendent function of the opposites. The confrontation of the two positions generates a tension charged with energy and creates a living, third thing—not a logical still birth in accordance with the principle *tertium non datur*, but a movement out of the suspension between opposites, a living birth that leads to a new level of being, a new situation. [Jung, *C.W.*, 8, para. 189]

Perhaps this is where the act of drawing has played such a vital role for Amanda, a way of activating the transcendent function.

Unlocking uroboric identification demands letting go of the "tail in the mouth": experiencing hunger and longing, managing a reflection and risking relationship at a profound level. Amanda let go of her "tail" in order to sink her teeth into therapy, but it seemed vital for some of the experience to remain within Amanda's absolute control—on the surface of the paper. The artwork then became a locus of transformation (Schaverien, 1991) where it was possible to track the evolution and healing of her internal world as if it were a dream series.

Amanda did not want to be completely "cured". She recognized that her inner struggle fuels her creativity, and her art is an essential aspect of herself and the meaning of life. As she leaves, she takes with her a stronger ego, a fitter body, a more confident sense of her self, a place in her family and a vision for a future. I, for my part, am left with a beautiful drawing for my wall and the enduring memory of the privilege and pleasure of working with the creative psyche.

References

Anzieu, D. (1990). *A Skin for Thought*. London: Karnac Books.

Bick, E. (1987). The experience of the skin in early object relation. In: *Collected Papers of Martha Harris and Esther Bick*. Perthshire: Clunie Press.

Fordham, M. (1957). *New Developments in Analytical Psychology*. London: Routledge & Kegan Paul.

Freud, S. (1960). *Inhibitions, Symptoms and Anxiety. S.E., 20*.

Glasser, M. (1979). Some aspects of the role of aggression in the perversions. In: I. Rosen (Ed.), *Sexual Deviation*. Oxford: Oxford University Press.

Guntrip, H. (1969). *Schizoid Phenomena, Object Relations and the Self*. New York: International Universities Press.

Kalsched, D. E. (1996). *The Inner World of Trauma*. London: Routledge.

Kohut, H. (1977). *The Restoration of the Self*. New York: International Universities Press.

Mathew, M. A. F. (1992). Stranded starfish. *Journal of the British Association of Psychotherapy, 23*, July: 111–112.

Moore, N. (1983). The archetype of the way. *Journal of Analytical Psychology, 28*(3), July: 240

Neumann, E. (1955). *The Great Mother.* London: Routledge & Kegan Paul.

Perry, C. (1991). *Listen to the Voice Within.* London: SPCK.

Piontelli, A. (1992). *From Fetus to Child.* London: Routledge.

Redfearn, J. W. T. (1985). *My Self, My Many Selves.* London: Academic Press.

Schaverien, J. (1991). *The Revealing Image.* London: Routledge.

CHAPTER SIX

The elusive elixir: aspects of the feminine in a male patient

Margaret Hammond

Introduction

I am in a department store, where an elixir has been advertised. I am
with a woman. The elixir consists of two phials, each containing a
substance, and they must be mixed together, to produce the potion. I
look at the ingredients, which are just spirits of salts and water. I am
doubtful, but try anyway. They fizz, and I drink the resulting liquid.
It tastes like Eno's. I am very disappointed.

This was the dream of a patient called John which appeared
nearly six years into his analysis. Jung placed the
psychology of the transference, and the mixing of analyst
and patient within it, at the centre of his thinking on the analytic
process. This dream, with its two phials, its two substances, the man
and the woman, the promise of the elixir, the *fermentio*, and
subsequent disappointment, sets the scene for the drama of mixing
and separating out within the analytic container, which I will try to
describe in this chapter. In the dream, the coming together of the
substances, the *coniunctio*, leads to loss and disillusionment. What
was advertised as the elixir of life, a magical feeding, turns out to be

a mere cure for indigestion. I will explore this idea of magical feeding, which was deeply embedded in an archetypal image of mother, in whom everything was encompassed, self, mother and anima, but which was, of course, indigestible and unattainable, and led to disillusionment and despair. I will describe how differentiations gradually emerged, heralded by events in the transference, and illustrated in a series of vivid dreams, which appeared at crucial stages in the work. The dreams describe the evolution of the internal situation, regulated by the operation of the self, and acted on, from the outside, by a great struggle in the transference, to separate out self and other, mother and child, lover and beloved. This struggle was painful and disturbing to both analyst and patient but formed part of the dialectical process of change as the internal and external worlds interacted.

The analytic container

In her chapter "The intersubjective nature of analysis" (1988), Mel Marshak outlined Jung's alchemical symbols for the process of the transference. I will emphasize three, namely the *vas*, the *coniunctio* and the *lapis*.

The *vas*, the container, can refer to two possible containers: first, the analyst as the container for the patient, and second, the analysis as the container for both analyst and patient. What I describe later concerns the struggle to move from the first situation to the second. The *coniunctio*, the union of opposites, was the treasure sought by my patient, but the difficulty in reaching this position lay, as I will describe, in the process of separating out, in order for there to be opposites which could creatively combine. The *lapis* is the metaphor for individuation, and the struggle for the actualization of the self. I suggest that within the vas, containing both analyst and patient, there is a struggle for actualization of the self of both. Or, to take this further, Warren Colman, in "Models of the self" (2000), referring to Fordham's statement that the self deintegrates and reintegrates, says, "We might see the self **as** deintegration and reintegration..." (That is, the self is the **process**.) He goes on, "The nascent individual may be a system, but it is perpetually in interaction with other systems, and is itself made up of myriad part-systems down to the level of genes, and further down to their atomic constituents ... The self emerges out of this primary wholeness and develops towards a discriminating consciousness capable of asking from whence it came". This self as process was active in both of us, within our analytic dyad, allowing the gradual release of material as it could be both experienced and tolerated.

The archetypes

Michael Fordham states in *Self and Autism* (1976) that, as the self deintegrates, it releases archetypal images. I have already mentioned the archetype of the mother, which must be present, in some form, in all analyses. Of this archetype, Jung says, "The mother is the matrix—the hollow form, the vessel that carries and nourishes, and it stands psychologically for the foundations of consciousness" (Jung, C.W., 16, para. 344). Into this vessel all experience is poured, experience of light and shadow, blissful oneness, or terrible entrapment, bountiful feeding, or being devoured. The carrier of this archetype is, in the first place, the personal mother, because the child lives at first in complete participation with her, in a state of unconscious identity. Edward Edinger (1960) speaks of the infant self being projected into mother, in this state of unconscious identity, and the eventual development of the self in relation to the growing ego, through what he calls the ego-self axis.

The task of separating from mother, personal or archetypal, is a massive one, and is the task of the hero. The idea of the hero is expounded by Neumann (1954a,b), with his quest to slay the dragon, standing for the Terrible Mother, to release the anima from the mother archetype. In Neumann, the hero is always male, but in line with Tatham, (1992), Covington (1989), and other modern thinkers, I think of the hero as present in both sexes. Both male and female need to achieve separation from mother, and when the analysis is with a female analyst and a male patient, the hero will need to be present in both parties. I am therefore including the hero among my aspects of the feminine.

In more personal terms, we can think of this separation as the task begun with the Oedipal conflict. Here, the child struggles to come to terms with the reality that it was mother's relationship with another that brought him into being. In this complex, the devouring mother may appear in the shadow as a projection, the product of the child's wish to stay safely in a two-person relationship, free of the pain and uncertainty of a threesome. Thus, a dragon may be constellated in the psyche, which will need to be slain later. For the negotiation of this stage, a child, boy or girl, will be helped, although in different ways, by a good enough relationship with the father.

Warren Colman discusses these links, emphasizing how the opposite sex parent embodies the contra-sexual archetype, while remaining distinct from it. The recognition of this distinction is vital for individuation. He says:

> At the height of the Oedipus complex, parental and contra-sexual images are fused and in a way, this creates the complex, since an intense longing for union with the oedipally loved parent is due to the fascinating power of the contra-sexual archetype with which they are identified. [Colman, 1996, p. 40]

The anima has been described in many ways by Jung and his successors. There has been much discussion whether she is present in both sexes, and whether she represents the soul. However, in Jungian theory there is a consistent concept of the dialectic of opposition, such that the anima represents and points to the opposite. For the masculine, this will be the feminine; for the conscious, the unconscious; for the ego, the self. It is important to note that, although the anima may provide a bridge to the feminine in the male unconscious, she is actually the complementary aspect of the hero, part of the male psyche, and not a separate entity.

My fourth feminine image is the heroine. I think the modern climate leaves the archetype of the heroine greatly neglected, and in some ways, despised. I will refer to Coline Covington's paper, "In search of the heroine" (1989) in which she makes the case for the heroine in her own right, not as the anima aspect of the hero, still stuck in the maternal nexus, but as a separate being with her own task to perform. The struggle of the hero is to become conscious, and he embodies the archetype of separation. The struggle of the heroine is to allow unconsciousness, to separate from the father, the logos, the ego, and presumably, to wrest the animus from the archetype of the father. This allows regression to a steady state, where the bridging of opposites can bring wholeness. She refers to Grimm's fairy story, The Handless Maiden, where a maiden, although handicapped, is compelled to leave her father's home, and languish many years in the forest, before undergoing a process of individuation, which enables her to be repaired and return to the world. Covington says, "Just as the hero has to be able to imagine something other or different, in order to be able to separate (from mother), the heroine must imagine what is within, to reintegrate matter, and in this way, regain her contact with the world outside". This is clearly a symbol for the process of pregnancy, but also for the process of analysis, for the containment and internal working, which may only be recognized when it is sufficiently complete, and able to emerge into consciousness.

In her paper, Covington suggests the idea of hero/heroine functioning together in dynamic interdependence, counter-balancing each other, in a reactive psychological process. She suggests that this pair constitutes a way of imagining the dynamics of deintegration and reintegration, and necessarily go hand in hand. In the rest of this chapter, as I explore some aspects of my work with a male patient, I will describe, how, as a female analyst, I embodied the mother transference in its many manifestations, including the anima. However, to effect transformation, it was necessary for the hero/heroine pair to play a vital part.

John

It's now time to introduce my patient, a man of middle years, who I will call John. He came into analysis with the aim of gaining a better rapport with women. John came from a large family where he was the only boy and one of the youngest, born to a mother coming to the end of her child bearing years. Mother is the one important figure in his early life, and inner world. Father is represented as weak, irrelevant, feminine, and symbolizes an inferior function. The image of mother is of a heroic figure, soldiering on grimly, through great adversity. She is a figure of action, not reflection, steely and tough. She encouraged her small son to fight in the rough environment in which they lived and any wounds which he suffered in the process were promptly taken to the hospital for treatment, with no feeling of sympathy or tenderness. However, inside this steely exterior, John intuited a helpless, neglected figure, empty and in need of his constant help, which became the recipient of his anima projection. In response to this, he became her constant helper in practical matters, mending things, earning small amounts of money, and certainly in his fantasies, father was virtually absent.

However, the tragedy was that he received no emotional reward for his labours from mother, apart from his own internal fantasy of being indispensable, in a world where mother and he were the only real people that mattered. So, in response to this negative experience of exclusion and deprivation, he took money from her, cut down her favourite tree, and internally entertained murderous fantasies. In the absence of a feeling of containment and affection, in his inner world he struggled with a whole range of ideas of how to get into mother by any means possible. This made it impossible to separate internally from this powerful, binding figure. Covington (1996), describes such a situation in the early relationship with mother where "her own feelings (mother's), particularly her own infantile needs for a responsive mother, make her frightened or over-whelmed by her baby's needs, so that she is unable to receive his projections and to differentiate them from her own. If this process goes wrong, then there is never a strong enough attachment which can support separation". Such was the situation with my patient.

The transference

For the first years of the analysis, I embodied this internal mother. In the transference, I was experienced as extremely powerful, and it seemed essential for me to "know", and to be experienced as "right". Anything else would induce panic, in which John would either need to take over the power himself, or suffer a dread, tantamount to falling apart. At this point, we were in the grip of the hero. I think this was necessary, because it was only a heroic analyst who could stand up to the negative power of the internal mother. If I embodied the hero John could allow himself to experience the dependent child, with powerful loving feelings, such as he never remembered experiencing before.

The other prevalent issue was containment. As long as I talked, and produced words, John could feel contained. As soon as I was silent, stopping to think, feel or wait, he felt excluded or in the presence of a great emptiness. He could feel this in the room between us, and would try to manage it by talking himself, trying harder and harder to get inside me with his words. If this failed, he would feel it in his body, with gnawing stomach pains, only satisfied by food. No wonder he dreamed of indigestion mixture! In this situation, the heroine aspect could not appear. She was experienced as empty, helpless, and no fence against chaos, and had to remain a barely conscious possibility inside me.

Enter the heroine

I take up the story on a February day, when the Oedipal issue resurfaced, as it had done many times before. This time it appeared in relation to his reluctance to recognize that I had any particular analytic orientation. This seemed to present a problem because of the implications—it would mean I read other people's ideas, that I might have supervisors, or an analyst, in fact, that I had other relationships important to me. This whole idea summoned up a great storm, out of which certain thoughts were distilled. It became clear that I was inflated as the one with all the knowledge as a defence against any idea of my having teachers, standing for father. To keep me in that place he had fantasies of wanting to chain me up, and keep me captive. I was first inflated, then rendered helpless. In the course of this, he reiterated how he could only achieve if it were in relation to me, like the boy who had to give all his earnings to mother, and that I was the only one with any value. It also became clearer that this involved a projection of the self into me, where he could then identify with it and share in the feelings of inflation.

There was something about this inflation which caused me to respond. I had contained it in the past, but this time I attempted to give something back, hoping it could be reintrojected. I commented on the great value of all the work he puts into the analysis. I have said such things before when they have gone almost unnoticed, not fitting in to the need of the time. This time the response was huge. At first, he was incredulous, and this quickly turned to anger, and a feeling of despair. I think he felt turned out of Eden, that I was attempting to return some of this projection of the self, through which I was supposed to look after all the meaning, while he looked after me. In my attempt to reverse his inflation of me, he felt I deflated him. But, as Edinger describes in *Ego and Archetype* (1972), in being turned out of Eden, Adam and Eve, very painfully, gained in consciousness. This was the case here.

In retrospect, I think the heroine was beginning to emerge, but I was not quite conscious of this. However, I was no longer holding the heroic inflation. I had made an independent comment, which showed that I could not be chained up, but I had also connected internally with all that I had been containing, and began a move towards reality. I was trying to let John know that his deintegrative behaviour had found a receptive mother/analyst, and been taken in, but he could not yet reintegrate any experience of that. He was still stuck in his system where I was the container of his self, and so any independent valuation by me was intolerable.

The first dream

John's response came in a dream, on the Friday night. It felt like a big dream, and unusually, he wrote it down to recount on Monday.

There is a Queen, although she wears no crown. She is with a group of maidens, wearing Roman type dresses, laughing and playing, answering her every whim. They are guarded by a patrolling lion, who notices me, and skirmishes with me. I feel guilty, that I have done something with my hands. They smell of fish paste, a smell from childhood that I don't like. The lion notices the smell, and is especially vigilant. They all go upstairs towards a chamber. There is an especially sensual girl, who would have gone in with the Queen, if I hadn't been there, but as it was, the Queen shut her out. The Queen knew I was there, and smiled at me a lot. But she smiled at everyone.

A man wants instructions to make and hang a door. I am explaining how to measure and fit it, and say I will phone him back. I lose the telephone number, and feel desperate.

In his associations to the dream, John felt the Queen was numinous, and stood for the feminine, and for me. The maidens reminded him of his sisters; the lion was a powerful male symbol; the fish paste reminded him of the smell of masturbating, or of being with a woman.

Indeed, the dream did seem to be telling us something about his relation to the feminine, at this point when he felt I had disturbed things between us. I thought that, as Queen, I was being put firmly back on my throne, with my chamber at the top of the stairs, although I had lost my crown, the symbol of my authority. There is a distinct sexual flavour to the dream, with all the focus on the Queen. There is a suggestion that the anima is represented by the maidens, and the sensual one in particular, who the Queen perhaps shut out in order that she might relate to John. However, they too are focused on the Queen, and of secondary interest. The lion, standing for the masculine, also seems to represent the John who would guard me vigilantly against any other males, including, paradoxically, himself, with his powerful instincts. This Queen is tantalizing and excluding. John is in thrall, with only his guilty attempts at contact, fantasies or masturbating, represented by the fish paste smell, for company. Any contact he may have had with another woman is a source of guilt.There is the feeling that he just might gain admittance, if he could get past the lion. The feminine is narcissistic, all encompassing, the mother, the beloved, the captivator, and the masculine is primitive and dangerous.

In the second part of the dream, there is some idea of the need for a door, providing separation, but the contact with the man who might fit it, is lost. The dream seemed to provide a vivid image of the internal situation in relation to the feminine, which had been so disturbed by the tentative appearance on stage of the heroine.

The second dream

For the next year, we worked with this material, with his feeling of exclusion, the difficulty of connection, and the powerful feelings of love and anger that this engendered. We then arrived at a period of vivid dreams, which appeared over a couple of months. The dreams were all to do with issues concerning the feminine. Some of these I will now discuss.

Again, we had returned to the topic of his idealization of me. This time it appeared more as a defence against a feeling of unfairness, for instance, the inequalities of the analytic frame. He got in touch with primitive feelings of aggression and greed, and spoke of the wall he erects to protect me from such affects.This led me to talk of the analytic container, within which we both are held, as opposed to the situation of me as the only container, which causes him so much anxiety. His first response was positive. This might dispense with the need for the wall, if I were contained too, and we were together inside something. This fulfilled his conscious wish. However, as in the previous year, the backlash was enormous. He felt both over-excited by the idea, and at the same time, isolated and lost. Again the idea of the frame stood for another, a symbolic father or mother, who contained me, which meant I was not omnipotent and neither could he be. Now, it did seem as if something had radically changed. He brought the image of being in the foundations of a castle, where the underground tunnels were getting narrower, and he was following a leader. It was too late to go back. His reactions veered to and fro. At one extreme he spoke of a terror that Samson had pulled down the temple, and Samson was sometimes me and sometimes him. At the other extreme, in a numinous session, he had an experience of feeling completely "known in essence and potential". He produced an image of meeting the "The Piper at the gates of Dawn". The piper seemed to stand for God, or the Self, a mysterious Other.

At this time, there was a sense of hero and heroine beginning to co-exist, in John, and in me. In the disturbance following my remarks about the analytic frame, there was definitely a fight, maybe a dragon fight, when the temple was pulled down by Samson, and rage and disillusion rumbled around for weeks. However, the heroine was also playing her part, giving birth to the image of the Piper, the numinous other, this time, wonderful, not threatening and terrible. The image did not stay. Its time had not yet fully come, and it vanished from whence it came, leaving John with no recollection of it by the next week.

The dream which finally emerged was the one I quoted at the beginning, but now I quote it in full.

> I am having sex with a naked woman, and doing what is required to please her. I am about to enter her, when I stop and go off somewhere else. The scene changes to a 16th century house with bay windows, but very dark. An old woman is working there, complaining bitterly, that she comes in at weekends and works,

but her life is worthless and there is no reward. Then, I am in an old street, and the house is on fire. Someone has torched it.

I am in a department store, where an elixir has been advertised. I am with a woman. The elixir consists of two phials, each containing a substance, and they must be mixed together, to produce the potion. I look at the ingredients, which are just spirits of salts and water. I am doubtful, but try anyway. They fizz, and I drink the resulting liquid. It tastes like Eno's. I am very disappointed.

He associated the old woman with his mother, who worked all the time, but also with himself, and the caring for which there is no reward. The fire, he associated with rage, and the fires he started as a child. The sex, with which the dream started, is a non-rewarding business, with all the emphasis on providing pleasure, rather than receiving it.

Taking the two parts of the dream together, there is a theme of disappointment and disillusion. There is no reciprocity, which is how he often experiences the process of analysis, and there is the difficulty of all the psychological work he has to do alone at weekends.There is no elixir, no magic, no reward. But, there is a separating out, two phials, a mother and lover, which provides a space in which feelings can be expressed, by the torching, or the effervescing, instead of being bound in idealization or inflation. But, at present, the old system has been torched, and the new one is disappointing. However, I remembered the piper, with hope.

The third dream

In the sessions that followed, we began to understand the importance of the lack of the paternal container, which came as the result of my referring to the analytic container, which had caused such panic. It was so threatening to try and cope with this emerging separateness without a satisfying identification with father. We struggled with his difficulty in coping with my independent validation of him, rather than the one he tried to induce. In retrospect, I think this was the equivalent of my rescuing the animus from the power of the father. My thoughts were based on my personal experience of him in the analysis, and my independent thinking. At one point, I referred to his creativity.

Again, this was experienced as a huge loss. He invested all the creativity in me, where he could admire it. If it was in him, it felt like a defence against futility. It is true that with John, I do feel creative and value that experience, but I also know it is partly because he encourages and wants this situation, as the only way to keep the creativity safe from devaluation. But, I began to feel we were moving from a situation of container/contained, to one of more mutuality. It felt as if the process of the self was active between us, rather than needing to be held so firmly inside me. After John's image of the Piper at the Gates of Dawn, the heroine was beginning to constellate in him too, and he could feel that something had changed. He began to think about the undesirability of actually trying to force his feelings into me, now that he did feel more contained. He was becoming increasingly able to wait in hope not despair.

The next dream in this discussion came the week before the Easter break.

> I am driving in a foreign country after the war. It is like the Steppes of Russia, grassy and rocky, with no roads. I am in a jeep or Mini Moke. I am looking for a woman, who has an address in heiroglyphs. I ask the way of peasants in scattered houses, and they send me on a wild goose chase. I ask someone who sends me down a steep path to a village. It's wrong, and I go up again. Finally, I reach a place where a soldier with a gun is guarding a gate. He steps aside to let me go in. I go through a series of rough gates with rough locks to a central house. There is the woman. She is a dark woman, with her eyes open, in a trance. She is upside down in a bath, in the lotus or foetal position. The people around her fade away. I don't know what to do to wake her, so I leave sadly, and drive off in the jeep.

John himself associated the woman with the anima. (He has considerable knowledge of analytic concepts.) He also thought that it stood for me, because we had been musing on the image of me that he would take with him into the break. His thoughts then quickly turned to a powerful image of mother, in whose bed he had only once slept, aged seven, before going to hospital. He was mortified that she turned her back on him, instead of cuddling him, and this has remained a potent symbol. He became depressed, wondering if the woman in the dream was dead, and turned for comfort to my cushion.

It seemed to me that, after his heroic journey across the steppes, after the struggle to find the way, in his macho jeep, with all the misleading instructions and such a foreign address, he reached this well guarded fortress, but was let in without a struggle. I imagine that this image could stand for the receptive mother, who does not require him to force an entry, but contains him, because inside the terrain is well differentiated, and there are many gates which have to be opened. In this situation, he was able to find the anima, who was separate from mother, but still deeply unconscious. He was not yet able to wait beside the woman, because she felt too strange and different, in her trance. In the dream he left, in his jeep, or Mini Moke, which introduced the idea that something was in fact, small and vulnerable. In the room, he managed his sadness by cuddling my cushon, which we know stands for me. In the present, he is now able to turn to the symbol of a body mother, to find comfort when his memories are so rejecting.

The fourth dream

This dream came in the middle of his Easter holiday, which was an extended break. The dream speaks for itself.

> I am in a big church, with a high atrium, like Liverpool Cathedral. There are galleries, each with a church window at the end. A ceremony is going on. My analyst is being given an award or promotion, and is wearing a shimmering blue dress. She is accompanied by an old man, an elderly sage. I am content to watch quietly, and am filled with good feelings.

John did not want to think about this dream or produce any associations. It just was. He had had a good holiday with little anxiety, and it seemed that I had been installed somewhere in his inner world. I could appear clearly in a relationship with this old man, the sage, maybe my teacher, which produced no reaction in John. The building was sanctified, large and differentiated, with galleries and plenty of light. I am wearing blue, which he associated with Mary's colour. There is a sense now of an independent but related me, not narcissistic and provocative, but clearly connected to him, and also to the old man, the other, a third. In the space provided by the break, something had consolidated, an award for both of us. Now he could truly reintegrate, under the influence of the heroine, and become conscious through the dream of what he had absorbed.

The fifth dream

After the break, the deintegrative process started up again. Now, I was more aware myself of feeling confused, scared, and helpless, especially in the wake of his powerful sexual feelings, which dominated the sessions, following the recounting of this dream. It seemed as if the question of mother had been settled, at least for now, which released the energy to engage with sexual matters. Now, I had to trust to the process, and survive his rage and frustration as there was nothing else I could do. Like the heroine, I could only wait. Eventually, the fifth dream appeared.

> I am in a camp of wooden huts. Some are dormitories and some are single. We are on the prairie, and a hurricane is coming. People are dashing around, wondering what direction it is coming from, and where to go. I go inside the huts. They are like changing cubicles, and insubstantial. I decide the only place to go is outside. The hurricane is all around but I must stay out in the open. Then suddenly, the clouds vanish, and the hurricane has dissipated.

This dream somehow produced a real disconnection between us. It was as if he had dreamed of what I had been experiencing the previous week, when I could only stay in the open, waiting for the storm to abate. His association was with yesterday's session, when he felt his unconscious fears had come to the surface and been dissipated. I could not connect with this thought, and my attention wandered. John picked this up intuitively, and returned to the powerful elemental feelings of last week. My response to this was to feel even more out of touch, as if I now could not remain conscious and thinking, but had to retreat inside myself, like the changing cubicles in the dream. John began to talk in an agitated fashion about the despair of not reaching me. The storm was blowing up in the room, as it had in the dream. He explained how he could not cope if I were not just the same as him, a state which would, he thought, make it impossible to be out of touch. This barrage of words brought me back into the room, thinking that actually we had been in touch, through this dream, but at a mutually unconscious level. I referred to the dream, in which the clouds vanished when John came out into the open, and waited. He said he could not risk that, he needed to shelter, and that the changing cubicle was inside me. He feared I would not wait with him, if he were outside. How could he trust that I would keep thinking, and try to reconnect, if I was different, female, not under his control. In this session, we had experienced an enactment of the dream, with John storming, and me temporarily taking cover. I was not at all sure where either of us were at the end of it, although I knew John had calmed down on the surface.

I discovered next day that, to his surprise, and mine, he went away feeling connected and creative, although he did not know why. Although his stream of increasingly desperate words stopped my logical thought, they strongly reached me at another level as a cry for help, when I had wandered off in my mind. This gave him the experience that he could get me back, and so he felt creative, because in some way, **he** had done it. Instead of an unresponsive, unreliable figure, I had become a temporarily distracted mother whose attention could be regained. For my part, under the influence of his dream, I could respond differently, by allowing myself to drift off into my own thoughts, with the confidence that we could reconnect. When the noise of the words ceased, in the quiet, we could hear each other, and it had a powerful effect.

The sixth dream

The next dream appeared just one day later.

I'm in an old car which is not mine, and am crossing a bridge over a huge chasm. The car is a khaki colour. I've been here before and got lost. There's a house on the other side, like a New England country cottage. A woman is inside waiting, and time is short. I think this road won't lead to the cottage. Sure enough, I end up down in a chasm. I get out of the car, which is an old Opel. I abandon it in the valley, but I'm lost.

John's thoughts were about the foreignness of the house, and how lost he felt. The car was old and outmoded, and stood for an old part of himself. The bridge stood for his old thinking, which was outmoded too, and now he knew it didn't link him to the woman, someone outside himself and his psychological systems. He was beginning to understand something that he had learnt from experience, rather than from thinking. I thought that the previous day, we had had an experience of being in the ravine together, and felt the need to meet down there, before we could reach the cottage. Maybe, we could now both tolerate feeling lost, and having to wait and trust to the process of the unfolding self.

The final dream

At the Bank Holiday, when he felt quite lost and alone, he had this dream.

> I am in the Navy, and on shore leave with a friend. We have been to the fair. My friend wants to chat up a girl we met, but I do not. However, my friend meets the girl, and I feel I should not be there. I stay to irritate them for a bit, and then I am transported up to my boat, the Queen Mary. Tucked under the prow of the boat is a tiny boat meant for me. I wonder how I can get it down to get into it. Then, I am turning the Queen Mary to face back up the estuary, away from the sea.

In this final dream of the series, the sexy girl and mother, the Queen Mary, are quite separated, and he has a sense of boundaries and of the possibility of intrusion. We still have the Queen, as in the first dream, and Mary reappears, a reference to the cathedral dream. But now, the Queen has become the mother, and there is a cosy place for John in his little boat under the prow, with just the problem of how to climb into it. But for now, he decides he does not want to face towards the sea, with the possibility of having to set sail, in his old heroic manner, so turns the boat round to face upstream, and allow time in the harbour for further developments to take place.

Discussion and conclusions

This series of dreams illustrates a gradual transformation in John's inner world, in his relation to the feminine. In the first dream, the self, the mother and the anima were all combined in the provocative queen, served by her maidens and protected by her patrolling lion. For any differentiation to be possible, we had to confront the shadow, with the rage and fire of the second dream, and the war zone of the third, before meeting a different woman in the centre of the many-gated town. However, she was in a trance and unavailable. This produced great sadness, but John could now find some comfort with me. This seemed to point the way for the installation of the analyst, in the holiday dream, as a good inner object, and one who could be allowed some separateness. We then had to face again the turbulence of the sexual issue, and in the course of this work reached a sense of deep relatedness, which heralded a new climate of reciprocity. The final dream illustrates clear differentiations and containment, but with the message, "Don't send me to sea too quickly like before!"

In this process activated by the self, we had to contain archetypal images of mother, self, and anima. I have argued that the transformation came about with progressive deintegration and reintegration under the influence of the hero/heroine. John could not separate from his mother because he had never felt sufficiently attached. In the analysis, he did not want to risk losing something he felt he had hardly attained. The dragon fight had to be initiated by me. I had to separate my self from his projections: that of heroic knowledge and creativity, which actually made us twin heroes, and of anima weakness, which enabled him to look after me. To achieve this, I needed to deflate myself, and experience myself as dependent, but on another, the analytic frame and all that means. To be effective, this had to happen at the level of the heroine, in the unconscious, with a real coniunctio, inside me. My responses then came from a different internal space, where my understanding was based on an experience of the opposites, the strength of letting go, and the space for creativity which is opened up by unknowing. I think this allowed a new atmosphere between us, in which a receptive heroine could begin to emerge in him, bringing about a transformation.

As for the elixir, it appeared briefly in the image of the Piper at the gates of dawn, then evaporated. In the end, it may turn out to be some more digestible state, in which internal images of the feminine are more differentiated, and in which hope is stronger than despair.

References

Colman, W. (1996). Aspects of anima and animus in Oedipal development. *Journal of Analytical Psychology, 41*: 37–57.

Colman, W. (2000). Models of the self. In: E. Christopher & H. Solomon (Eds.), *Jungian Thought in the Modern World*. London: Free Association Books.

Covington, C. (1989). In search of the heroine. *Journal of Analytical Psychology, 34*: 243–254.

Covington, C. (1996). Purposive aspects of the erotic transference. *Journal of Analytical Psychology, 41*: 339–352.

Edinger, E. (1960). The ego–self paradox. *Journal of Analytical Psychology, 5*: 3–18.

Edinger, E. (1972). *Ego and Archetype*. Boston and London: Shambala Publications.

Fordham, M. (1976). *Self and Autism*. London: Heinemann.

Marshak, M. (1998). The intersubjective nature of analysis. In: I. Alister & C. Hauke (Eds.), *Contemporary Jungian Analysis*. London: Routledge.

Neumann, E. (1954a). *The Origins and History of the Unconscious*. London: Routledge & Kegan Paul.

Neumann, E. (1954b). *The Great Mother*. New York: Bollingen Series.

Tatham, P. (1992). *The Making of Maleness*. London: Karnac Books.

Further reading

Christopher, E. (2000). Gender issues: animus and anima. In: E. Christopher & H. Solomon (Eds.), *Jungian Thought in the Modern World*. London: Free Association Books.

Izod, J. (1996). The piano, the animus and the colonial experience. *Journal of Analytical Psychology, 41*: 117–136.

Weisstub, E. (1997). Self as the feminine principle. *Journal of Analytical Psychology, 42*: 425–452.

CHAPTER SEVEN

Excretions and interpretations: some thoughts on the contamination of psychological space and its effect upon psychological capacity

Elizabeth Richardson

Introduction

The purpose of this paper is to look at the effect on the analyst of containing and carrying the patient's poisonous projections. The importance of the analyst's capacity to imagine the patient imagining, so that growth may be facilitated is discussed in connection with the effect on the infant's psyche, when the mother may have been unable to imagine her infant imagining.

Conscious awareness of the patient's use of projective identification can provide a means of perceiving and eventually interpreting the transference. Ogden describes projective identification as the dynamic interplay of the intrapsychic and the interpersonal (Ogden, 1982). This can be likened to the amniotic fluid surrounding the foetus *in utero*. This fluid contains elements of the mother's and the infant's physical inner and outer world state. The developing foetus excretes into this fluid during the last trimester of pregnancy.

It is possible for the analyst and patient to experience a state which is an unknown time, a kind of archetypal time which can be activated in the present, and experienced as an "is" and not as an "as if". The "is" and the "as if" have merged.

The ability of the analyst to be able to recognize the "is" moments in analysis may enable the patient to experience an early infant state in the transference. This can lead to the patient beginning to be able to use metaphor and the "as if" in the analytic setting.

This phenomenon is defined by Fordham, in his description of the primary self. He says,

> I conclude with a reflection on the "ultimate". I take it to represent a state in which there is no past and no future, though it is present like a point which has position but no magnitude. It has no desires, no memory, no thoughts, no images, but out of it by transformation all of these can deintegrate. There is no consciousness and so no unconsciousness—it is a pregnant absence. [Fordham, 1985, p. 33]

In his description of deintegration and reintegration, Fordham describes the interplay of the archetypal and the external, which occurs from before birth.

I offer a personal example of the kind of moment I am describing. Before I had any notion of the theories of inner world experiences or object relations as a young adolescent, I was involved in looking after a four year old autistic girl called Donna. I had been present in her peripheral world for several months, and she was vaguely aware of my existence. On the day I am thinking about she was fractious, slapping her face and grinding her teeth in her usual repetitive ritual. In an attempt to calm her, I sat with her on my lap facing me, on the swing in the garden. She seemed to become quieter, and then began to chant, a wordless intonation, as she often did. I joined in, quite unconsciously, humming my own rhythm, day dreaming in the sunshine, slowly swinging backwards and forwards, hardly aware of what I was doing. We happened to sing the same note at the same moment. Our eyes met and Donna stopped and gave me a long, deep look. She began to chant again and before long, the same thing happened. Donna stared silently at me and into me, then she touched my lips with her hand, and stared at her fingers, touched her own lips and gazed again at her fingers. It was as if she was trying to identify from whose mouth the note emerged, and whose sound it was. She seemed mystified that we could have both sung the same note at the same time.

Looking back, I can see that just for an instant, our two selves had met and we had communicated in the same language together. We were not harmonizing, but singing the same sound. It was not "as if" we had sung the same note, we *had* sung the same note. For Donna it may have been a moment of non-threatening togetherness in a world of virtual isolation. It was symbolic of an earlier merged state. We were two children together on a swing, in the warm sunshine, each in our own separate world and who happened to tune in together.

This describes an "is" moment. To be in it allowed for the field of echo to be heard, like the rest in music, ... waiting for the reverberation. Being in it is more important than interpreting it. Interpretation comes later.

Bion (1967) wrote of the mother's state of reverie in relation to her infant's primitive emotional communications, and something similar is needed for the analyst to be able to hear the patient's "is" in the analytic setting. This requires a space in the mind where thoughts can begin to take shape and where confused experiences can be held in inchoate form until their meaning becomes clearer (Rustin, 1989). This kind of mental functioning requires a capacity to tolerate anxiety, uncertainty, discomfort, helplessness, and a sense of abandonment. All these capacities are demanded of a good enough mother and a good enough analyst.

Unconscious projected fantasies often evoke congruent feelings in others. It is unsettling to imagine experiencing feelings and thinking thoughts that are not entirely one's own (Ogden, 1982). The lack of a vocabulary with which to think about this seriously interferes with the analyst's capacity to understand, manage and interpret the transference.

Both therapist and patient struggle to find words to describe pre-linguistic experiences. The feelings involved in this stage of the work are very powerful, and are often communicated on a pre-verbal basis in a somatic form. These feelings and sensations are connected with the infant's very early part object, pre-verbal stages of development, and the infant's instincts and impulses, and relations with bits of mother, and fantasies of mother and her insides (Clark, 1996).

Amniotic fluid and psychological fluid space

The mother's uterus can be likened to the *vas bene clausum* frequently mentioned in alchemy (Jung, C.W., 12, para. 219). Jung writes that the well-sealed vessel is there to protect what is within from the intrusion and admixture of what is without, *as well as to prevent it from escaping* (my italics). Nothing enters into it (the stone) that did not come out of it, since if anything extraneous were to be added to it, it would at once be spoiled.

Within the sealed vessel of analysis is a fluid psychological space where the patient's previously unintegrated, psychic experiences can be floated, reconciled and transformed. This is similar to the amniotic fluid in the intra-uterine space which the developing foetus swallows, digests and excretes into. As well as being nourished via the placenta whilst *in utero*, the developing foetus is surrounded by amniotic fluid which is dynamic, and reflects the hormonal state and, as a plasma filtrate, the mother's diet. During the last trimester of gestation the composition of this fluid is further altered by the foetus swallowing it and excreting into it (Lev & Orlic, 1972; Alberts & Cramer, 1998).

Amniotic fluid changes constantly as a consequence of the mother's physiological state and as a result of foetal swallowing and excreting *in utero*. Maternal anxiety and depression may affect the biochemistry of this fluid (Piontelli, 1992). Equally it is possible to conjecture that foetal affects may contribute to changes in the fluid's biochemistry. A physical or physiological change in the uterine environment may precipitate foetal distress, resulting in the distressed foetus passing meconium into the amniotic space, thus contaminating what was there to protect him.

I find myself wondering if there is a kind of amniotic fluid between analyst and patient in the analytic setting. A dynamic, constantly changing fluid space where patient's and analyst's thoughts and ideas can be floated, reflected upon, swallowed and excreted, an intermediate fluid, changing environment, between two minds. The physical fluid contents of the mother's uterus are taken in and assimilated by the foetus. This fluid contains elements of the mother's diet of inner and external world experiences. These elements are digested and excreted, and then taken back in again— a process that could be likened to Fordham's ideas of deintegration and reintegration (Fordham, 1973). Foetal studies which demonstrate deintegration *in utero* also support this view. Verney describes "how the unborn becomes an active participant in intra-uterine bonding" and supports the idea that "bonding after birth ... [is] actually the continuation of a bonding process that [begins] long before, in the womb" (Verney & Kelly, 1981, pp. 61–62, cited in Urban, 1992).

Foetal distress is a condition frequently encountered when there is a problem during delivery of the infant. When an infant is experiencing foetal distress, it may open its bowels and pass meconium into the amniotic fluid. Foetal distress can cause the infant to gasp before it is born. If meconium is inhaled by the infant, it causes severe lung irritation and infection, leading to acute breathing difficulties after birth. By excreting meconium into the fluid that bathes and protects him, the infant has contaminated the safe nurturing container, and turned it into a dangerous threatening place, which he must get out of as soon as possible.

Fordham states that if the baby is submitted to noxious stimuli of a pathogenic nature (*in utero*, and during or after birth) a persistent over-reaction of the defense system may start to take place. This over reaction may become compounded by projective identification. If the foetus excretes meconium into the amniotic fluid when it is distressed, during delivery, it may then inhale the meconium that it has expelled from its own self, thus compounding the distress, and causing a life threatening situation. A distressed patient may excrete poisonous projections into the fluid space in the consulting room, and then ingest the projections that he has expelled from his own self, thus compounding the distress.

This kind of auto-immune reaction sets in and would account for the persistence of the defense after the noxious stimulus has been withdrawn. Not-self objects, even if they are internal objects experienced as not-self, then come to be felt as a danger to or even a total threat to life, and must be attacked, destroyed or their effect neutralized. The focus is therefore on the not-self and thus little or no inner world can develop (Fordham, 1976, p. 91). In defining damaged developmental events in the transference, Clark (1996), describes the simultaneous feeling of murderous hate and envy out of which the patient creates a place full of inactive oceanic reverie and bliss; and an active battlefield of bullet like projections and psychic germ warfare. I understand this to be similar to the place of oceanic reverie and bliss that the foetus might experience whilst floating in the amniotic fluid within the uterus. This same place could be turned into an active battlefield of bullet-like projections of meconium excreted by the foetus, or toxic viruses from the mother that have entered the amniotic fluid by the process of diffusion. Both are life threatening to the foetus.

Patients who somatize find the analytic situation difficult because it is one where feelings are talked about rather than put into action. They may complain that they are more unhappy, more hopeless and more angry than ever before. They are fearful of accepting any knowledge that might precipitate a psychic change. Interpretations may be experienced as poisonous meconium intrusions causing psychic wounding, rather than a source of help. There seems to be a wish to destroy the analyst's attempts to try and make unconscious feelings more conscious. This can be understood if symptoms are viewed as techniques for psychic survival, as a means of preserving an unconscious sense of self and maintaining some kind of personal integrity (McDougall, 1982). Jung stressed the positive value of a symptom which he regarded as an unconscious attempt in the here and now situation to correct something that was going wrong in the person's life (Jung, C.W., 8, para. 548).

Sidoli (1984) speculates that patients who somatize have split the two polarities of archetypal experience into body and psyche. The instinctual part has become lodged in the body and the spiritual part has become an empty image. Clark (1996) suggests that these not-wholly-human animating images derive from later psychic fantasy, and are symbols of pre-image experience, even of foetal relations.

In analysis, there are some patients who may produce a somatic explosion as a defence against understanding or remembering conflictual situations which may stir up painful or exciting feelings. They seem to be unable to imagine, they lack affect, and have no words to describe their emotional states. There is difficulty in distinguishing one emotion from another, whether it be differentiating anxiety from depression, or excitement from fatigue. It seems as if the feeling has become neutralized, and attempts by the analyst to verbally explore this are avoided by the patient.

Sarah

Sarah had been diagnosed as suffering from chronic fatigue syndrome. She explained how she would feel faint, and get to the point of actually losing consciousness whenever she had to wait for something exciting to happen, such as spending a holiday with her grandchildren. She was able to enjoy all the preparations leading up to the holiday, and then two or three days before the event she would begin to experience nausea, dizziness and feel faint. She would go to bed and cancel the arrangements. Her family were then angry and disappointed with her, and she felt abandoned and frustrated by them. We explored what might be happening and what Sarah's body was trying to communicate to her over many sessions.

At first she was angry because she felt I disbelieved her and was saying it was all in her mind. The importance of the analyst believing the patient's somatic pain has been discussed by Bennett (1997), and Taerk & Gnam (1994). Sarah expressed her anger to me by "closing down", and refused to go on talking about her physical symptoms.

One day, she remembered a time when she was eleven years old, at the end of the second world war. She described sitting in the class room, where, over a period of several days, the school secretary would come in and call out a girl's name, saying, *"Your daddy has come home, he has come to collect you"*. Sarah dreamed of the day her name would be called.

She knew her mother had different feelings about her husband's return. She did not want him back. There had been constant rows and the marriage had been failing before he left to join the army. Sarah was unable to display any feeling of excitement or anticipation about his homecoming. The day he returned, she was playing netball in the school team and he appeared on the side lines and called her name. The surge of feeling that she experienced at that moment were uncontainable. She was overwhelmed, and fainted. Her father found this highly amusing and frequently teased her about it, whilst her mother was annoyed with her for showing any reaction at all. Sarah said she was devastated and embarrassed.

Three months later, her parent's marriage broke down and her father left without ever saying "Good-bye". He disappeared as suddenly as he had arrived, and once again there was no one to contain Sarah's feelings and help her come to terms with his loss. She felt that he had been driven out by her mother, although she dared not show her anger in case she, too, would reject her.

There seemed to be a link between the remembered past, waiting for father's return, and the experienced present, waiting to go on holiday with the family. Both had been exciting events to prepare for. Both events brought the family together. I found myself wondering about the over-exciting object/father. Sarah's fantasies of him had built up in his absence. When the fantasy became reality and father returned, Sarah's excitement was uncontainable. Her feelings went into her body. She was in a state of hyper-arousal and she fainted away, driving her bodily self and her psychic self into momentary unconsciousness. I tried to put Sarah's physical reactions into psychological, feeling words by saying things like, "You had waited for so long to see your father and you were overwhelmed with excitement when you saw him. It all felt too much and you blanked out". Sarah would appear not to hear me and did not respond.

She told me there had never been much closeness between her and her mother, and from the age of eight she had been expected to look after her younger siblings after school until mother returned from work feeling tired and "cross". Once Sarah complained that it wasn't fair, and her mother became furious, bemoaning the fact that she had to get married because she was pregnant with Sarah. She had not wanted to marry her father or to have the baby, and it was into this unwanted marriage that her brother and sister were born. Sarah's angry, guilty feelings about what her mother had told her were displaced onto anger about the household chores. She now began to experience frequent "tummy aches". Mother then became concerned about Sarah's abdominal pains and would put her to bed, taking some days off work to look after her. Initially, this felt like a treat, but then the guilty feelings began again when mother started complaining that she was missing time at work and losing money that they all needed.

During the first two years of her three times a week analysis she idealized me. She was gushingly grateful that I cared about her and in the transference I was her idealized father. I was aware that in time this would change and I would need to receive and contain her projections of the denigrated mother if she was going to be able to work through her feelings of rage . If I could hold her projections of good and bad objects, she might be able to internalize a sense of being able to link the two.

I experienced a jumbled confusion of feelings when she was in the room. When I struggled to identify a feeling within me, it would quickly change into another. There was a paradoxical mix up of longing and of hating, of interest and scornfulness. She wanted me to feel as she did as a child with warring parents whom she could not comprehend, and to experience her warring internal objects who attacked her capacity to make sense out of what was happening.

I struggled to maintain my privacy and separateness as I experienced Sarah's intrusiveness into my inner and outer world. She would park her car so near to my front door, that it was impossible for my children to get into the house after school because she had left no room for them to squeeze past. I frequently interpreted her need to be close to me, and suggested that she would like to drive her car right inside my house, and right inside me, so that I could experience what it was like for her to be a child living with an intrusive mother. My interpretations were usually met with a hurt look or a simpering smile. Sarah longed for me to tell her what to do, and would invent things that I was supposed to have said, or slightly alter things I had said so that I became confused. I could not think of what to say, and when I did say something she would misinterpret it. I would feel as if I had been drawn into a verbal web of treacle in which we both became stuck. She would then berate me for confusing her which made her even more exhausted. Nothing I said seemed to reach her and nothing seemed to change.

I was feeling incapacitated, incompetent and sick and tired of trying to be the soothing, containing mother I had a sense of disquiet within myself, yet I was unable to think about what I was feeling let alone put the feeling into words. I had become immobilized. Unwittingly, I was colluding with Sarah's feelings of helplessness. Sarah's inner world of internalized maternal hate, and the mix up of both the mother and the child's wish to destroy each other were being projected into me. If we both were paralysed we could not kill each other. I began to realize that Sarah's mother had complained that she was sick and tired of looking after the family, and Sarah's main symptoms were of feeling sick and tired. This is a remark that many mothers make to their children when expressing angry feelings. Sarah had internalized it in a concrete way and was living in a physical "sick and tired" state—a somatized anger.

The change in our work came at the time of the year when I raise my fee. The increase I proposed was minimal but Sarah was angry and felt exploited. She wept inconsolably, and cried out with the pain she said I was causing in her legs. She called me a bare-faced bureaucrat, threatened to vomit on my carpet, and after sitting up on the couch and swearing and shouting words of vitriol at me, she stood up to leave the session and virtually fainted onto the floor. I was taken over by a surge of anger that rose up from my gut. My heart was pounding and I could not trust myself to speak, fearing that I would have retaliated and shouted. I felt quite powerless and persecuted by her. Reluctantly, I helped her back to a sitting position on the couch, and was surprised by my hoarse shaky voice when I commented somewhat tersely that she was letting me know how angry she was feeling and that I too felt angry. I pointed out that she was a professional person earning a full salary, and that I too was a professional person and felt I was charging a reasonable fee. I was flushed with indignation and was quivering with rage.

What seemed to be happening was that I was experiencing the raging mother that Sarah had internalized, and which was now projected into me. I felt my rage rise up from my gut which was precisely where Sarah had located her angry feelings as a child. Sarah had unconsciously attempted to get some of the mothering she longed for by developing tummy aches, and for a while this worked. Then mother complained that she could not go to work to earn money that they all needed. It was when the issue of money was raised in her analysis that this whole scenario became re-enacted. I found myself wondering who was incapacitating whom at these times. Did Sarah need to incapacitate her mother in order to have her needs met, or did Sarah's mother need Sarah to be incapacitated before she felt able to mother her?

I needed to be like the firm husband/father able to stand up to a powerful manipulative wife, and able to contain an adolescent daughter's angry outburst. But at the same time, I had to be a caring mother who could understand the feelings of confusion and anxiety that she was experiencing. Because I had expressed some of my own helpless angry feelings, she could then experience conflict and a difference of opinion with me. She was forced to know that we were separate.

When Sarah felt a little better, I interpreted her fainting in connection with her ambivalent feelings towards me, and suggested that she was experiencing me as a strong father figure. I linked these feelings with the return of her absent father, fainting when she caught sight of him, and her ambivalent feelings towards him. Sarah was able to stay to the end of the session and left in a sullen silence. She returned the following week saying that she was feeling full of energy and wanted to replant her garden.

The fee remained a bone of contention between us and I noticed that it was at times when she felt particularly depleted of energy that this issue would be raised again. She would bring carefully documented accounts of her outgoing expenditure, and appeal to me to read them, saying that she could not possibly afford to pay me and I was bleeding or sucking her dry. She complained that she was exhausted and attempted to thrust the pieces of paper into my hands. I suggested to her that she wanted me to grasp how important raising the fee was, and how exhausted she was feeling with trying to work out a way of satisfying my demands. I linked this with the way she had tried to satisfy her mother's demands when she was a tiny baby, and she felt like I was sucking her emotions dry. Sarah needed me to experience the way she felt as a child with a mother who seemed to feed from her instead of the other way around.

I felt sure there was a link between Sarah's feelings about having insufficient money to pay me and insufficient energy to do what she wanted. Initially she had been diagnosed as suffering from neurasthenia, and later the diagnosis changed to chronic fatigue syndrome. One of the symptoms of both of these conditions is that patients experience extreme tiredness, sometimes to the point of being totally incapacitated. In the recovery stages they have an anxiety that they will use up all their energy and return to this incapacitated state. I realized that in these circumstances, it was very important that I did not reduce my fee and thereby become the anaemic one, exhausted by Sarah's attacks.

Sarah was able to rebel, threaten and attack, knowing that I could remain separate from her and survive. She was free to choose whether she continued to come to the sessions or not. If I had reduced the fee, I sensed that it might be as if she *had* bled me dry, I would be an anaemic, weak, exhausted mother who could no longer stand on my own two feet, or stand up to her demands. This could have precipitated a psychic mix up. Which one of us was suffering from C.F.S.? Who was doing the milking and who was doing the feeding? C.F.S. can be used by the psyche as a very protective suit of armour because it can render the patient too "sick and tired" and exhausted to take anything in.

Each time I had a break, it seemed to excacerbate her somatic condition. She felt abandoned and alone, and took to her bed. This was similar to the way she would go to bed with tummy ache when she had insufficient attention from her mother. She said she felt persecuted by me and threatened to leave. I was indeed the wicked, uncaring mother, and the abandoning father. Interpretations were useless, I had to bear her venomous outpourings of how cold, cruel and calculating I was to leave her.

I felt Sarah might need some help to create a me/not me transitional object that she could make use of during the breaks. I have a few stones in my consulting room and she chose one to take with her. She told me she kept it in her pocket and would check if it was there and touch it for reassurance. She had mixed feelings about the stone as it reminded her that I was not actually there, but that she had a reminder of me.

One day she was able to convey to me the depth of her furious attacking self. She told me how she had talked to the stone every day when I had been away, then, as she returned it to its place, she hesitated and then turned to me and said, *"Right now I could throw it right through your window"*.

At this moment Sarah was moving from the concrete to the symbolic. She was able to be in the "as if", space in her imagination, rather than the concrete place of actually throwing the stone. Whilst I was away, the stone became the object that had received and contained her need to attack me, instead of her turning her fury into a somatic assault on her body that immobilized her uncontrollably. Sarah was beginning to be able to imagine and to symbolize. Towards the end of her analysis she no longer needed the stone. She forgot about it. She was able to express her angry feelings directly to me and was able to BE angry, instead of having to DO angry things.

An identifiable process of development had occurred. There was a gradual movement from a state of unintegration, in which she was able to use neither language nor symbols to describe how she was feeling, through to a greater state of integration in which psychic opposites could be contained and transformed.

Sarah expressed her feelings by complaining through her body with more and more physical symptoms, and at these times she needed me to accomodate her complaining feelings and uncomfortable physical sensations in much the same way as a mother holds and transforms the intense emotions of her infant. As I tried to link her physical discomfort with her psychological discomfort, I would find myself wondering if I had over-fed her with indigestible interpretations causing her analytic colic, or if I was under-feeding her and she was suffering from hunger pangs. It was then I realized what the problem might be. For months I had been making interpretations that she could not digest. What she needing was for me to say nothing, just hold her projections, and contain and process them until such time as her psychological digestive system was sufficiently developed for her to accept them in a more swallowable form. Slowly she began to trust and feel contained by our relationship in the analytic setting and to take over the task of holding herself. This was made possible by the development of her capacity to symbolize and the transformation of her bodily symptoms into a language that she could verbalize. Language became the new container for the pain that had been previously expressed in her bodily symptoms. Finding words to express previously unintegrated psychic contents can lead to feelings of transformation and reconciliation (Browne, 1988).

Ned

Ned was married, had a young family, and worked as a priest. His presenting problem was an obsessional fear of defaecating when feeling trapped in public places. Ned had undergone medical investigation for this condition, and no physical cause was found. He seemed to be devoid of emotional feeling and would ask me, "How does it feel to feel?" He seemed to have neutralized the subjective element in his personality and this was a severe hindrance to him in his personal life and in his work.

In his family of origin, Ned was the youngest child. His elder brother died when a baby, and his sister was four years old when he was born. Ned's mother had been severely depressed throughout the time she was expecting him and his delivery had been painful and difficult. She may well have experienced mixed emotions on his arrival, as her first baby son had died.

Mother's depression continued and was exacerbated by the death of her husband when Ned was three. She could not bear her son to be close to her, or separate from her. She needed to know what he was thinking, what he was doing and where he was going, whilst at the same time saying that she could not cope with him. He was sent to boarding school at the age of seven.

Very early in his analysis, Ned told me how he had always loved the sea. He wanted to stand on top of the cliffs and look down into it, but he dare not go too near to the edge because of an irresistible urge to jump into the swirling, crashing waves below. I felt he was being pulled by the archetypal, devouring, suffocating power of his mother, that could potentially kill him off. He may have been letting me know about his unconscious desire to return to his mother's womb, although the image he presented was that of a consuming, asphyxiating place, rather than that of a warm nurturing container in which to grow.

I can imagine Ned as a foetus swallowing the amniotic fluid of his depressed mother and taking in her inner world state and her diet of outer world experiences. In analysis the patient is surrounded by the analytic space in which ideas are floated, possibly swallowed, and unconscious communications are shared. There is an encountering of inner world states and outer world experiences.

Ned had experienced severe intestinal cramps and a desire to empty his gut whenever he felt trapped inside a container such as a lift, a train, or in the "belly" of the church conducting a service. I might speculate that this may have been an unconscious re-enactment of his mother's ambivalent, depressed feelings towards her developing foetus, or even an archaic re-enactment of his birth and his mother's psychological and physical labour pains replayed in the present.

It is significant that Ned wanted to empty his bowels whilst conducting a wedding service or administering the Eucharist, both services with deep symbolic meaning, depicting a marrying together of man and woman, and a marrying together of the actual and the symbolic. The Eucharistic feast symbolizes transformation and transubstantiation, a change from one state to another via a concrete object, the Eucharist. It is possible that Ned could have been caught in an unconscious archetypal repetition of bringing his internal parents together in an act of union in order to recreate himself so that he could begin again. Yet in so doing, there may have been a feeling memory of being in the uterus and unconsciously experiencing his mother's angry depressive attack upon him, and his need to shit on her and then get out to save himself.

Ned had felt a "call" to the ministry three months after his mother had died. I think this might have been a call for help to the absent archetypal father. It seemed that he had attempted to create a new womb in the guise of the church, and attempted to recreate himself by bringing together the archetypal mother church and saviour father.

In "Concerning Rebirth" Jung states that by witnessing or participating in some rites of transformation, such as the Mass, the individual feels vouchsafed immortality (Jung, 1939). However it seemed that Ned had become an observer of rituals rather than participating in them. He seemed unaffected and remained outside of the experience. The ritual had become an end in itself rather that an expression of symbolic meaning. This idea has been explored by Plaut in his paper "Where have all the rituals gone" (Plaut, 1975).

Ned frequently complained of life being boring. He was an outside observer of life, unable to participate in it. In the counter-tranference, I experienced a different kind of boring. I felt as if his steely blue eyes were boring right into me, riveting me to my seat so he would know where I was, just like his mother had wanted to know where he was and yet was unable to bear him being close to her or separate from her.

Ned was obsessive, and thrived on structure. He described long catalogues of events, weddings, funerals, deaths and births. He needed to be identified with an institution, first boarding school, and then the church. Both were establishments where he could exist in an impersonal way as a part of a team, secure in a social group that offered a pseudo-intimacy, a safe alternative to getting closely involved with anyone. The rituals of the church were routines that Ned could take part in, but never felt part of. They had no deeper significance or meaning for him. Ned would take part in the routines of his analysis, but for a long time was unable to allow either of us to feel part of the analytic relationship. Jung (C.W., 12) stated that "so long as religion is only faith and outward form, and the religious function is not experienced in our own souls, nothing of any importance has happened. The *mysterium magnum* is not only an actuality but is first and foremost rooted in the human psyche".

Ned's way of relating on parish committees, or to prayer book words in ritualized church worship, was totally impersonal. He described a poor relationship with his parishioners, and did not feel liked or valued by them. He had been looking for an alternative place to work before seeking analysis, and told me that he could not settle anywhere. Recreation and holidays were rituals to be endured. Sleeping was a task and sexual activity, a meaningless chore to keep his wife happy. He complained of not being able to remember anything I said within a few minutes of leaving the session, and I found it difficult to remember what he was saying even a few minutes after he had spoken it. I felt helpless, and realized that Ned was projecting his helpless anxiety into me. I was also experiencing the power of the archetypal devouring mother, killing off my ability to think or remember, and aborting my thoughts before they could fully form.

Ned seemed to feel threatened whenever I tried to make any sense of his experience. My interpretations would be scoffed at. I felt ridiculous and stupid. It seemed as if he had a wish to destroy my capacity to hold thoughts in my mind and to link them with his experiences so that together we might be able to attach some meaning to them. This attack on linking prevented either of us from being able to create or to imagine (Bion, 1967).

Ned could not allow me to be of any use to him. I was not allowed to be potent or penetrating. It seemed as though he used me as a lavatory for his words, which would go straight through me like the diarrhoea he so often suffered from. At the end of each session he would flush me away, out of his memory. Neither he nor I seemed to be able to absorb or digest each other's words or contain each other's thoughts. I felt blank and confused. Ned was caught in a somatic functioning state. There was no psychic intercourse.

My interpretations felt like mistakes that robbed him of his omnipotence. It seemed that if Ned took anything in from the analytic space, it had to be immediately excreted or aborted. I would feel demolished and useless, but I learned that at these times, although I could make little sense of what was going on, I had to hold on to myself, and silently wait until some feeling of equilibrium returned.

On reflection, I wonder if my words were being experienced as meconium, contaminating the fluid space between us. These words that I should have contained within my gut, my intuition, until Ned was in a safe enough psychological place to hear them, could have been the links between us. Bion (1967) states that the mother's denial of the infant's projective identifications is experienced as an attack on the principal linkage between them. This linkage-attacking mother is internalized, and in time becomes part of the patient's defence against experiencing or understanding anything that is unacceptable to them.

Ned's mother had been unable to give him physical, containing warmth, or to mediate and contain his projections of love, hate and destructiveness in infancy. She was unable to digest, to process what Ned had been trying to convey to her. As a result of this, he had not developed his own capacity to contain these feelings within his mind. He could only contain them in his body, and then react to them by defecating. I realize now how difficult it must have been for Ned to allow himself to feel contained anywhere. Instead he remained in an unsettled restless state. In the analysis, it seemed that as soon as he caught a whiff of being contained by me, e.g. if he had any sense of being understood even for a moment, he felt trapped. The well-sealed vessel of analysis, and the sense of being held in mind by me, were experienced by him as imprisoning and persecuting from which he needed to escape.

During a break, Ned went off on his own to a religious retreat. He found he was unable to relax and was anxious and agitated. He decided that the only answer was to move to another parish to work. He returned to the sessions telling me that God had intervened and he had applied for a post that was going to be wonderful. It was by the sea in a place where there were plenty of lavatories!

He was in fact aborting me, and sending me away just as he had been sent away as a young child. Despite weeks of attempting to interpret this, he was still determined to go. It was only when I accepted that he was definitely leaving me, that he began to experience feelings of sadness. There was a change in the way he started to accept interpretations, and he remembered interpretations that I had made. He realized that he could be separate from me, whilst at the same time relate to me and still feel potent and alive.

A day came when he was able to link a physical feeling he had in his gut with the emotional experience of sadness. He had been telling me about conducting a funeral service of an infant baby boy, and described the tiny white coffin carried by the baby's father. I was feeling extremely moved by what he was telling me, yet he seemed unaffected. "This feels so sad," I said. "How do you mean?" he asked. There was a momentary silence, and then he pointed to his gut and asked me, "Is this how sadness feels? Is this the feeling I have got here?"

At that moment I had imagined how sad Ned was feeling, and the pain he was feeling in his gut. He then allowed what I had imagined to affect him. He made the link between his psyche and his soma. This was the first time that he had been able to do this as far as I knew.

It is striking that this feeling emerged with the image of a father carrying his baby son's coffin, at a funeral service that Ned was conducting. For Ned this was a connection with his own father who had lost his first born son, the baby that would have been Ned's older brother. He had experienced so many losses, the safety of his mother's womb, his older brother, his father, and his depressed mother. For the first time, Ned had an experience of a safe enough containing place with a safe enough analytic mother to expose himself to the feelings related to these losses. The containing rituals of the church and the funeral service, coupled with the rituals of the framework of analysis and my efforts to try and imagine and to contain what he might be feeling had reached him. His inner world and outer world, his sadness and his aching gut, suddenly made sense to him. Ritual can bring together very powerful forces of past, present and future within the containment of a collective and historical experience.

Ned had never been able to differentiate between his own pain and that of his mother. It was as if he was experiencing colicky cramping labour pains and felt he needed to visit the lavatory in an effort to get rid of the bad object mother who had lodged herself in his bowels, and at the same time give birth to himself.

When Ned felt safe knowing that his analysis had a definite

ending, he could then allow himself to become attached to me. It was during this time that he began to gain some understanding of his somatic condition, his fear of being trapped, and of defecating. He told me that at his boarding school, tears could only be cried in private, in the lavatory. It was too shameful to be seen to cry. Ned had kept his feelings trapped inside his body, in a somatic form, where they would not be seen and he would not feel ashamed. I tried to put his physical reactions into feeling words by suggesting to him that boarding school and church were both places where he had to hide his feelings in the lavatory when he was all by himself. Analysis was a different safe place where feelings could be seen and felt with someone who would try to understand.

Ned was unable to attend his final session due to a severe attack of diarrhoea. He was unable to acknowledge the ending and the final separation from me. I felt he was re-enacting his boarding school days when he could not bear to say goodbye to his mother, and after she had gone, he cried his tears of rage and sadness in private, in the lavatory. I too felt very sad and just a bit angry that he had prevented me from saying goodbye to him. I shed the tears and he had the diarrhoea.

Ned contacted me a few months later to let me know that he had resumed his analysis with someone else because he wanted to try and find out who he was. I believe he was struggling to find a way of expressing a pain he could only experience as a void or an ache, or in watery tears of diarrhoea.

Discussion

It can be assumed that in infancy, Sarah and Ned had each experienced inadequate responses to their feelings of anxiety and abandonment. Mother had been unable to contain her infant's projections, and unable to imagine her infant's fear. She may have retaliated to these projections in an angry attacking way rather than trying to imagine and contain how her infant might be feeling. This angry, attacking mother was then internalized, creating the sense of a poisoned unsafe, uncontained inner world, which affected the capacity for thinking and imagining. Both patients projected the poisonous rage of the internalized mother/object into me, and it was crucial that I was able to imagine, contain, process and most important of all, survive this. In experiencing the projections I felt poisoned and my capacity to think and to make links with what was being said was greatly affected. Both patients needed me to try to make sense of, and to try to find, words for the chaotic disorder in which they both found themselves entrapped. It seemed important in the initial stages to be able to carry the projections, and to be in a place of *not imagining* what their experience was like. Thus in the transference I was able to experience how it might have been as an infant with a mother who lacked the capacity to imagine, or to understand, and, as a mother, not being able to understand.

Both Ned and Sarah had a need to replay early contaminated or contaminating experiences in their analysis, and their anxiety regarding intimacy made forming an in-depth analytic relationship extremely difficult. In a replay of early contaminated or contaminating experiences, some patients seem to have an unconscious need to contaminate the analytic space, in such a way that their analysis is seriously threatened. This could be activated by unconscious poisonous projections by the analyst into the analytic space thus causing distress to the patient, or by a serious problem arising with or within the analytic container, or by the patient becoming more aware of overwhelming unconscious material, which may precipitate extreme anxiety.

This is similar to contamination of the uterine space by meconium excreted by the foetus when in distress. Meconium is poisonous if it is inhaled. Foetal distress can be caused by physiological or biochemical changes in the mother, physical changes in the uterine environment such as the cord causing a constriction of the infant's neck, or in the process of birth itself when the infant becomes exhausted or traumatized during the process of delivery. The heart rate increases rapidly, and it is impossible to know or to imagine the extent of the anxiety that the infant may be experiencing at this time.

In either situation, contamination of the uterine space, or contamination of the analytic space, the security of the developing self is seriously threatened. Contamination of the analysis may take the form of an attack upon the analytic relationship, the setting, or the process itself. Trying to understand the distress that may have provoked this attack can provide valuable insight into the patient's underlying personality structure and techniques for psychic survival.

Redfearn (1992) proposes that what the patient's actual somatic body is *really* doing is what the mother of his fantasy is, in fantasy, doing to him. Sarah felt sick and tired, and Ned suffered bouts of diarrhoea when trapped in a confined space. These are physical experiences of something uncontainable within the body needing to be ejected. Neither Sarah's or Ned's mother had been able to contain their infant's projections of love and hate, nor been able to process feelings for them.

Both patients had experienced relationships with their mother that were intrusive and abandoning, and their father was weak or absent. There was no one to mediate the feelings engendered between them, and difficulties with mother were present from birth or even earlier, as described by Simpson *et al.* (1997). Ned and Sarah had experienced loss as a sense of shame when they expressed strong emotion as children. They were trying to deal with the persecutory feelings that had led them to develop a massive defense of the self.

Sarah was afraid of separation and Ned was afraid of the imprisonment that closeness would bring. What I was attempting to find was a space that did not feel too impinging or too distant, similar to the space between mother and foetus in the sealed vessel of the uterus—a dynamic, fluid space where the patient's and the analyst's thoughts and ideas can be floated, reflected upon, swallowed and excreted, an intermediate fluid changing environment between two minds in which, between us, we could develop a way of relating and understanding.

Winnicott (1971) suggests that the use of ritual and transitional objects are ways of managing and containing distress and separation. For Sarah, one of the factors that seemed to set the healing process in motion was finding and using a transitional object, in the form of a stone from my consulting room. When people and objects which have been differentiated come together in co-operative play, the object becomes a potential symbol because the meaning of the object can be shared with a person (Trevarthen, 1980). When Sarah realized that the object could endure her angry attacks she began to believe that I too might be able to survive her rage.

Ned had become ensconced in a rigid self structure in an unconscious effort to manage his obsessive anxiety. There was a similarity between Ned and the autistic child that I described at the beginning of the paper. Both had a need for repetitive ritual as an attempt to contain an obsessive, controlling, fragmented self. Rituals, including repetitive compulsive acts, serve mainly to preserve the status quo, to stabilize a self threatened by disintegration, as described by Plaut (1975). Within the containing framework of analysis, transformations may and do occur more or less spontaneously without, or regardless of, attempts at active intervention. Ned was telling me about the performing of a religious ritual, a funeral service marking the passage from one state to another, and I felt sad as I listened and was able to tell him so. Ned experienced a transformation in that he was able to connect with the sadness I was feeling, recognize it as his own, and then experience a shared moment of sadness between us, linking psyche with soma. In the past Ned had experienced difficulties whilst conducting a wedding service or celebrating the Eucharist. These rituals of marrying together, of transformation and renewal, may have had an unconscious effect upon him.

Despite few "good enough" experiences, some patients manage to hold on to an archetypal image of a good enough mother. It is possible for these patients to regress to the collective archetypal experience that we all have deep within us, of being a mother, being mothered and of being an infant, all at the same time. When the archetype is activated in the present, it can be felt as an overwhelming "is" experience that can be unbearable, and painful, but also wondrously awesome.

It is as if the analyst is required to hold and contain the patient, the overwhelming immediacy of feelings, and the archetype, like holding the primal self of the newly emerged infant for a moment, as well as holding and containing *his or her own* archetypal and actual sense of mothering which will also have been evoked. The simultaneous meeting of all and each of these elements is likely to cause a psychic explosion that the analyst must be strong enough to survive and contain. This can be the first experience of "actual" mothering. The "as if" becomes the "is". The analyst at that moment *is* the actual mother, and is experienced in the reverie of resonating silence, and encountered in the echo of feelings.

This is a *now* happening, not a past memory. In the transference, it is as if the past, the present, and a potential future are all present in the same moment.

Summary

In this paper I describe two patients who have experienced mothers who were unable to contain their infant's need to imagine, which led to the infant identifying with and internalizing the mother's inner conflicts. These conflicts were manifested in a somatic form. It was as if the infant was experiencing mother's conflicts as an internalized poisonous meconium rage.

In analysis, feelings that represent the poisonous meconium mother may be projected out into the analyst. It is crucial that these attacks are endured, and the projections of poisonous hate are contained, thus enabling the patient to see that they have not destroyed the analyst. If the patient feels that the analyst cannot cope they might decide to leave, in much the same way as the distressed foetus must get out of the contaminated uterus in order to save himself from being poisoned by what he has excreted. A patient in a preverbal state may experience inappropriate or untimely interpretations by the analyst as the excretion of waste products into the analytic space, rather than as ideas floated in the hope of facilitating change and growth.

In this kind of situation words are useless and interpretations are experienced as poisonous intrusions like meconium. The patient feels attacked and musters a massive defense to try and save himself. Hopefully, there just might be a moment when there is a fleeting communication between analyst and patient where there is a merging of ideas, and the patient senses that the analyst is trying to understand.

Ned and Sarah used bodily symptoms to express emotions and feelings to communicate something they had no words for. Analysis enabled them to begin to transform somatic doing into psychological feeling, and to embark on the journey towards symbolization.

Analysts try to mediate an ever-growing capacity for symbolic experience which involves the emergence of both symbol and language. Within the sealed container of analysis is a fluid psychological space where previously unintegrated psychic experiences can be floated, reconciled and transformed. This is similar to the amniotic fluid in the intra-uterine space which the developing foetus swallows, digests and excretes into. A fluid space between foetus and mother, between patient and analyst that contains excretions from both, excretions which can be absorbed and changed, and then re-assimilated by each of them. There is a kind of interplay between the internal world and the external world which begins before birth is made explicit.

It then may become possible to survive the opposing psychic forces with their paradoxical impulses for fusion and for separateness. Gordon (1978) suggests that this may lead to the emergence of creativity and personal growth. The patient can then begin to imagine himself imagining.

I have much to thank Donna for, the autistic child I mentioned at the beginning of this paper. She never uttered a word, but for a moment in time we merged and spoke the same language. This child lodged herself in my inner world and taught me that sometimes, when working with patients, we swing backwards and forwards, between past and present, outer world to inner world, rage to sadness, and occasionally, and unexpectedly we might come across that moment when we will sing the same note at the same time, and our separate worlds will happen to tune in together, the "as if" has become the "is".

References

Alberts, J. R., & Cranmer, C. P. (1988). Ecology and experience. Sources of means and meaning of developmental change. In: E. M. Blass (Ed.), *Handbook of Behavioural Neurobiology, Volume 9: Developmental Psychobiology and Behavioural Ecology* (pp. 1–35). New York: Plenum Press.

Bennett, A. (1997). A view of violence contained in chronic fatigue syndrome. *Journal of Analytical Psychology*, 42(2): 192–199.

Bion, W. R. (1967). *Second Thoughts. Selected Papers on Psycho-Analysis*. London: Karnac Books.

Browne, A. (1988). Language and the emerging symbol. *Journal of Analytical Psychology*, 33(3): 277–297.

Clark, G. (1996). The animating body: psychoid substance as a mutual experience of psychosomatic disorder. *Journal of Analytical Psychology*, 41(3): 353–368.

Fordham, M. (1973). *Analytical Psychology. A Modern Science, Volume 1, Library of Analytical Psychology*. M. Fordham, R. Gordon, J. Hubback, K. Lambert & M. Williams (Eds). London: William Heinemann Medical Books Ltd.

Fordham, M. (1976). *The Self and Autism*. London: Heinemann Medical Books.

Fordham, M. (1985). *Explorations into the Self*. London: Academic Press.

Gordon, R. (1978). *Dying and Creating: A Search for Meaning*. The Library of Analytical Psychology, Volume 4. Frome and London: Butler and Tanner Ltd.

Jung, C. G. (1939). *C.W.*, 5, 2nd edn. Princetown University, 1967, pp. 39–78.

Lev, R., & Orlic, D. (1972). Protein absorption by the intestine of the foetal rat in utero. *Science*, 177: 522–524.

McDougall, J. (1982). *Theatres of the Mind*. London: Free Association Books.

Ogden, T. H. (1982). *Projective Identification and Psychotherapeutic Technique*. New York and London: Jason Aronson.

Piontelli, A. (1992). *From Fetus to Child. An Observational and Psychoanalytic Study*. London: Routledge.

Plaut, A. (1975). Where have all the rituals gone? *Journal of Analytical Psychology*, 20(3): 3–17.

Redfearn, J. (1992). *The Exploding Self. The Creative and Destructive Nucleus of the Personality*. Wilmette, IL: Chiron.

Rustin, M. (1989). Encountering primitive anxieties. In: L. Miller, M. Rustin, M. Rustin & J. Shuttleworth (Eds), *Closely Observed Infants*. London: Duckworth.

Sidoli, M. (1984). The availability of the analyst. *Journal of Analytical Psychology*, 29(4): 335–372.

Simpson, M., Bennett, A., & Holland, P. (1997). Chronic fatigue syndrome/myalgic encephalomyelitis as a twentieth-century disease: analytic changes. *Journal of Analytical Psychology*, 42(2): 197.

Taerk, G. & Gnaw, W. (1994). A psychodynamic view of the chronic fatigue syndrome. The role of object relations in etiology and treatment. *General Hospital Psychiatry*, 16: 319–325.

Trevarthen, C. (1980). The foundations of intersubjectivity: development of interpersonal and cooperative understanding in infants. In: D.

Olson (Ed.), *The Social Foundations of Language and Thought*. New York: Norton [quoted in Urban, E. Out of the mouths of babes. *Journal of Analytical Psychology, 38*(3): 241].

Urban, E. (1992). The primary self and related concepts in Jung, Klein, and Isaacs. *Journal of Analytical Psychology, 37*(4): 418.

Verney, T., & Kelly. J. (1981). *The Secret Life of the Unborn Child*. London: Sphere Books.

Winnicott, D. W. (1971). *Playing and Reality*. Harmondsworth: Penguin Books.

CHAPTER EIGHT

Psychotherapy as a two-way process

Nathan Field

Introduction

P sychoanalysis was invented just over a century ago by Freud and Breuer, both of whom were doctors. Inevitably the analytic relationship became based on the time-honoured doctor–patient relationship, which assumes that the doctor is healthy and the patient is sick. Analysis likewise presupposes a mentally healthy, well-analysed psychoanalyst engaged in the treatment of a mentally ill, unanalysed, patient. It assumes, furthermore, that just as the doctor knows more than the patient about the functioning of the patient's body, so the analyst knows more about the patient's mind.

While this is a reasonable assumption, a hundred years of clinical experience has increasingly exposed the medical model as not quite fitting the psychological facts. As analyses have become progressively longer, and probed more deeply into unconscious, inter-subjective, processes, the relation between the two parties is seen to be rather less unequal. Indeed I would argue that a long therapeutic relationship, at least in its culminating phases, becomes rather more of a *reciprocal* healing process. If this is the case, then we may be advised to view the whole analytic relationship from a somewhat different perspective. The idea is not new. Back in 1923 Georg Groddeck wrote:

> And now I was confronted by the strange fact that I was not treating the patient but that the patient was treating me ... It was no longer important to give him instructions, to prescribe for him what might be right, but to change in such a way that he could use me. [Groddeck, 1923]

Jung made a similar point in his observation that "when two chemical substances combine, both are altered" (Jung, C.W., 16, para. 358).

To illustrate my theme I shall first describe my attempt to treat analytically a seriously disturbed young woman I shall call Rachel. The second section looks at the dynamics of early trauma, which played a crucial part in Rachel's illness. In the third section I describe the change of attitude that was forced upon me through her resistance to getting better. In the final section I shall discuss some implications of the view that psychotherapy is more of a reciprocal process than has hitherto been assumed.

I am aware that in recounting the vicissitudes of Rachel's therapy it may read like a catalogue of errors and fortuitous recoveries. In my defence let me quote what Jung said regarding a taxing case of his own:

> (It) is not in the least a story of triumph; it is more like a saga of blunders, hesitations, doubts, gropings in the dark, and false clues which in the end took a favourable turn. But all this comes very much nearer the truth and reality of my procedure than a case that brilliantly confirms the preconceived opinions and intentions of the therapist. [Jung, C.W., 16, para. 564]

Portrait of a victim

I first saw Rachel in the early years of my practice. She was then in her middle twenties, unattached, and had never had a relationship with a man. She lodged with a divorced woman friend whom she had met during her two-year stay in mental hospital. In the case notes Rachel had been described as a "depressive schizoid, with paranoid features", and that was how she looked as she shuffled into my room, putting one foot in front of the other. Her head and jaw were thrust forward like someone about to explode, in marked contrast to her large blue eyes which had the most dreadfully hurt look. Around one eye was a large bruise. I remember thinking: "O Lord, this girl looks really sick. What am I getting into?"

I said hullo, and there was a very long silence. Eventually she managed to say that she didn't want to be here and did *not* want psychotherapy. Instead of asking what she *did* want, this remark virtually stopped my thinking processes and the remainder of the hour was spent in a mutually tormented silence, punctuated by my tentative questions which she barely answered. Eventually, in desperation, I said: "Who gave you that black eye?"

There was another long, potentially explosive silence. I had a sudden image that out of a black lake some huge prehistoric serpent would rear its monstrous head and eat me alive. Eventually she muttered: "I get very angry".

I countered with: "Are you warning me?"

There was the faintest glimmer of a wolfish grin. I knew the first crisis was over and we arranged to meet. But there were many more crises in store. In the following months she came to each session as if it were that first meeting: her averted gaze, brooding antagonism, and silent lip biting conveyed how desperate she was—yet when I spoke to her, she would hardly respond. I found this phase agonizing in a way I had never experienced before: most of the time I felt utterly useless, mentally paralysed, and full of some obscure dread. After some weeks I began to wonder if this was the mental state Rachel herself habitually lived in and that she had somehow managed to induce in me? If so, I don't know how she endured it. I too felt locked into an unbearable trap: it was as if she silently screamed for relief from dreadful mental pain but forbade me to make the least move to help her.

Gradually I managed to piece together, from the case notes and her barely audible utterances, something of her history.

Even in the womb Rachel had a traumatic start in life, since her mother had tried to abort her. At birth she was nearly strangled by the umbilical cord and took two days to be born. She was barely a few weeks old when her brother, then aged two, swallowed an unknown quantity of his mother's sleeping tablets and nearly died. For months afterwards he occupied her mother's whole attention and she continued to dote on the older brother throughout Rachel's childhood. She was a very docile child, desperate to gain her mother's attention and invariably failing. On the rare occasions she showed any temper her mother said: "That's not really you".

Rachel's father was a security guard: she said she could not remember a time when she was not terrified of him. As a child she felt he could not stand the sight of her, because she was fat, slow and stupid. But she slimmed down in her later teens and his attitude took a marked turn. She noticed he would kiss her on the lips and, if she stood by his chair, he would idly run his hand up her thighs as he read his newspaper. She said she did not know this was in any way sexual but she was so grateful for these gestures of affection she would have done anything to please him. Such attentions also meant that she "put one over" on her mother to whom she always felt immensely hostile. She had never forgiven her for the abortion attempt.

Her mother now became openly reproachful about Rachel's closeness with her father and began to blame her for the fact that she and her husband no longer "acted like man and wife". Rachel's memory of this period is scanty and confused: she remembers being very depressed, having weird thoughts about merging with trees, and was subsequently admitted to mental hospital. While there, according to the notes, she went through a psychotic episode, "with terrifying visual delusions", which she said she never remembered. She stayed for nearly two years. After discharge she lived on government benefit, did no work, and attended a psychiatric day hospital. Her prognosis was very poor.

Although she attended her therapy sessions regularly she hardly uttered a word. After several months of this intense yet stultifying silence I was forced to the conclusion, with my supervisor's agreement, that the basis for analytic work did not yet exist. In desperation I decided that since we could not work together perhaps we could just play together? I knew, again from the notes, that she had once shown some interest in art, so I bought a large drawing pad and some crayons and suggested she might wish to draw? She flatly refused. Perhaps she could just doodle? With the greatest reluctance she conceded she might co-operate if I doodled first. So I drew some pink flowers all round the pad and handed it to her. With a fiendish glee she defaced my flowers with black jagged lines, and handed it back. My heart sank, but after a while I responded with green leaves growing from each of her jagged points ... so it went on, and at least it gave us something to talk about. By now, at her insistence, we both sat on the floor, like two children at play.

The drawing lasted a few months, then she got bored, so I introduced plasticine which she would mould with great skill, while I fumbled like a clumsy child. Once she produced a perfectly formed little dog and placed it on the mantelpiece with its muzzle up against the breast of a figurine that sat there. I asked her what she was trying to tell me, but she ignored the question. The plasticine also petered out, but she still liked to play. Indeed she became so playful it became difficult to control her: she turned the chairs around, covered the face of the clock with plasticine, or brought black plastic spiders to the sessions and threw them at me. I would interpret each of these actions, but they never seemed to register.

After several months I was allowed to return to my chair and again tried to get some sort of analytic dialogue going. I took up her refusal to use the couch. I suspected it had to do with repressed sexual anxieties, but it felt impossible to discuss the topic. What she did readily talk about was how much she hated therapy. This was confusing because she never missed a session and invariably resisted leaving. It was painfully clear that she found it even worse when she couldn't come. During each holiday break she developed quite painful physical disorders, such as septic abscesses under her teeth. Were these the poisonous words she dared not utter? Yet her complaints always left me feeling in the wrong: I was wrong when I saw her and wrong when I didn't. I had to work hard at not feeling more than a little crazy, but it helped to speculate that I was vicariously living out Rachel's own intolerable double-bind.

Since her verbal responses were minimal, I found myself pressing her with, first, one question, then another, then a third ... to each of which she grudgingly responded. But I persisted and her replies were those of someone helplessly yielding up layer after layer of protective armour. I would sometimes catch the tone of my own voice: it sounded triumphant and inquisitorial. I realized, to my discomfiture, that I was enjoying a certain excitement in pursuing her hidden thoughts and forcibly intruding into her private world.

Under further questioning, it emerged that she was indeed repressing sexual fantasies. Their disclosure was especially difficult because they involved being hunted down and anally raped. I got the impression that she often fantasized this scenario, while at the same time feeling that it was shamefully perverse. I interpreted that, although it depicted an abusive form of contact, reminiscent of her connection with her father, it *was* a form of contact, something she had been deprived of by her mother. She responded with a non-committal shrug.

She never made it clear if I was her imagined rapist, but then I realized that she and I were actually re-enacting her fantasy in the therapy itself; her evasiveness provoked my insistent questioning, which turned me into a hunter and her into my prey. As her rape fantasies disclosed, she derived a masochistic excitement from imagining herself in subjugated states. She found this very difficult to accept, but I insisted that she recognize how, throughout her life, she had repeatedly contrived to become a victim, originally her father's and now, apparently, mine. I wanted her to understand that she actually felt much safer when she was a victim: better the devil she knew than the devil she didn't. Even more puzzling: better the devil she knew than the *angel* she didn't. By angel I meant good experiences, such as feeling safe, loved, valued, successful or happy.

I felt that my recognition that she actually preferred to be a victim was an important insight, and I reminded her of it more than once. But it did not seem to help, and gradually I understood that to be labelled a "victim" made her feel even more persecuted. It was also chastening for me to recognize that, from the time we had first met, she had succeeded in making me *her* victim: she tantalized me with her evasiveness, she ignored any insights I might offer, while I utterly failed to alleviate her unabated misery. With considerable dismay I had to accept that we were deeply enmeshed in a reciprocal sado–masochistic relationship.

I was wrong, too, about her fear of the couch. It had less to do with sex and more with a deeper fear. I puzzled over the meaning of a fantasy she kept having that, if she lay down on the couch, her body would involuntarily perform a bizarre backwards loop-the-loop and vanish through the wall behind her. Years later I learned that this is a characteristic psychological defence of children who have been sexually abused. But there also existed the very opposite desire. She imagined that lying on the couch was something so blissful she would simply melt into it and be lost for ever. It took me months to grasp the intensity of her longing to enter into a state of fusion with me. It was as if the bed was my body and she would return to the womb. Whether she simply melted into me or magically escaped via this strange loop-the-loop, either way she would disappear for ever, lost in infinite space. Both prospects filled her with dread. It now became clearer why she was always so angry and resistant. By comparison with her underlying dread, these habitual states of anger, anguish, humiliation, regret, yearning, grievance, complaint, frustration and failure, however painful, were almost like old friends. Any alternative threatened the dissolution of her very self. What I saw as the path to her getting better, she saw as the road to annihilation.

The dread of the good object

The tenacious resistance, in many patients, to getting better comes as a shock to us all, as it did to Freud: "One becomes convinced", he says in *The Ego and the Id*:

> not only that such people cannot endure any praise or appreciation, but that they react inversely to the progress of the treatment ... They exhibit the so-called negative therapeutic reaction ... (arising) from a sense of guilt, which is finding atonement in illness and is refusing to give up the penalty of suffering. [Freud, 1923]

Freud himself became so shaken by encountering this deep unconscious resistance, with its attendant "compulsion to repeat" self-destructive behaviour, that he eventually formulated the much-contested notion of the death instinct. By this he meant that there is a power at work in all of us that opposes the life force, and therefore opposes the therapy. In those early months, when I sat in agonized silence with Rachel, I really felt in the presence of something deathly. Object relations theorists offer an alternative hypothesis. They assume that we are endowed at birth with a pristine, undivided, self which Fairbairn calls the Central Ego (Fairbairn, 1952). With good-enough parenting this basic self reacts to the inevitable traumas of life by developing a strong but flexible ego.

But when early trauma happens to be excessively severe, which was certainly the case with Rachel, the ego barely develops, leaving only an archaic, neo-biological, survival system as the sole defence of the self.

Let me clarify what I mean by trauma. It ranges from actual life-shattering mistreatment in childhood to the more subtle spectrum of "cumulative trauma", which includes such ongoing experiences as parental rejection, misattunement, emotional deprivation, impingement, instability, failure, criticism, and even actual hatred. Trauma may also occur in the womb, due to attempted abortion, as in Rachel's case. Birth experiences, again like Rachel's, can be traumatic; some infants are born prematurely and need to be incubated, others are born with a serious physical or genetic defects, and all these may leave lifelong damage.

The archaic defensive formation that early trauma activates, was described by the Jungian analyst, Donald Kalsched, as the "self-care system" (Kalsched, 1996). It has quite a different character from normal ego defences. He compares it to "a kind of inner 'Jewish Defence League' (whose slogan after the Holocaust was 'Never Again!'). 'Never again', says our tyrannical caretaker, 'will the traumatized personal spirit of this child suffer this badly'", p. 5. Kalsched goes on to identify some of the drastic methods it uses to "protect" the trauma victim: " '... before this happens, I will disperse it into fragments (dissociation), or encapsulate it and soothe it with fantasy (schizoid withdrawal), or numb it with intoxicating substances (addiction) or persecute it to keep it from hoping for anything from life in this world (depression) ...' ", p. 5. Most of these defences could apply to Rachel.

As Kalsched describes it: "Once the trauma defence is organized, all relations with the world are 'screened' by the self-care system. What was intended to be a defence against further trauma becomes a major resistance to all unguarded spontaneous expressions of self in the world. The person survives but cannot live creatively", p. 4. Nor is this all. "This diabolical inner figure is often far more sadistic and brutal than any outer perpetrator, indicating that we are dealing here with a *psychological* factor set loose in the inner world by trauma—an archetypal traumatogenic agency within the psyche itself", p. 4 (Kalsched, 1996). The self-care system first changes from a protector to a gaoler, who then actively terrorizes his prisoner;

that is, the self-care system breaks loose from the psyche and actually wreaks deep damage on the imprisoned spirit from within.

But there remains a complication in understanding this "diabolical inner figure". Sadistic it may well become, but its original task was to protect the individual from the ultimate catastrophe of schizophrenia. In fact Ferenczi, observing the way it functioned in the case of his horrendously abused patient Elizabeth Severn, actually called it her "guardian angel". Unfortunately the price of her protection proved almost as damaging as the madness from which it saved her (Stanton, 1990). In brief, early trauma places the victim between the "devil and the deep blue sea", and in most cases they cling to "the devil they know".

Giving up

About the end of the third year, after a period of limited co-operation, Rachel became again persistently negative. Every intervention that I made was ignored, ridiculed, and ultimately nullified. I felt we were back where we started: in fact, it felt worse, and my goodwill was beginning to run out. In my more benign moments I compared her to Rapunzel locked up in her tower, guarded by a fearful witch. When I went to rescue her, I was horrified to meet not Rapunzel but the witch and, like the Prince in Grimm's tale, I became blinded in making my escape. By now I could see no way forward, and indeed, I was barely capable of thinking at all. But I kept trying.

Some time in our fourth year I reached the conclusion that we were hopelessly stuck. In one bitter exchange Rachel herself clinched it by actually saying to me: "Say what you like, I'm just not going to give you the satisfaction of making me better..." I recall that, as I heard these words, I had a distinct sense of a demonic force speaking through her lips. Several times I decided to tell her of my decision to finish, but I knew that with her minimal income she could never find another therapist. Feeling utterly feeble and demoralized, I just could not quite bring myself to end it, and we carried on. But in admitting defeat, something must have changed in me. I gave up trying to cure her: I gave up trying to analyse her, because I seemed to have run out of new interpretations, and the old ones had simply become tired clichés. But once I stopped trying to change her I found, to my surprise, that I could begin to accept her more or less as she was. Not only accept, but I realized I could begin to learn from her. In learning more about *her* inner world I found I was learning more about my own—my *own* sadism and masochism and narcissism. Working with Rachel in this spirit, with a minimum of my own preconceptions, was becoming a continuation of my own therapy.

Yet the work remained very difficult. Even though I was beginning to accept Rachel just as she was, her protector/persecutor obstinately resisted accepting that acceptance as her own. The trust that might briefly develop in one session invariably disappeared by the next. It was as if the witch, once she got Rachel alone, whispered in her ear: "You know that was not real, just therapy. He's paid to make you feel better ... He can't possibly value you, nobody could. How can he, when he knows you have such depraved thoughts ... And even if he does accept such awfulness, what can that say about *him*? Perhaps he's perverted too? Perhaps he actually wants to abuse you? ..."

Sometimes in the session itself, whenever there was any hint of closeness developing between us, she defended against it by virtually going into a trance. I could see it happening. A shudder went through her, her eyes drooped and almost closed. It was quite eerie. But there were occasions when the same thing happened to me. No matter how hard I fought it, I found myself afflicted by an anaesthetic condition so overwhelming that I virtually lost consciousness. The experience was very unpleasant.

Drowsiness and sleep in the analytic session, whether it occurs in the patient or the therapist, is professionally regarded as counter therapeutic; the nullification of the analytic work. Yet what followed suggested a different possibility. On one occasion during a long silence the room began to disappear into a blur, but this time I let it happen, almost out of curiosity. I felt I was passing out but managed to ask her what she was thinking.

She replied: "I keep thinking I want to eat your foot".

My head cleared instantly. I repeated, in astonishment: "You want to—*what*?"

She laughed. As she laughed I registered that, for the first time since I had known her, she briefly looked *normal*. I could have made an interpretation that my foot represented my penis, and that my penis represented ...? But I simply laughed with her. The next time the drowsiness came upon me I just let it take over. Then something strange followed: the room became very peaceful, filled with a dreamy, warm, yet energized feeling of connection. Eventually I dozed off. This happened on several occasions and it was after one of these episodes that Rachel said: "You fell asleep again". "Did I?" I replied defensively. But I registered that she was smiling: she said "So did I". I realized she regarded it as a breakthrough. It was as if she had briefly escaped from the witch's tower to join me in some unknown realm of the unconscious. These shared "sleeps" began to happen regularily, just a few minutes of blissful quietude.

In Jungian terms our experience could be described as a *coniunctio*. Later I came across its equivalent in the literature of psychoanalysis. Marion Milner wrote that she could reach this state in the company of certain patients: "I suspect that the adjective 'divine' ... can be an accurate description ... of what happens when the consciousness suffuses the whole body" (Milner, 1987). I think it is what Michael Balint described as a "harmonious and inter-penetrating mix-up" (Balint, 1968). Margaret Little calls it, "primary undifferentiation" (Little, 1986). In everyday life it is the state an infant can enjoy in its mother's arms, when both drift off into a contented nap. In Masud Khan's opinion, "the need for the achievement of this state of undifferentiation is the source of these patients most crucial seeking and their most adamant resistance and negativity" (Khan, 1996).

The mutative effect of skilled interpretation, especially transfer-ence interpretation, cannot be disputed. But I think that a patient like Rachel, before interpretations can carry any real conviction, needs the mutative effect of the "primary undifferentiated experience". It helps to create that basis of trust, in the absence of which an interpretation may be at best a cerebral exercise, at worst a wounding criticism.

Orthodox analysis tends to emphasize the need to accept pain. Again, this is perfectly valid: we most certainly need to face painful truths about ourselves. But with masochistic patients like Rachel there is the risk that there can be not so much "gain in the pain" as pleasure in it. It can become a perverse gratification. I suggest that we need to supplement the tolerance of pain with the acceptance of healthy pleasure, otherwise we starve our internalized good object while the bad one grows fat.

This is not to prescribe a diet of positive reinforcement. I mean simply to sustain an awareness of *whatever* was happening in the present, whether painful or pleasurable, and not try to change it; not even to interpret it, simply to register it. The same acceptance of both joy and desolation is recognized in Fordham's "de-integration —re-integration" cycle, in Winnicott's "illusion–disillusion" process, and in Bion's treating both positive and negative "realisations" as integral to development. The wisdom of living mindfully in the present, whether joyful or dreadful, is hardly a revelation. Every form of spiritual exercise advocates it, but it is very difficult to sustain in everyday life. I was now discovering that this phase of our therapeutic work offered an opportunity for what came close to a shared spiritual practice.

It occured to me one day that it had been a long time since I had become anaesthetized. I could only assume that Rachel's mind-numbing rape fantasies, together with her dread of dissolving and disappearing, had just been forgotten. Because I had long before given up trying to make her better, most of this went unnoticed until I began to register certain positive remarks she let slip. Once she interrupted a discussion to say: "You're a strange man ... you're really pleased to see me". Or she could manage a back-handed compliment: "You don't always understand. But you do try ..." Another time she said: "I'll say this for you, you never gave up on me".

On this occasion I replied: "That's not quite true. I did".

"You gave up?"

"About a year ago".

She looked shocked, then went quiet for bit. "But you carried on?" "Yes". Again she was quiet, then said: "I'm going to find it hard to leave you". I said: "I didn't know you were thinking of it?" By way of reply she told me that the friend in whose house she still lived was apparently having another breakdown. "It made me realize something", Rachel said, "Actually, compared with her, I'm in a different league. Deep down I'm alright. Well ninety percent alright ..."

I asked her: "How do you know that?"

She shrugged: "The way I am with you, I know I'm alright".

I realized this was true. I just hadn't recognized it. Outwardly her life was the same as before: she was still on income support, she had no job, no partner, and still lodged with her now-sick friend. But I was using the wrong yardstick. Nothing had changed, but everything was different, because Rachel felt profoundly different about herself. Previously her ongoing experience was contaminated by a pervasive sense of unreality, as if her life had not yet begun. But now, by sharing with me her awareness of the present, good and bad, it had begun to feel real. Previously, you might say, she had been dying, now she felt she was living.

Actually she didn't leave for another year, and it was a very stormy one. We went through a reciprocal "release of bad objects", where we both said all kinds of confronting things to each other. For her this was very important: she realized she could openly voice her anger and not destroy me or our relationship. For my part, having previously learnt to give up being a persecutory therapist, I now managed to stop patronizing her by being the all-accepting one. Thanks to Rachel I lost much of my fear of my own anger. We both survived these open confrontations and parted with mutual warmth and regret.

She left on the understanding that she could come back after a year away. She never did, except for a cup of tea from time to time. For three years her circumstances remained unchanged, and I seriously wondered what the whole struggle had been for? Then she took her first job in a nursery for small children, and kept it. Much later she became a practitioner in one of the alternative therapies. The last time I met her she had a practise she could live on; she said that she now felt ready to meet a male partner, but it didn't seem likely, and that was sad. So it was not exactly a fairy tale ending, like Rapunzel, but we both knew that, after all these years, she "had a life".

Discussion

I began this paper by presenting Rachel as a patient who refused to get better. This became a self-fulfilling prophesy in that I tried to make her better; instead I made her worse because, as Balint (1968) explained, she possessed insufficient ego to take in interpretations;

at least the kind that I chose to offer. In spite of prolonged efforts I was forced to give up *trying* to change her; instead I focused on tuning in with her, and that seemed improve matters.

Was this a case that turned out to be another demonstration of a shared "breakdown–breakthrough" process which I have explored elsewhere? (Field, 1996). In essence, yes. But, while I think that giving up played a decisive part, it doesn't comprise the whole story. Without the years of struggle that preceded it, my giving up would have been a non-event, and no breakthrough would have come out of it. This seems to be the way that all creative achievement comes about: long years of struggle, until you are forced to admit defeat—whereupon something emerges, seemingly out of nowhere; because by giving up you make room for something new to enter. In retrospect I can see that I gave up many times, and each time a new solution presented itself. But only when it was ready. It didn't work until I was driven virtually to the despair that Rachel herself experienced. This sounds a very painful process but with a patient as damaged as Rachel, it may have been the only way.

Did I actually give *up* or did I actually give it *over* to some unconscious healing process we had mutually generated; a process that, only when it had reduced me to a trance-like state,could get on with its job? When Rachel too could give in to it, a third stage was reached. The form it happened to take was an intense, silent, heartfelt mutuality. There is a precedent. Something even more intense apparently took place between Jung and Sabina Spielrein. As she wrote to Freud, "we could sit in speechless ecstacy for hours" (Carotenuto, 1984). In spite of Jung's over-involvement with his young patient, I suggest that it was, in great part, his capacity to enter with Spielrein into an experience of *coniunctio* that transformed her severe mental illness into the creative capacity she later demonstrated.

Jung's involvement with his patient requires us to take a closer look at the idea of the two-way process. We need to take careful note of the possible danger that it could lead to a reversal of the therapeutic relationship, one where the therapist *uses* the patient for his or her personal healing. This would constitute what Galipeau (2001) called a *perversion* of the therapy relationship. But with this danger in mind, I have little doubt that if I had been incapable of learning from Rachel and remained the analyst with all the answers, she would have remained implacably resistant to learning anything from me. The two-way approach was finely demonstrated in Casement's clinical study, *Learning from the Patient*, first published in 1985. The more radical idea that healing heals the healer can be seen to operate regularily in different therapeutic settings: for example, in therapy groups. Again and again I saw how affirming it was for one group member to be told by another how helpful they had been, even when they thought they had been aggressive or confronting. Reciprocal learning and healing is a basic tenet of marital therapy, where it is very clear that the more one partner can change the more the other can. The individual analytic relationship is also a partnership, capable of a special intimacy that, at its height, goes beyond the personal and seems to initiate a mutual healing process.

The idea of reciprocal healing was most fully developed by Harold Searles (1975), culminating in his paper, "The patient as therapist to his analyst". Searles argues that there is an innate need in every child to heal its parents; and that in a like manner the patient has an innate need to heal the analyst. He demonstrates in detail the therapeutic strivings of his very ill patients towards him. Indeed he attributes their original schizophrenic illness not only to early trauma, but to the unconscious sacrifice of their personal integration in a failed attempt to heal their own damaged parents. In Searles's view his patients slowly got well to the extent that, at the same time as he healed them, they could heal *him*.

Searles' view seems diametrically opposed to one that sees the child's love for its parents simply as a form of reparation. He acknowledges the role of reparation, but points to the fact that the healing impulse can be found in very young children, or in massively disintegrated patients whose ego organization could not encompass the notion of reparation. Searles says: "Innate among the human being's potentialities, present in the earliest months of post-natal life, is an essentially therapeutic striving". In a concluding "Comment" on Searles's paper Flarsheim says:

> Freud frequently stressed that he was constantly learning from his patients, learning from them eagerly, and it is my impression that this was perhaps the most important thing he offered to many of his

patients, and that it remains quite frequently the most important thing we offer to our patients today. [Flarsheim, 1975]

This is a far cry from the conventional role of the masterful analyst who takes the malfunctioning patient apart and puts him together again.

I have drawn attention to two distinct, but linked, processes: the first is the breakdown–breakthrough cycle; the second is the recognition that therapy at a deep level is a two-way process. Jung was an early, and passionate, advocate of this approach. He declared that: "A genuine participation, going right beyond professional routine, is absolutely imperative ... The doctor must go to the limit of his subjective possibilities, otherwise the patient will be unable to follow suit" (Jung, C.W., 16, para. 400). Given this orientation, it was no accident that Jung made the unique discovery that psychotherapy is the heir, not only to medicine, but to alchemy. The phrase "solve et coagula"—break down so that you may build up—is the watchword of the spiritual alchemists. But equally in the spirit of alchemy is the notion of the two-way process. Jung said that: '... often the doctor is in the same position as the alchemist who no longer knew whether he was melting the mysterious amalgam in the crucible or whether he was the salamander glowing in the fire ...' (Jung, C.W., 16, para. 399).

Freudian psychoanalysis, which aspired to be a branch of science, has proved one of the most fertile ideas of the twentieth century. Is it foolhardy to speculate that in the twenty-first century the Jungian perspective, reaching back into alchemy with its roots in the spiritual domain, will prove to be the next creative development in depth analysis?

References

Balint, M. (1968). The Basic Fault. London: Tavistock.
Carotenuto, A. (1984). A Secret Symmetry. London: Routledge and Kegan Paul.
Casement, P. (1985). On Learning from the Patient. London: Tavistock.
Fairbairn, W. R. D. (1952). The repression and return of bad objects. In: Psychoanalytic Studies of the Personality. London: Tavistock.

Field, N. (1996). *Breakdown and Breakthrough*. London: Routledge.

Flarsheim, A. (1975). Comment on H. F. Searles, "The Patient as Healer". In: *Tactics and Techniques in Psychoanalytic Therapy, Volume 2*. New York: Jason Aronson.

Freud, S. (1923). *The Ego and the Id*. London: Hogarth.

Galipeau, S. (2001). Perversions in the temenos. In: *Journal of Jungian Theory and Practice, Volume 3*. C. G. Jung Institute of New York.

Kalsched, D. E. (1996). *The Inner World of Trauma*. London: Routledge.

Khan, M. (1996). *The Privacy of the Self*. London: Hogarth.

Little, M. (1986). On basic unity. In: *Transference Neurosis and Transference Psychosis: Toward Basic Unity*. London: Free Association Books.

Milner, M. (1987). The concentration of the body. In: *The Supressed Madness of Sane Men*. London: Tavistock.

Searles, H. F. (1975). The patient as therapist to his analyst. In: *Countertransference and Related Subjects*. New York: International Universities Press.

Stanton, M. (1990). *Sandor Ferenczi*. London: Free Association Books.

CHAPTER NINE

Life gives and life takes—therapy in the waiting room of birth and death

Arna Davis

"Waiting can be the most intense and poignant of all human experiences—the experience, which above all others, strips us of affectations, and self deceptions and reveals to us the reality of our own needs, our values and ourselves"

W. H. Vanstone, 1982, p. 83

Introduction

The course of life has a certain beginning—birth—and a certain ending—death. This statement becomes loaded with poignant meaning for a person moving into a waiting space where there is no escape from giving birth or when the approaching death can not be shrunk from as an illness is reaching its terminal state. In a symbolic way death and rebirth, loss and fear of the different separation experiences, need to be faced as an essential part of the individuation process at each stage of a life cycle.

As therapists we are used to sitting quietly in a waiting space. At the beginning of each session we are in a place of not knowing where our patients will lead us. It is, at times, almost unbearable to remain waiting, to be still and inactive when we, with our patients, enter into messy periods of transitions, the uncertainty, the bewilderment and the out of control feelings that belong to the therapeutic process. There is an urgency to hasten the process, as staying in that not knowing space becomes intolerable. A writer friend, who has had to learn to wait, voices his experience: "The journey through waiting travels through the territories of loose ends and jagged bits of life that should not too readily be tidied up" (Eadie, 1999, p. 6).

What are the special issues in a therapeutic relationship where the physical reality dictates the time available for the work to be done and the changes, happening in the body, tell of the ticking of the clock? The uncertainty, the forced inactivity and the help-lessness to hasten or prolong the process of life coming to an end or giving birth to a new life arouse deep feelings of insecurity and fears. Memories of separations and earlier anxiety states are activated and defence structures are weakened. In the stillness of the therapeutic space and relationship there is a chance to gain access to cut off parts of the self. The waiting space becomes a transitional phase, giving a chance to re-assess the journey travelled so far and giving a time-limited opportunity to prepare for the journey ahead.

In this paper my intention is to explore the special issues that coloured the therapeutic relationship with two patients, Anna and Otto. In both therapies there was an urgency of time running out and a separation to be achieved. Birth and death do not wait. The fictitious names have a symbolic meaning, deriving, in my mother tongue, from the verbs *to give* and *to take*. Anna is the command: Give!, Otto the noun: Taking out.

The common task for both Anna and Otto was to re-unite with the core of the self that had been split and sealed off. Each patient had experienced a breakdown in the maternal container in infancy and each had needed to provide "self-holding" and had developed a primitive "self-care-system" (Kalsched, 1996) to protect an essential core of the person from unbearable anxiety.

In the first part of the paper I shall discuss how pregnancy and the birth of a real baby affected the therapeutic relationship. In the second part of the paper the implications for the therapeutic relationship of an approaching death will be discussed.

Anna's journey was towards motherhood, separating her from being tied to a mother, unable to protect her child, and separating the infant's delusional fantasies from her adult reality. The core issue in therapy was uniting the split-off nursing couple within her and gaining trust in herself as a mother who would be able to meet the needs of her real baby, a new life in her care.

Otto, terminally ill, needed a space to reflect on his life and to know what life, in its unfairness, had taken away. In his preparation for death there was a painful return journey to be made to the lost self as well as a journey of separation to accomplish, a hero's journey of fighting the final enemy, death, in order to feel freed to die.

Life gives—in the waiting room of birth

It frequently happens at the very beginning of treatment that a dream will reveal in broad perspective the whole programme of the unconscious. [Jung, C.W., 16, para. 343]

Jung's statement of the importance of the initial dream is often quoted as a tool in the assessment process, both in understanding the patient's problem and seeing the patient's unconscious aiding the therapist in her thinking of the task ahead. The dream does not need to be an actual dream. I have learned to trust the opening story as a kind of dream. By listening to it as the patient's unconscious communication, the therapist is guided in her thinking. It is telling of the core difficulties and shows the internal archetypal structures and object relationships of the psyche and gives an indication of what the centre theme and the task in therapy will be both for the therapist and the patient. "It is all important for a disciplined imagination to build up images of intangibles by logical principles and on the basis of empirical data, that is, on the evidence of dreams" (Jung, 1963, p. 341).

Anna, aged thirty-six, newly married for a second time, referred herself, as she explained, as a preventative measure. She was frightened that her second marriage might end in a failure, as had her first one. She wanted to gain an understanding of herself and her part in the destructive interactive patterns that had been repeated in her relationships. Her wish was to conceive a child and, in this very concrete way, to cement the new marriage. She was asking for a safe space where we could gain a sense of the events in her life, and that through that unfolding a new reading would be made, helping her in her desire to make the future different from the past. I note that the trigger for her seeking help is that she is frightened. Her security structure has been threatened by a major change in her life, a new marriage.

Anna's story

Fourteen years ago, living then in North of England, I gave birth to my baby son in a hospital where the Maternity unit was quite close to the Psychiatric unit. I was happily relaxing, my baby had been put into the baby room, when suddenly there was a sound of an alarm and panicky running of the nurses on the ward. I did not take a lot of notice at first but soon discovered that a baby had been stolen from its cot, and then, that it was my baby son that was missing. I became frantic and hysterical, my first thought was that my baby would be starving and then the real panic set in. Several hours later it was discovered that a mad woman from the psychiatric unit had sneaked in and stolen my baby and wandered off.

In listening, I asked myself what is Anna telling me in our very first session and what do I need to remember as we start our work together? I made the hypothesis that, with her opening story, Anna was not only telling me about her experiences with her first born baby, she was also giving me a clue to her internal object relationships and their interactions within. Was she preparing me for the drama that would be acted out in therapy? Had Anna referred herself to a "maternity unit" that, in her mind, would be contaminated with the nearness of a "psychiatric unit"? Would I become the mad psychotherapist who would steal her baby and separate the mother/baby couple? On the conscious level she hoped and was asking for the presence of a thinking other to protect the new marriage and the not yet conceived baby. By coming to therapy she wanted to ensure the baby's delivery into a safe world. She was also asking for a containing space, where her internal drama could be re-lived and understood.

In exploring the content of the story, I noted that, on an archetypal level, there are two leaking containers. The first one is the maternity unit that fails in its task to protect the new-born baby and the mother/baby couple from unwanted intruders. The second one is the psychiatric unit whose task is both to offer a place of safety for the mentally ill patients as well as to protect the public from the actions of a disturbed mind. I then asked what are the consequences of these two leakages for the mother/baby couple, for the baby and for the mother? One can presume that the neo-natal state of attachment has been violently torn apart. There is a state of an emergency, externally, in the maternity unit and in the mother, and, internally, panic, confusion and fear both in the mother and in the baby. The new-born baby has been catapulted from the continuation of the womb-like existence and the blissful state of security into a hostile world at a stage when there is no internal boundary between the outside and the inside. How would a primitive system deal with this ripping apart and the threat to its survival? What happens to the mother? She has lost trust in the authority of the archetypal container and, in personal terms, she has also lost trust in her own capacity to be a protecting mother for her baby.

The security of the original attachment has been lost, cut off. A too early detachment on one hand and an overprotective separation anxiety on the other hand, has permanently damaged the perfect fit. The leaks in the two containers have introduced madness into the mother/baby couple interactions. The mother and baby that come together after this catastrophe are not the same two they were before the event. Would this violently experienced loss mean that a hard shell had to be erected around the feeling core of the self and some kind of primitive self-management system created as survival strategies in a hostile, threatening world? The mother, having lost trust in her capacity to be a protecting mother, might turn the baby into a critical other, looking at her with accusing eyes, thus feeding the emergency strategy of self-management in the baby. Outwardly together again, but having been torn apart, before an outside the womb separation had been achieved, one might presume that the relationship between the baby and the mother would be coloured by mistrust and chronic disturbance and confusion. The baby can no longer trust the mother to do her job, the mother can not trust herself and too early gives the thinking to the baby, misreading signals as thoughts.

History

In the first three months, as a working alliance was being established, Anna described her background history and her current life situation. I shall outline briefly the main points, before going on to describe the therapeutic process.

Anna was the only child of parents whom she saw as two lost and frightened people. They came to London from the country, knowing no one, and lived in poverty and isolation. Anna did not know much about her birth, but she has been told that she was literally starved as a baby, because her mother herself was starving and had not enough milk. Her parents elevated Anna, from an early age, to their rescuer and mediator in their dealings with the outside world. Anna became her own authority, an omnipotent little grown up, managing her life and her parents life, detached from her dependency needs and feeling contempt for her child-like parents. She was praised for her independence, she was bright and clever and felt contained in the school environment, she did well and gained a university place and obtained a good degree.

During Anna's final year at the university she met a student from a foreign country. He was a charmer, seductive, warm and full of trust in himself and in the world. Anna fell deeply in love for the first time in her life, her steel-hard defences melted in the attention and love she was shown. She became pregnant and the couple decided to get married. While her new husband went back to his own country, preparing for them to return there, their baby son was born. Anna felt let down by her absent husband. The traumatic events of her son's birth she described at our very first meeting.

The move abroad and escaping from the responsibilities she carried for her parents was exciting. Her husband's return home was the celebration of a prodigal son. Anna described how their baby son was snatched from her arms and whisked away to be shown off to all the relatives and friends. It did not take long before Anna's happy dreams of a new beginning were shattered. The sunny south changed into a menacing, nightmarish place. Anna felt isolated and unprotected and not wanted, she did not know the language nor did she understand the customs and traditions in her new country, she was in a strange world she did not belong to. She felt threatened by, and envious of, her mother-in-law's overflowing love, already having captured her husband's heart and about to steal her baby son's affection. The mother-in-law, with milk pouring out from her big breasts, became in her mind the archetypal good mother of boy babies, whilst she, the baby girl, was abandoned into the care of an attacking Witch Mother. She could not voice her bad, unreasonable feelings, nor did her husband understand the change that was taking place in Anna and in their relationship. The love in his eyes turned into a hostile, critical glare.

Anna's story of her marriage read like a fairytale, with its archetypal figures. There is a "Sleeping Beauty" behind a fence of thorns, woken up by the Prince, full of his masculine power, then the return of the prince to his kingdom, ruled by the widowed Queen Mother. There is the starved orphan, driven by feelings of envy and jealousy, fleeing back to a cold, barren world. The penis, that had initially seduced Anna and filled her with goodness, had now become the hated and envied object.

Anna returned to England and gained, after a complex legal battle, the custody of her child and, later, a divorce. She worked as a marketing manager and moved close to where her parents lived. The old defences of self-management were re-erected but with the difference: she now had her son as her security object she could clutch and control. Initially her son had little contact with his father, but as he approached adolescence the contact increased. The son, in his separation process from a controlling mother, became critical and rebellious and identified with his absent, idealized father. Anna felt robbed, devastated and rejected. She started an affair with a married man, and, as a result, the conflicts and battles between Anna and her son increased, as he, in turn, felt abandoned by his mother and demoted by the new man in Anna's life. The carefully created safety structures were breaking down. Anna had entered her lover's family system as a disturbing outsider and an intruder, stealing the father from his children and breaking up their family.

At the point of the referral Anna had recently married her new man, with chaos in both family systems still raging. Anna's son was sulking and refusing to relate to his stepfather, her husband's children were resentful of the new marriage, with the ex-wife in the background fuelling feelings of anger and jealousy.

Anna's background information confirmed my original hypothesis of her early infant experiences. There was no external support, no archetypal container, for the parental couple. They were struggling with their own survival, leaving the starving, panicky infant in the grips of archetypal experiences not mediated by the parents and these experiences became part of her internal structure. I quote Mara Sidoli:

> in the de-integrative phases of early infancy, when the primal self de-integrates, archetypal drives are activated and because of the fragile and fragmented state of the infant's ego the opposites are constellated, and produce in the infant a kind of experience which could be described as archetypal. Thus in the absence of the real flesh and blood mother, who may perform the function of mediator of such experiences for her baby, the infant finds himself in the grip of archetypal experiences, good and bad. [Sidoli, 1983, p. 203]

One can presume that primitive defenses came into operation to ensure that the overwhelming affect of the loss of a maternal container is not experienced. Winnicott emphasizes in his discussion of the concept "false self" how essential it is to take into account the mother's behaviour and attitude, as the infant's dependence on the mother is "near absolute" (Winnicott, 1972). A "false self" is created to manage with the external world, terrified of the breakdown that has already been experienced but cannot be remembered. Being elevated to an omnipotent child/adult and admired by her parents gave Anna confidence and trust in her capacity to manage. The initial falling in love and defending herself against that loss of her loved one, by transferring her dependency needs into the symbiotic relationship with her baby son, indicated that some mediating of the original archetypal structures had taken place.

The therapeutic relationship and the therapeutic process

Having a safe, containing framework and setting up an adult to adult contract, where the responsibilities of the therapist and the patient are clearly defined, is essential in all therapies. Anna had no internal trust in an outside authority, and, I knew, she would be looking for inconsistencies and breaks in the frame. She needed to feel held by the structure from the very start. The fact that she had made a self-referral and had chosen me as her therapist was an indication that she did want the therapeutic relationship to work. She accepted, on a conscious level, the contract as outlined in the first session: the commitment to therapy, her responsibility for coming to her sessions and for how she used them, her agreement to paying the fees monthly and by cheque. We agreed to two sessions a week. I suggested the use of the couch, as a good working tool, separating the therapeutic relationship to something unique and special. This she accepted.

Listening to her current life situation, I understood that Anna needed a place of safety on many levels. The image of the Russian "Babushka" doll with layers of maternal figures inside another came to my mind. I felt that it would be the combination of the reliable therapeutic space and I as the reliable therapist together, that would provide the firm and constant archetypal container needed to hold both the internal and external chaos. I was also concerned about the projections and fantasies that the hoped for new baby might have to carry.

My first task was to simply be there and give Anna an experience of being firmly held. In practise this meant accepting that initially I would be working with the controlling "manager" part in Anna, with no access allowed to the feeling baby within her. I needed to wait, join her, not enter into power struggles, not intrude and cause her to feel sudden jerks by my interventions. At the same time, each time the opportunity arouse, by clarifying and separating what was her task and what was mine in the therapeutic relationship, I hoped to reduce the power of the omnipotent "manager" in her. The theme of each session was set by Anna, and in listening to the material she brought I concentrated on the archetypal patterns of her internal and external interactions. In feeding back to her what I had understood, I needed to find the correct words, based on the evidence gathered from her story in each session. Jung, in the interpretation of dreams, speaks of "spontaneous amplification of the archetypes", and these "availing themselves of the existing conscious material" (Jung, C.W., 8, para. 403). I link this "principle of amplification" into seeing the archetypal patterns and hearing the unconscious communication in the manifest material.

Being a container for the infant who had been thrown into a hostile world meant avoiding separation between that part of Anna and me, and allowing her an experience of blissful safety, a feeling of being firmly held by a thinking other. My hope was that the experience of me joining with her in her world would counteract the too early detachment of the nursing couple. I was mindful that, in the transference, I was dealing with a baby who had no trust and who had defended herself against "unbearable psychic pain" by delusional fantasies of omnipotence and "self-holding" (Kalsched, 1998). Those fantasies would not disappear by words, and the pain would not become accessible unless she had an experience of constancy in thought and care.

In each session some work was done with the stories she brought, often confirming the confusions between madness that leaked from outside, contaminating and becoming madness within, which in turn poisoned the outside world. For example, she allowed me to explore with her the meaning her unreasonable mistrust of her husband and her work colleagues. She was allowing me to enter her world of fear and terror so that we could begin to separate what was the adult reality and what was her primitive defence system and the archetypal structures created by an infant thrown into a hostile world. We had glimpses of an inner space being created, where she could begin to think of her feelings of emptiness and of the meaning of that empty space for a hungry, crying infant. She understood how that emptiness might have needed to be filled with delusional and omnipotent fantasies of self-holding, of not needing any one.

Pregnancy

After four months in therapy Anna announced that she was pregnant. I felt the timing was interesting, as just when she had allowed her defences to slip a little, she needed to protect herself from becoming dependent and vulnerable. Her empty feeling would be taken away by a real physical feeling that something good was growing inside her. She felt triumphant, she was now pregnant and would manage without me. We had a crisis in our work, as Anna failed to come back to her sessions after a short break in the therapy. She was five months pregnant. I wrote to her, firmly indicating how important it was for her, and for the baby she was carrying, to come back so that we could explore the meaning of her action in words. She did return and settled down again. We discovered that her mother had nearly had a miscarriage in the fifth month of her pregnancy with Anna, and so were able to avoid an unconscious repetition from the past. I was also convinced that it was the "omnipotent" Anna who was reluctant to give up her power and felt threatened by her growing dependency on me.

The work in the sessions changed. We had now moved into a time that was limited by the pregnancy, a waiting space. The job of separation became more urgent, the foetus inside her was moving, giving Anna a strong sense of reality. At the same time her triumphant feelings receded, and she expressed envy and ambivalent feelings towards the baby inside her, who was taking some of her space in our sessions. She felt guilty that she had these hating, envious feelings. The unresolved conflicts and anxieties from earlier stages of Anna's psychic development resurfaced. She remembered how her feelings towards her first husband had changed because of her envy of the love he received from his mother. As an only child she had never been faced with rivalry. She became aware of the effect the new arrival might have on her son, who already felt abandoned.

My task was twofold, both to contain the inner child and to prepare Anna for motherhood. Anna needed help in gaining trust in her capacity to protect and take care of the new life and to separate her adult reality from the cut-off, lost and hungry baby within. At times I also felt like a grandmother and a container of the collective anxieties in the whole family, as both her son and husband were acting out their fears of exclusion and their infantile feelings of being abandoned by the mother. Helping Anna to understand the acting out allowed her to give up her omnipotent need to control. Instead, she was able to help her husband to understand both her son's acting out and her need to withdraw into a state of reverie.

Birth of the baby

Anna had been in therapy just over a year when her daughter was born. There had been a short break, then Anna came back with her baby girl, Cara. In the first sessions Anna was holding Cara in her arms and offering her breast at frequent intervals. I was observing the nursing couple and noting the anxiety in Anna's handling of her baby. After a few sessions Cara was brought in a carry-cot, placed close to Anna. Every time Cara made the slightest whimpering sound she would be picked up and put to the breast. I could see a startled expression on the baby's face, her space was intruded upon and her blissful state disturbed. She was in no way ready for a feed. I wondered if the memory of hunger was triggered within Anna. I could see that she was neither able to separate what belonged to her or what belonged to her baby, nor to contain her anxiety. I suggested that she could leave the carry-cot next to my chair and, instead of immediately picking up the baby, she could try to put into words the feelings aroused in her by Cara's first sounds at waking up. In this way the real baby and the thinking "grandmother" together helped Anna in the separation process between the unmet needs of her internal baby and what was the reality in the here and now. Having the courage to stay with her anxiety and wait for Cara to give clear signals of her needs built Anna's confidence as a good mother. After a while Cara was left in Anna's mother's care, allowing the grandmother a redeeming experience in caring for her grandchild. Our work now continued undisturbed. Anna became more conscious of the hungry, needy parts within herself, and at the same time she felt safely held and allowed herself to feel fed.

Three months after her birth, Anna brought Cara again to a session. Anna was concerned that Cara was not holding her head up properly. I felt I needed to intervene on the reality level and suggested that Cara is taken to a paediatrician. He saw the whole family. I was impressed by his psychological insight. He had understood that this baby had been born into an emotional position in the family, predetermined by multiple factors that had little connection to the new infant or her needs. He seemed aware of the problems of a re-constituted family. He noted Anna's anxieties and encouraged the father to be firm in helping Anna not to pick Cara up constantly, and for both of them to trust the baby to hold her own head up. He included Anna's son in the interviews. Thus the family now had a father and a mother at the archetypal level, containing them in their separation process from the past and supporting the new family and parenthood.

During the first year Cara was shown to me at regular intervals, so that I would confirm Anna's success as a mother. My long summer break occurred soon after Cara's first birthday. Anna did not return back to therapy. She wrote a letter saying all was well and "please, this time do not ask me to return". I understood her message, the mother/baby couple no longer needed an outside "maternity unit".

Anna's opening story told of broken archetypal containers, the safety of a maternity unit being contaminated by madness that sneaked in from outside, and the confusion that followed. The trigger for Anna in seeking "a place of safety" was the fear of her new marriage being contaminated by unresolved conflicts of the past and the confusions in the present interactions. Her hope and fantasy was that a new baby would be the healing force and cement the new marriage.

In the waiting space Anna experienced a feeling of safety and being firmly held. The thinking presence of the therapist enabled a separation from the infant's delusional world of omnipotence to take place as Anna's fantasies were challenged in the adult reality. The actual experience of pregnancy, of something good growing inside, and the giving birth to a new life and caring for her baby, helped Anna in her separation from childhood to motherhood. The real baby, with her signals, and the "grandmother" therapist, using the baby's signals, together cemented a trusting relationship between mother and baby. The gift of a new life allowed a new beginning after hurt and losses in the re-constituted family.

*   *   *

I now move onto the second part of this paper where life seems to be cruelly taken away rather than given.

Life takes—therapy in the waiting room of death

And so it is—death is indeed a fearful piece of brutality; there is no sense pretending otherwise. It is brutal not only as a physical event, but far more so psychically: a human being is torn away from us, and what remains is the icy stillness of death. There no longer exists any hope of a relationship, for all the bridges have been smashed at one blow. Those who deserve a long life are cut off in the prime of their years, and good-for-nothings live to a ripe old age. This is a cruel reality which we have no right to sidestep. The actual experience of the cruelty and wantonness of death can so embitter us that we conclude there is no merciful God, no justice, and no kindness.

From another point of view, however, death appears as a joyful event. In the light of eternity, it is a wedding, a mysterium coniunctionis. The soul attains, as it were, its missing half, it achieves wholeness. [Jung, C.W., 14, p. 346]

Reading this Jung's statement, I have had to ask myself which is more brutal: death in all its finality; or living in that waiting space of death, seeing its shadow day by day drawing nearer.

Otto's story

Otto, aged fifty three, chronologically in mid-life, but with a death sentence already written on his face, needed a space for rendering an account of his life as he was approaching the final stage of his earthly journey. Otto had contacted a colleague of mine, who knew him well, for her to suggest a therapist. From the referring colleague I learned that Otto was born with the hereditary disease, haemophilia (a tendency to uncontrollable bleeding through deficiency in the blood of the normal clotting substance, a disease transmitted through the mother to her male children). I was also told that a few years ago Otto, in need of a blood transfusion for his haemophilia, had been given blood contaminated by the HIV virus. Haemophilia had threatened Otto's life from his birth; now the fight against the HIV virus had reached a point of no hope of cure. Otto's health was deteriorating rapidly and he felt there were issues he needed to work with whilst he was still mobile enough to get to a therapist. My first response to this referral was to suggest that Otto might need a male therapist. This was not to be, and, in accepting the referral, I needed to acknowledge to myself that there was a fear in me that I would not be strong enough for the task ahead. Had I already, in my counter-transference response, identified with the mother who could not protect her child from the pain that was in his body? Or had my unconscious informed me of the task in the therapeutic relationship: to be a thinking father in Otto's separation process from a too involved mother? Possibly both.

Otto was a small, thin, frail looking man with a beautifully shaped head and an open, intelligent look in his eyes. When we met for the first time, I needed to acknowledge that it was not an accident that Otto became my patient. There was a journey we needed to travel together, a journey, I sensed, that, at times, would be full of unbearable pain. What this journey would mean for me, I had no way of knowing, but we did know that for Otto there was no false hope of healing, of becoming better. My task, as a therapist, I understood: to be there and not shrink away from his anguish of the brutality of death, the raving against the untimely taking away of his life, a life that had already robbed so much from him. The unfairness of that life needed to be shared, the pain, anger, fears and frustrations voiced. The reality of death was already present, it was in the room and the denial of this fact, from my side, would simply be my lack of courage. Could the therapeutic space and relationship give the containment for his "final stage of growth"? (Kubler-Ross, 1975).

Otto had had intensive psychotherapy before. That experience had changed his life in a fundamental way and led him to both study psychotherapy and work in the helping professions. He had recently given up his work for health reasons.

A working alliance on the adult to adult level was easy to establish. He was a highly intelligent man, thoughtful and curious, and there was an urgency in him to do the work. We met once a week for nearly two years, all the time conscious of playing with the opposites of an approaching death and needing to return to his birth for him to re-unite with a part of himself that had been sealed off.

Otto, his life threatened from birth onwards, had never know what it was to live an ordinary life. He had never had a healthy body to be there for him to use freely, to be strong enough to defend him against attacks, to stand firmly and take some knocks and bumps or to simply have a body to love and be proud of and to enjoy its strength. His cry from the heart, often repeated in the sessions, was to be "vin ordinaire", not to be special or singled out, have healthy red blood running through his veins. He was born a victim, physically carrying his grandfather's illness in his body, trapped into a body he could not trust nor love, and born into the arms of a mother, whose father was the only surviving male out of six brothers, all victims of haemophilia. This father, himself crippled with pain, with the threat of his death hanging over the family, offered no security or reliability to his children. How could Otto's mother, carrying the unprocessed feelings of a frightened, abandoned child, be a trusting, containing mother to her son, particularly as she carried the guilt of having given her child her father's hated, frightening illness? Even for a mother, free from guilt and separated from her past, there would be no way of protecting her child from the pain of internal bleeding within his body. Otto's mother did know, from the terrors of her own childhood, how excruciating the pain was. Her way of dealing with Otto's bleeding attacks was to abandoned him into the care of others, leave him in the hospital, detaching herself from thinking of her baby's needs, and, once he was back, being over protective and clinging and anxiously watching her child.

Otto's first hospital admission was when he was only six months old, and through his childhood, almost yearly, these hospital admissions were repeated. At six months, how would a primitive system deal with the physical abandonment of the holding mother, whilst at the same being left alone to endure the unbearable physical pain in his own body?

We know that early separation is an experience that causes a deep trauma, affecting the emotional development of the infant. Kalsched states that "Early trauma is by definition an experience that causes the child *unbearable* psychic pain—pain so severe that it cannot be processed by the psyche's symbolic and integrative capacities, owing to the ego's immaturity" (Kalshed, 1998, p. 83). Kohut (1984) describes this as "the deepest anxieties" experienced by a person whose very self is beginning to disintegrate, threatening total fragmentation and estrangement from body to mind.

When a breakdown in the transitional processes occurs and "the terrifying archetypal experiences" are not processed, the infant needs to bring into force primitive survival strategies, by creating an omnipotent fantasy image that provides "self-holding". Kalsched notes that rarely are these defences seen as having accomplished anything in the preservation of life for the person whose heart is broken by trauma. "While everyone agrees how maladaptive these defences are in the later life of the patient, few writers have acknowledged the miraculous nature of these defences—their life-saving sophistication or the archetypal nature and meaning" (Kalsched, 1998, p. 85).

This defence system allows normal development to continue. This might operate like the body's immune system, but at the cost of autistic encapsulation and the person becoming an emotionally detached observer of his own image. Would this be true also when the infant has to deal with not only psychic pain but real physical pain? Having frequently had to relive the physical pain, Otto certainly had not forgotten the feelings of being in a place worse than hell and the relief he felt, at the age of seven, when was given morphine. Anna Freud writes:

> a child in pain is a child maltreated, harmed, punished, persecuted or threatened by annihilation ... young children react to pain not only with anxiety but with other aspects appropriate to the content of the unconscious fantasies i.e. on one hand with anger, rage and revenge feelings and on the other with masochistic submission, guilt and depression. [Freud, 1969, p. 272]

For Otto and his family there was no protection from the reality of his haemophilia, there was no normality to return to after an attack or hospitalization, his defences did not shield him from the pain of feeling isolated, being special, in a negative way. For example, he remembered the humiliation of having to sit, for his own protection, in a wheelchair in a corner of the school playground during breaks, having to be an observer of the rough and tumble of normal childhood play. Now, years later in the sessions, he could express his envy of those healthy ones and his anger and disgust with his own feeble body.

His adolescence was a nightmare. He was frightened and ignorant, could not understand what was happening in his body, terrified of his wet dreams and the fluid pouring out of him in his sleep, frightened by his own urge to touch his penis and frightened to masturbate, unable to share his fears and fantasies with anyone. Eventually he gained factual information from reading a book on sex and felt confident enough to think of an actual sexual relationship. He met his wife when he was twenty and, to his surprise, they enjoyed, right from the start, a mutually satisfying sexual relationship. His deep frustration was that now he was no longer able to make love, but he had not given up hope of his potency returning.

The therapeutic relationship

Although the adult to adult working alliance was established immediately, I knew without any detailed background information that from the beginning on the unconscious level Otto would have no trust in a containing other. Having worked with many patients who have been left far too early to "self-manage", I have learned the importance of the therapeutic space as a container that simply is there, firm and constant. In that space my task is, for a long while, to be a non-intrusive presence, joining the patient and gaining his trust by listening to the repeating patterns in his stories, and then, by using the patient's own words, feeding back the patterns, giving them a creative meaning. For a child, abandoned by a real protecting mother, the creation of an internal vicious circle is a defence and a safety structure and a survival mechanism against the unbearable abandonment, an abandonment that has already taken place. The negative, repeating pattern, where every creative effort by the internal child is attacked and mocked by the witch mother, needs to be challenged as useless and outdated in adult life. De Bono (1986) uses the concrete images of different coloured hats to describe different modes of thinking. He calls the vicious circle thinking, offering no change, "black hat thinking". In helping my patients to look with adult eyes at their primitive, often delusional, thinking patterns, the black hat, that blinds new visions, has become a remembered and comic image.

In gathering information and re-living his history together, Otto and I understood that he was indeed a powerless victim of fate twice over, first by having been born with an inherited blood disease and then, a second time, by having a supposedly life saving transfusion that gave him a deathly virus instead. He also carried in his internal psychic system "viruses" that had seeped into his system at a time when there was not sufficient ego strength, or boundaries between him and the outside world. Together we identified archetypal patterns that Otto was trapped in: the omnipotent hero/the powerless victim, in a never ending dual; the abandoned Child/the Witch Mother in a vicious circle; the detached Child/the overprotective, clinging Mother in a tug of war. The separating archetypal Father was missing. A real father, who would have mediated between these opposing forces, was absent, a father, whose task would have been to trust his son, help him leave the clinging mother and encourage him to move on towards the journey to manhood.

Where was Otto's father? It seemed that, married for a second time, he was already an old man at the time of Otto's birth. His father, disillusioned with life, detached himself from the anxious closeness of mother and son, withdrew to his study and was an absent figure in Otto's life, ending up as an alcoholic and a recluse. No wonder I had wanted to pass on the referral to a healthy, strong male therapist.

I understood the movement in the first year of therapy in terms of Fordham's (1976) concept of de-integration and re-integration in the presence of a holding, thinking other, as well as the separation of reality from fantasies by using the evidence of the patterns in his own stories that he could not deny. As these archetypal patterns started making sense, Otto could see and acknowledge them still operating in his internal world as a defence and in his interactions within his family and in particular with his wife. She was left to carry the role of a powerless, overprotective mother in her real anxiety concerning Otto's health, which he chose to deny with his flights to manic fantasies and, at times, with his reckless actions.

About nine months into therapy, something had shifted in the therapeutic relationship. I sensed that there was trust, that Otto felt understood and firmly held, and that he was also more united within himself. The energy that had been trapped in the useless fights of two opposing forces of equal strength was becoming released and, even physically, his blood count improved temporarily. This new release of life forces manifested itself in his obsession about flying, flying a very special plane, a single-seat fighter, a war plane, a "Spitfire". He had in his youth wanted to become a pilot, and had learnt to fly, but was not accepted for pilot training due to his illness. Now he not only wanted to fly the plane but actually to buy one. He brought a picture of the "Spitfire" for me to see and I learned that the Battle of Britain, in 1940, was won by these "Spitfires", the fastest fighter planes in the squadron service anywhere in the world.

We might have explored the symbolic meaning of this obsession, but putting thoughts into words did not seem relevant. With unbelievable sadness in my heart I simply listened. We knew that this was a battle for life, Otto needed his Spitfire, his single-seat war plane, to live with his ailing body, to fight the enemy, the impending threat of death, and to give him, at least in fantasy, a chance to become a hero, a war hero. Few weeks before our first long break in therapy, Otto brought this dream to his session:

> I am standing on an airfield, there is only one plane on it, a "Spitfire". I step into that plane, turn the engine on. It speeds along the runway and takes off, gathers more and more speed, accelerates through the clouds up into the sky, so high that finally the engine cuts off. The plane glides gently towards the earth, and lands on the west coast of Scotland, in a remote area. I survive unharmed, and live there, feeding myself with wild berries and flowers. Nobody knows who I am, for the local people I become this recluse and their wise, revered mentor.

In his numinous dream the fight was over. Otto had united with the archetypal Father, the sky, the fighter "Spitfire" was no longer needed, the engine's power was redundant, the plane could glide back to earth, to the nourishing archetypal Mother. A transformation had taken place. Otto was no longer a needy child but a Wise Old Man with no personal desires and free to spiritually nourish the local people. The dream had prophetic significance and was a forewarning that time was running out, but not yet. There were battles to be fought in the struggle to separate from the bonds to his parents, that tied him to his childhood interactions in his adult world, and to free him internally from unprocessed feelings that were still attaching him to his victim position.

In the final stage the sessions were filled with roaring rage and anger towards the hospital that had given him HIV, hate towards the unfairness of his life, towards his wasting body, all beyond his control. There was bitter envy of healthy, strong men, of his tall young son, of people who had no need to think about death or pain, who could take life as granted. His abusive shouting filled the consulting room, and I must admit that it was, at times, extremely hard not to become a controlling mother. There was fear, panic and separation anxiety not only in him but, more acutely, in his wife. The marriage went through a very difficult phase, his wife, one moment, wanting to leave him, run away, and the next moment feeling guilty and remorseful for her death wishes, then angry and attempting to powerlessly control Otto's reckless actions, his final acts of defiance, such as getting inebriated or driving his beloved sports car too fast, with the radio blasting away, and spending money they did not have. She was convinced that the HIV virus was affecting Otto's brain and could not see that he needed to hold onto his autonomy as life was being taken away. I can not find words to describe how distressing it was to watch Otto's body wasting away. I listened, with the heart in my throat, as he climbed the one step into my waiting room, anxious that he might fall. It became difficult for him to get off the couch, I struggled with the conflict should I offer to help him or not. In the end I simply sat still, with tears in my eyes, watching this proud, independent man slowly get himself upright. He could no longer drive and started missing sessions until his wife agreed to drive him. He brought me photos of himself as a child, and cried bitterly in the sessions for the suffering of the little boy. He understood, finally, the courage and bravery of the child in having to carry both his physical and psychic pain. Shortly before my annual break Otto's final battle was fought in the dream:

> I was taken prisoner by a group of homosexual men who tried to rape me. I saw there was a half-open door and a woman stood in the doorway. I was fighting for my life and thinking that the woman might help me. Finally I managed to free myself from the grip of these men and run out of the door. I turned to look at the woman and saw that she was old and had a wrinkled face. I knew she could not have helped me in my fight against those men. I walked out and felt a sense of freedom I had never experienced before.

The therapeutic relationship had come to an end, I was going away, not knowing whether Otto would still be alive on my return. In his dream, he dismissed me, his spirit was free, he had won the battles within himself, he had reached his final stage of growth. The journey had lead him to the source of peace and strength, to his inner self. In practical terms he now needed the loving care of his family. After my break Otto did not come back, he had died two days before in Scotland, his wife fulfilling Otto's dream and listening to her husband's request when he announced: "It is time to go north".

*   *   *

Who was I in the transference, a bisexual parental figure? A containing mother and firm father, proud of his son, a father who encouraged Otto to play and fight? Is it necessary to analyse what took place in the waiting space of death? All I know that there was an urgency for the work to be done and that being there in stillness was at times unbearable and the pain and sadness in the room tangible. The pain was not only about life coming to an untimely end. It was as much Otto's need to discover the lost self and opening himself up to the infant's terrors, abandoned to cope with his attacking body, to the unbearable pain, transferred into a hate of that body that took away his right to be ordinary "vin ordinaire". In the final stage of life Otto found the loving compassion for that suffering child and the suffering body, now with sores weeping in his ailing legs.

Six months after Otto's death followed my own husband's death, after a prolonged illness. Was this why I needed to make the journey to the valley of death? Was it the unconscious knowing my need for the Wise Old Man, Otto, to prepare and guide me on the painful journey to the final separation from a loved one? Who was the giver who the taker in this exchange?

Ending

Being the travelling companion with Anna, for her to give birth to a new life, and with Otto, to meet the end of his earthly journey, leaves me with a deep sense of gratitude. Both therapies took place in a time limited waiting space, both ended in a separation where I, as their companion, was no longer needed. The external reality of birth and death was part of the context colouring the two therapies. I saw as my central tasks, firstly, to offer a secure and safe space in which the original drama could be understood and to explore the nature of the primitive defence structures, created as an emergency to protect the injured self; secondly, as a therapist, I needed to offer both non-intrusive holding and an experience of a thinking, containing presence, where signals could be heard, understood, re-framed and given a new meaning. The separation from the archetypal patterns that entrapped both Anna and Otto was helped by the urgency of time running out and their creative need to take leave of the defensive habit of the destructive "self-management" in order to move on and unite with the brave infant within.

Why have I written the stories of Anna and Otto? It is true that the most rewarding experiences I have had, as a therapist, have been the work I have done with women who have suffered an early trauma and have needed to become "self holders". Then, using me as an archetypal container, these women had become pregnant, feeling safe to move towards motherhood and give birth to a new baby. It is also true that being in the waiting room of death with Otto has been the most painful experience for me as a therapist. Perhaps I needed to share the joy and the sorrow, perhaps these stories needed to be told, in the hope of giving them a universal meaning. Life and death are part of the cycle of life, each transition from birth onwards moves us closer to death. In our need to be healers who help to promote psychological growth and change, we may sometimes forget the reality of death.

References

De Bono, E. (1986). *Six Thinking Hats*. Harmondsworth: Viking (Penguin Books).

Eadie, D. (1999). *Grain in Winter*. Peterborough: Epworth Press.

Fordham, M. (1976). *Self and Autism*. London: Heinemann.

Freud, A. (1969). The role of bodily illness in the mental life of children. In: *Indications for Child Analysis*. London: The Hogarth Press.

Jung, C. G. (1963). *Memories, Dreams, Reflections*. New York: Pantheon.

Kalsched, D. E. (1996). *The Inner World of Trauma, Archetypal Defences of the Personal Spirit*. London: Routledge.

Kalsched, D. E. (1998). Archetypal affect, anxiety and defence in patients who have suffered early trauma. In: A. Casement (Ed.), *Post-Jungians Today: Key Papers in Contemporary Analytical Psychology*. London: Routledge.

Kohut, H. (1984). *How Does Analysis Cure*. A. Goldberg (Ed.). Chicago: University of Chicago Press.

Kubler-Ross, E. (1975). *Death The Final Stage of Growth*. New Jersey: Spectrum Book, Prentice-Hall, Inc.

Sidoli, M. (1983). De-integration and re-integration in the first two weeks of life. *Journal of Analytical Psychology*, 28: 201–212.

Vanstone, W. H. (1982). *The Stature of Waiting.* Darton, Longman and Todd.

Winnicott, D. W. (1972). *The Maturational Process and the Facilitating Environment.* London: The Hogarth Press.

CHAPTER TEN

The difficulties inherent in having your own mind

Geraldine Godsil

"Good metaphors appear as the indispensable instruments for reweaving new *webs* of belief-desire"

Fiumara, 1995

Introduction

I n this paper I am going to discuss work with a young woman called Nina who had great difficulty in thinking about her emotional experience. She presented me with many theoretical and technical dilemmas. A feature of her analysis that was extremely difficult for me to understand and tolerate was her absence. This included both her silence when she *was* there and her regular absence from sessions, particularly the first one of the week. Something psychic disappeared into a negative action: not speaking or not coming. Parallel to this was that psychic experience often disappeared into a somatic complaint.

The title of the paper refers both to Bion's theories about thinking and also to Jung's depiction of the individuation process as a series of perilous coniunctios establishing positions that constantly succumb to the pressure for new development (Jung, C.W., 16; Bion, 1967). For both thinkers the symbol had a crucial role in bringing about transition from one state of mind to another. The post

Kleinian and Jungian traditions share much common ground and both make connections with Freud's earliest work in *Studies on Hysteria* (1893–1895) where the dissociation of aspects of the mind was explored in vivid detail. In his early work on hysteria and later on disavowal and its function in perversion, Freud was fascinated by symbolizing and *difficulties* in symbolizing which he connected with the wish not to know.

Through his alchemical metaphor Jung illustrated that the generative force of the archetype drives the development of the mind and its continuing if fraught integration. Ronald Britton, building on Bion's work on projective identification as a communicative function, writes, that he regards, "the epistemophilic instinct (Wissentrieb) to be on a par with and independent of the other instincts" and that "exploration, recognition and belief" are components of this "desire for knowledge" (Britton, 1998). In both Jungian and Kleinian theory archaic image schemas linked to instinct generate the mind's development.

Having your own mind is not something to be taken for granted. As analytic theory has moved more into the exploration of psychotic states, new accounts of primitive object relationships and their connection with thinking have been outlined. Establishing symbolic structures derived from primitive objects in relationship with each other is necessary before you can have your own mind. It is these primitive and nebulous representations of self, father, mother and their couplings that establish structures that eventually generate thoughts.

I found it useful in thinking about these early structures to employ the metaphors of circular space and triangular space. The experience of the nipple in the mouth and the mother's holding physical contact gives the baby a sense of an encircling skin that can then be internalized as a container inside which experiences and thoughts can happen. Establishing this secure link represented by the circle gives the baby the mental capacity to establish further links. The parental couple link, which has created the baby, can then be observed if the mind is capable of achieving a position from which this can be tolerated. This achievement of circular and then triangular space has immense significance for the development of a capacity to symbolize.

These archetypal image schemas of circular and triangular space and their generative relation to the development of symbolizing appear in Freudian, Kleinian and Jungian theory and practice (Jung, C.W., 16; Fordham, 1957; Bick, 1968; Britton, 1989; Rupprecht-Schreyer, 1995; Yarom, 1997) I will use classical and contemporary writing from these theoretical traditions to frame an exploration of some of my patient's difficulties in thinking. The first part of this paper will review theoretical contributions in the following three areas.

- Freudian: Classical and contemporary work on hysteria and triangular structuring at oedipal and pre-oedipal levels.
- Kleinian: Bion's conception of an obstructive and terrifying super-ego which exists as an internal object that is hostile to all links.
- Jungian: Jung's concepts of the coniunctio and the syzygy.

In the second part I will present aspects of the clinical work which link with this theoretical discussion.

Theoretical overview

Classical and contemporary work on hysteria

In the theoretical work I shall review here a spectrum of *defences against knowing* are explored. These range from primitive and unconscious to more developed and conscious strategies.

In Freud and Breuer's *Studies in Hysteria* (1895) Freud describes and discusses *dissociated states* akin to a hypnotic trance. These states contribute, along with psychic trauma, to the double consciousness observed in the hysteric. Anna O's daydreaming—her "private theatre"—lays the foundation for a "dissociation of her mental personality". Under the influence of intense emotions of anxiety and dread, the daydreaming becomes an "hallucinatory absence". Freud writes that

> It is hard to avoid expressing the situation by saying that the patient was split into two personalities of which one was mentally normal and the other insane. [1895]

This insane part of the personality was referred to by Anna as her *"bad self"*.

Freud explains that the motive for the splitting of consciousness is to defend against psychic pain through the mechanism of conversion. In place of the mental pain, physical pains make their appearance. Freud elaborates further on the connection between the conversion and the disappearance of ideas of a "distressing nature". These ideas are forced out of consciousness and out of memory: "The hysterical patient's *not knowing* was in fact a *not wanting to know*".

For Freud, the wish not to know in *Studies*, involves a *conscious* repression and a *conscious* disavowal "the blindness of the seeing eye" (p. 181, Penguin edition footnote). The splitting of consciousness at this stage in Freud's work refers only to those ideas that are capable of entering consciousness and those that are not (Grubrich-Simitis, 1997).

Far more primitive and *unconscious* forms of *not knowing* have been explored since then in analytic theory. Green (1998) gathers them up under the general heading of "the work of the negative" and he also draws attention to Freud's addition in 1911 of a radical distinction between repression and abolition/foreclosure. In abolition/foreclosure the symbolizing processes are annihilated or erased. This Green sees as an alternative way of describing the fragmenting attacks and emptying of the mind by evacuation of the type described by Bion.

Recent work on hysteria tries to integrate pre-oedipal and oedipal levels of experience and sees the use of the body in hysteria both as an attempt at and a failure to symbolize (Rupprecht-Schampera, 1995; Yarom, 1997).

Rupprecht-Schampera (1995) attempts to unify pre-oedipal and oedipal conflicts present in hysteria by focusing on problems of separation/individuation. The future hysteric has difficulties in triangulation arising from problems in the mother–child relationship, then further compounded by an unavailable or disappointing father. Where early triangulation has not been established, symbolizing is affected and the body will be used in particular ways, for example:

- To distract from an unbearable internal world.
- To give a sense through sensation of continuing existence when fragmentation threatens.

- To give an illusion of independence so that the more threatening object related feelings can be avoided.
- To act as a substitute for the early third object.

In this last case the body is used as an object to effect a "substitute triangulation" so that a false third object is created represented by the body itself. The body is used in a desperate attempt to solve failures in psychic structure. However, this approach does not address the possibility that primitive emerging structures might be actively attacked because they represent awareness of a couple. The damage caused by a hostile internal object that attacks all links is better explained in post-Kleinian work.

The collapse of triangular space, caused by the removal of links that create that space, traps the individual in a concrete claustrophobic world where no new life can form. From this perspective, relationships with primitive objects are inseparable from the development of psychic structure and implicated in its failures. The classical and contemporary Freudian work places the emphasis more on real life events, past and present.

Yarom uses a matrix with three axes to try to map different perspectives that may illuminate the problem of hysteria. Her approach retains the classical focus by identifying the three axes as: (1) conflicts over sexuality and gender; (2) repression; and (3) conversion. A range of personality structures may be implicated. Her paper provides a matrix that can be used flexibly as a guide in the analysis of narcissistic and borderline patients with hysterical features. Her central position is that sexual conflict is at the core of hysteria. It must not be understood primarily as a defence against psychosis or concealing a more fundamental level of maternal deprivation.

Recent books by Mitchell and Bollas (2000) have sought to explore further the importance and relevance to contemporary culture and clinical work of hysteria. Both note that it disappeared from psychiatry as a diagnostic category in the 1950s and that in clinical work diagnoses of borderline and narcissistic personality disorder have gradually eclipsed hysteria.

Bion and the post-Kleinians, Rupprecht-Schampera and Yarom come from different theoretical positions which give their work different emphases but here I will focus on the common ground.

Failure to establish oedipal triangulation and separateness affects the symbolizing function.

An internal object hostile to links

Bion's development of a theory of thinking which makes emotional experience central to the growth of the mind takes Freud's interest in the hysteric's "wish not to know" a stage further. Bion's work with psychotic patients focused his attention on thinking and failures in thinking. He draws a qualitative distinction between psychotic and non-psychotic functioning. In psychotic functioning, the ego and the means by which it knows reality is splintered and projected by "the fragmentation and expulsion of the senses, consciousness and thinking" (O'Shaughnessy, 1992).

In *Attacks on Linking* (1959), Bion extends Melanie Klein's concept of projective identification so that projection of bad parts of the self can be seen as more communicative and purposeful. However, if things go wrong in this process, then there is a resort to projective identification "of all the perceptual apparatus including the embryonic thought which forms a link between sense impressions and consciousness".

In this paper Bion gives examples of attacks on the link between two objects which include, in the analytic situation, attacks on the words which are the chief means of communication and on the functions that connect the mind with internal and external objects, such as feeling, thinking, perceiving.

Bion's explanation for these sustained attacks on the links that make analytic work possible is the presence of an internal object that is hostile to curiosity and actively destroys any emotional communication. This hostile internal object is partly caused by failures in the primary relationship and partly created by the distorting effect of the projection of a greedy devouring part of the patient. This amalgam operates malignantly. When the personality is under its sway, all understanding and emotion is hated. The analytic process is perceived as an attempt to drive the patient insane and the analyst often feels in the same position that the child may have occupied: trying to communicate with a mother who doesn't want to know and who hates the child for disturbing her.

In normal development, the capacity for dream thoughts that

underpin the development of thinking, stems from early passionate emotional experiences. Thought and thinking can only emerge if the mother's alpha function, her ability to take in and meditate on the meaning of her baby's communications, is available. The internalization of a thinking mother is essential if symbolizing is to develop. Without the mother's capacity for reverie what Bion calls the infant's "harvest of self sensation" would be incapable of being thought (1962). The experience of being understood produces alpha elements which we could think of as generative structures that lead to the development of the mind and thinking. If a thinking mother has not been sufficiently available for the baby to internalize, a link attacking object becomes active in the baby's mind. This attacks the baby/breast link; the intercourse between the parents and the sensory and perceptual links that connect with internal and external reality. This hostile internal object omnipotently denies all reality, claims moral certitude and omniscience and manifests itself as an obstructive force that seems to hold up progress and migrate between patient, analyst and people in the external world.

As Bion developed his theory of thinking further the link attacking object became -K. In Bion's theory of links (LHK) he describes the emotional experience present when two people or two parts of a person are related to each other. The K link involves an active relationship: there is a subject who tries to know an object and an object which can be known. Mental pain and frustration are inevitably present in this relationship. When the -K link is active mental pain is avoided and the psychotic part of the personality dominates. The predominant characteristic of the internal object in -K is its "withoutness" which perhaps suggests its alien, hostile, empty quality.

> It is an internal object without an exterior. It is an alimentary canal without a body. It is a super-ego that has hardly any of the characteristics of the super-ego as understood in psycho-analysis: it is "super" ego. It is an envious assertion of moral superiority without any morals. In short it is the resultant of an envious stripping or denudation of all good and is itself destined to continue the process of stripping described [previously] as existing, in its origin, between two personalities. The process of denudation continues till $-\female$ $-\male$ represent hardly more than an empty superiority-inferiority that in turn degenerates to nullity.
>
> There is a reversal of symbolizing. [1962]

Bion's theory of alpha functioning which accounts for the transformation of alien, unthinkable aspects of experience through the activity of maternal containment and supports the development of the K link, is a theory of imagination that has many parallels with Jung's alchemical analogy. The wish to get to know oneself and another person is present in Bion and Jung's work as a major drive. In Jung's alchemical formulations of the stages of relating, or coniunctios, the putrefactio stage of each coniunctio also has parallels with the -K state of mind that seeks to evade and destroy knowledge. I turn next to explore some of these parallels in Jung's major work of 1946, *The Psychology of the Transference* (C.W. 16).

The coniunctio

Jung's major contribution to an understanding of the mind's structure was in his work on the archetype and the complex. Jung had no need to invoke a concept like the death instinct or conflict over a forbidden wish to account for the lack of unity in the psyche. For Jung, the divisions in the psyche are the result of the activity of the archetypal images. He provided an evolutionary perspective on the development of mind and an account of the mind's structure where splitting was the major defence and integration of the ever-changing complexes the goal. Jung's theory of archetypes postulates a deep reservoir of *irrepresentable* structures in the psyche. These archetypal structures generate symbolic forms and meanings that influence the construction of the complexes. Archetypal influence takes place in its most primitive form at the psychoid level (C.W. 8). At this level matter and mind are indissolubly linked. Like Bion, Jung thought in terms of a primordial mind in which the psychological both preceded and accompanied the physical. (See Bion's reference to Jung in his 1976 Los Angeles' seminar, 1980.) The most primitive, inaccessible area of mind, split off from developed representation, Jung called the psychoid and Bion called beta elements. Both these concepts involve psycho-sensory elements of a primitive, not quite thinkable, nature.

Jung brings to the mind an infinite dimension, which again links him with Bion rather than other object relations theorists. Both assume there are aspects of the mind that are alien and cannot be known and that the mind has archaic areas that affect symbol formation. Both developed theories to connect this primordial mind with human development. For Jung the symbol had a generative power to heal splits in the psyche and transform energy. As early as 1916 he wrote about the transcendent function which arises from the union of conscious and unconscious contents and brings about a transition from one state of mind to another through the mediation of the symbol (C.W. 8). This symbolic functioning was perceived by Jung to be inherent, a natural capacity. Initially he thought that the symbolic life of the mind could be studied through active imagination and this gave the patient some independence from the analyst. But in 1946, in the *Psychology of the Transference*, he fully explored the relational context in which symbolizing develops through the alchemical imagery of the *Rosarium*. Here, he makes it very clear that

> the human connection ... is at the core of the whole transference phenomena, and it is impossible to argue it away, because relationship to the self is at once relationship to our fellow man. [C.W. 16, para. 445]

There are four cycles in the *Rosarium*: every coniunctio phase is followed by death and rebirth (Fabricius, 1971). Jung discusses the first ten woodcuts in the *Psychology of the Transference*. I want to refer particularly to woodcuts 5–10 which show the process of the second phase of coniunctio. This second stage is called the nigredo. The womb like container (5) gives way to the sarcophagus (6–9) in which the fused couple experience the departure of the soul as linking function (7). Then follows the purifying and clarification of the healing dew (8), the return of the soul (9) and the establishment of a new position in the form of the hermaphrodite (10). In spite of Jung's misgivings about the hermaphrodite as regressive, the alchemists saw this as a great achievement, indicating the development of new relationships within the self (Schwartz-Salant, 1992).

In his commentary, Jung makes clear that the experiencing and integration of psychotic states is an essential part of the individuation process and makes the analytic relationship inevitably fraught with danger. This is especially true of the putrefactio stage. The individual's "specious unity" breaks down and the analyst has to contain an experience so overwhelming in its intensity that, like the alchemist, it can be difficult to know

> whether he {is} melting the mysterious amalgam in the crucible or whether he {is} the salamander glowing in the fire. [C.W. 16, para. 399]

The nigredo stage is experienced as dismemberment of the body and Jung employs powerful imagery to suggest psychic fragmentation:

> The painful conflict that begins with the nigredo or tenebrositas is described by the alchemists as the separatio or divisio elementorum, the solutio,calcinatio, incineratio, or as dismemberment of the body, excruciating animal sacrifices, amputation of the mother's hands or the lion's paws, atomization of the bridegroom in the body of the bride, and so on. [C.W. 16, para. 398]

Unlike Bion's theory of -K, Jung does not consider fragmentation to be the result of early maternal failure or excessive hostility but is seen to be inherent in the structure and organization of the mind. However, Jung agrees with Bion that the safe traversing of these states is wholly dependent on the analyst's transcendent function.

The putrefactio stage of woodcuts 6 and 7 is particularly dangerous and critical.

In Woodcut 6, the king and queen are dead and "have melted into a single being with two heads".

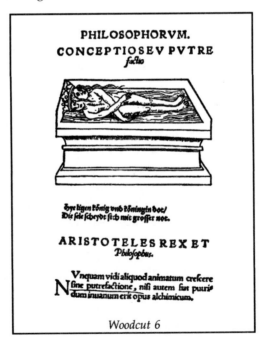

PHILOSOPHORVM.
CONCEPTIO SEV PVTRE
factio

Hye ligen könig vnnd königin boe/
Die sele scheybt sich mit grosser noe.

ARISTOTELES REX ET
Philosophus.

Nquam vidi aliquod animatum crescere
sine putrefactione, nisi autem fiat puuris
dum inuanum erit opus alchimicum.

Woodcut 6

Alchemists think this is a necessary stage, but Jung recognizes that it is also highly dangerous when development can become paralysed or a psychotic breakdown may occur. The next step would be to reverse the fusional process, and to separate out, which means thinking about the projections and taking them back into the self, releasing the fused other into separate life. However, this process can be experienced as overwhelming as Jung emphasizes:

> With the integration of projections—which the merely natural man in his unbounded naivete can never recognize as such—the personality becomes so vastly enlarged that the normal ego-personality is almost extinguished. In other words, if the individual identifies himself with the contents awaiting integration, a positive or negative inflation results. Positive inflation comes very near to a more or less conscious megalomania; negative inflation is felt as an annihilation of the ego. The two conditions may alternate. At all events the integration of contents that were always unconscious and projected involves a serious lesion of the ego. [*C.W.*, *16*, para. 472]

As the psyche begins to develop towards integration, mania or depression may cause disintegration rather than growth.

In Woodcut 7, the dead fused couple have changed places but not position and the soul ascends from the lifeless corpse.

Woodcut 7

Jung calls it a "soulless" condition where disorientation and collapse threaten. The mind has gone missing. Jung reminds us of the possibility of psychosis and in Bion's terms, this is the moment when -K functioning may appear. In this condition the patient must be held by the analyst's mind which is also paradoxically the object of attack and hatred. It is striking how close Jung is to Bion's theory of alpha function in the formulation below.

> The waters must be drawn together and held fast by the one water, by the forma ignea verae aquae. The kind of approach that makes this possible must therefore be plastic and symbolical, and itself the outcome of personal experience with unconscious contents. [C.W., 16, para. 478]

Jung uses alchemical metaphors whereas Bion hovers between religious and scientific territories with his wish to find an empty category that is not already filled up with associations. Jung's alchemical metaphor refers to the "aqua permanens" which is directly connected to Mercurius, the agent of transformation. Jung refers in Psychology and Alchemy to the suitability of Mercurius as a symbol to represent "the 'fluid' i.e. mobile, intellect" (1953).

The understanding mind of the analyst is the critical factor if the movement forward is not to falter and disintegrate. Jung links the movement with religious imagery of the resurrection, the second coming and the birth of the divine child.

Clinical presentation

Introduction to the clinical work

Nina was a young woman who had been born in the United States and moved to England as a child. Early on in the analysis she asked me if I knew a case history of Jung's where a woman came to him and confessed a murder. I was intrigued by the meaning of her reference. Later, I thought that her concerns about the violence of her inner world were indicated by her question. Her work and personal relationships were always marked by strong ethical and humanitarian concerns. It was herself she treated badly. Often at breaks, she was involved in accidents and injuries of a very worrying kind.

Her self destructiveness gradually became active in the analysis as a powerful counter force sometimes mute, sometimes highly articulate. She strove, with great rhetorical power to blind me to the emotional realities of her plight. Her undeniable intellect and imagination served her omnipotent wish to be "top dog" and to extinguish any potential creative space between us. This was never absolute. With this patient being able to maintain several points of view about her and resist my wish to be right with *my* point of view was as important as not caving in. For my part, retaining some flexibility of mind, not letting different perspectives vanish or movement get paralysed could, at these moments when dimensionality was threatened, restore some vitality to the analysis.

Hysteria and the body

Nina's body and its suffering were central in the analysis. At the first interview she was recovering from a debilitating illness. During her analysis she had two long-term relationships. Both her partners were seriously ill and seemed at times, to function as objects into whom she could project the ill parts of herself. Archaic and classical forms of hysteria seem to have been present in these vicarious identifications . The distinction between hysterical conversion and psychosomatic symptom was never clear cut. There was a complex layering and intertwining of developmental levels. Sexuality appeared sometimes to be removed from the picture so that a regressive archaic fusion with the mother could be enjoyed

In the third year of Nina's analysis there was a three-month period either side of the Christmas break when she missed every Monday session. She put a hiatus between her analysis and the weekend. On one occasion when she returned to her next session, fifteen minutes late, she talked about the theft over the weekend of her brand new saddle from her bicycle and its replacement with a shabby man's saddle. Her partner had been away and on returning had telephoned her after making other calls first and at midnight when she was tired and wanted to sleep. This looked, on the surface, as if she had experienced a narcissistic blow in the separation from both analyst and partner at the weekend. She was "fourth in the queue" as she put it, relegated from brand new to shabby. I was invited to sympathize. However, this would have been insufficient. The image of the saddle/bicycle link revealed the difficulty in triangulation and the distortion of her body image and the sexual organs. She had projected herself into aspects of the parents' bodies creating a confusing and bizarre mix up. The material about her bicycle and the theft of the saddle mixed up oral and genital imagery and suggested a relationship of control and omnipotence to the bicycle wheel breasts. The saddle seemed to be both mouth, vagina and penis. Her "brand new saddle" is a phantasy of a penis that is better than father's but all the bodily parts of breast/penis/vagina were very confused.

By removing the Monday session and projecting herself into parts of the parents' bodies, she removed the triangular situation from her so denying the difficult feelings that might have accompanied awareness of a couple together and excluding her. When she returned to three sessions at the end of this period we entered a very stormy phase.

I found it very difficult to think or speak and felt afraid to say anything in sessions. Initially, she would come on Monday and then miss Wednesday. She would also argue that two sessions were better than three. In two sessions she could think but if she came for three she felt terrible. I finally said "Three is a harder number than two". She came back into three times a week analysis steadily until the Easter break. Although she came, she filled the space with detailed accounts of a dying friend. The experience of separation and exclusion was sexualized as she savoured her descriptions of suffering bodies with morbid pleasure. It was as if she wanted to thrust a dying body into my mind like a spectre at the feast, to disturb any chance of intercourse.

Two episodes of serious illness during the analysis illustrated attacks on her own body and her identifications with certain aspects and functions of her internal objects. In the first episode, her friend, mentioned above finally died after a long and painful illness. This precipitated bouts of vomiting and diarrhoea in J. that lasted for a month. I want first to outline a complex sequence of events during this month, before commenting on it.

- Her friend dies.
- While away for the weekend she thinks that my husband and I may have gone away too and that she might bump into me.

- On the Monday morning she has acute diarrhoea and is half an hour late for her session.
- A week later she cancels because of an attack of food poisoning after drinking too much and going for a curry with two friends.
- The following week when she is at dinner with some friends she is overcome with an attack of vomiting in which she vomits blood. She is not drunk. The attack happens when they are discussing comings and goings in the flat. Several people are leaving and she will need to find a new home. She rings to tell me about it the next day and to cancel her session. She has also rung a friend who is a doctor for a medical opinion. She is told she's probably burst a blood vessel.

The death of her friend with whom she had been very identified left Nina with no way of externalizing in another body primitive anxieties to do with death and dying. These were now experienced with psychotic intensity. On the following weekend she thinks of me and my husband. Bumping into me is a verbal expression of the rage and the acute diarrhoea expresses on a somatic level that pulverizing rage as well as the wish to get rid of it and the knowledge of the couple that provoked it. The disorientation and dissociation that she reported in the session to which she came thirty minutes late indicates the split in her ego. The thought of the parental couple is retained but the aggression in relation to them is denied. The innocuous word "bump" suggests that dangerous feelings have been got rid of (expurgated).

The attack of food poisoning seemed to be more connected with identification with a "lager lout and curry" culture. It followed a drinking orgy at work while she and colleagues were moving premises. Here she identified with a careless father who created messes through abusive, uncontrolled activity (she knew her birth had not been planned). The attack of vomiting and the graphic details of blood and mess suggested a gruesome abortion.

In the sequence reported above, the capacity to symbolize varied. Sometimes there was a sense of a symbolizing process at work, however primitive, for example in the use of the word "bumping". At other moments, the blood and mess of the vomiting which came on in the restaurant seemed to be at a pre-symbolic psycho-sensory level: elements that Jung described as psychoid and Bion as beta elements.

Throughout this month psychic reality and the analytic container were attacked by absence, lateness and phone calls instead of sessions. I had to retain a thinking capacity that could withstand the pressure to depart from an analytic stance and try to make links with her feelings of pain and anger that reached psychotic intensity in the context of loss of home and exclusion.

The second episode was not related to her internal organs of stomach, bowel and blood vessels—the visceral organs—but to her bodily frame of bones and muscles. She developed back trouble that meant she had to take three weeks off work. At this stage she and I were more able to think about her emotional experience. Again, there were external circumstances that seemed to play a part. There were two Monday holidays during this month when I cancelled sessions, her position at work was also under threat. She found that her job, which she was doing on an "acting" basis was to be advertised and she would have to go through an interview process. She had understood that her appointment would just be confirmed automatically. She was very angry and took time off work. Uncharacteristically, she attacked me openly when I interpreted her anger over my Monday holidays as having a similar source. It seemed, I suggested, as if Mondays too, were hers by right. If she chose not to come that was different. What I had deprived her of was her ability *not* to come. Her fury was now out in the open. Her narcissistic illusion of omnipotent control and entitlement had been painfully shattered.

The establishment of triangular space, is a difficult developmental task. Where failures in the primary relationship have occurred this is particularly so. At this point in her analysis, Nina remembered, when she was little, her mother leaving her and her brother, threatening never to come back. She was very distressed although she didn't show it but acted tough unlike her brother who had cried.

The back trouble which emerged at the same time as the Bank Holidays and the disappointment at work seemed to represent many different aspects of her emotional experience. It was her back that was in contact with the couch: that touched it and separated from it. She came relentlessly to her analysis throughout her three weeks off work, by mini-cab if necessary. She forced me to witness her pain and how she suffered as she lay down on the couch and struggled to get off it at the end of sessions.

But also her back was linked with the phallus, because it is the spine that holds us erect. She revealed that she had made the back strain worse quite deliberately by going to a Shiatsu Master at the weekend who had used his feet on her back so that she was nearly crippled by the subsequent bruising to her muscles. I thought about *who* was being trampled under foot and *by whom* and how complex and many faceted the identifications were.

At the end of this period she brought a screen memory which her back pain had evoked, of a holiday in France when she was a child. A driver had turned out of the campsite and quite deliberately knocked her and her mother down. Her father had managed to partly pull them out of the path of the car and into a ditch. He had also taken the car number so the driver had been caught, tried and convicted. The emergence of a discriminating, quick thinking father who could protect mother and child was quite new. She could also see that there were aspects of her that could be like that. Just as there were aspects of her that resembled the driver. However, she found it quite difficult not to be dismissive about the father's appearance as a potent figure. "Why do you think that's so significant?", she said in a contemptuous tone.

The psychic became unknowable yet at the same time spoke in its own cryptic language. The splitting and projection into the body was sometimes partly conscious and could be worked with, sometimes she refused to know. At other times it seemed as if there was no other way in which she could communicate primitive emotional elements except through this archaic bodily language.

Death, absence and loss may distort the primal scene. Difficulties in relationships in infancy may compound such distortions. Sometimes, later trauma can cause a reversal of an oedipal position that has been established but is now threatened. Many of these factors were present in Nina's history.

A terrifying internal object hostile to linking

When Nina began to experience powerful feelings of anger, love, hate and jealousy and move from absence and withdrawal into turbulent relatedness, an internal object of malevolent destructive force was activated which claimed that evacuation was better than digestion. My patient was not psychotic; the non-psychotic part of the personality was still alive and in contention. But it was a very difficult period. As with the exploitation of physical suffering, there was sometimes an element of masochistic pleasure in being on the edge of breakdown.

Mindlessness began to appear as an addictive alternative to the pain of thinking about her emotional experience. This period of the work overlapped but extended on either side of the three months of missed Monday sessions. She seemed to lapse into a drugged world of hallucinatory gratification in the last sessions of the week. In this state the weekend didn't exist, time and space were nullified and no boundaries existed as she found a method of avoiding thinking about the separation. She existed in a dangerous dream world of self-induced narcosis where there was only deterioration and death. She removed self-knowledge. As a later dream revealed, the real crime was in the deception, the covering up of her need for help and the pretence that there were other methods that worked better than analysis. In the dream she took a drug and then was relieved when the evidence was destroyed so she wouldn't be found out. What she couldn't stand was any vulnerability or dependence on the analysis. In the same dream, there was a sick man who had an abscess on his leg which had been plastered over. Her feelings about the forthcoming break (absence) were again to be covered up. The part of her that was addicted to mindlessness was always arguing that analytic work is bad for you, it's difficult, it doesn't get you anywhere, it's painful so what's the point. There must be easier ways. The rhetoric was seductive and intended to make us both despair.

However, there was always a part that could work and think and discriminate, even though at times she was overwhelmed. Towards the end of this period in the analysis I drew her attention to the recurring theme of propaganda versus truth and that she now seemed more able not to succumb. As the attack on psychic reality waned she was better able to acknowledge her deep unhappiness and her pain.

The attack on linking was at the psychotic end of the spectrum. However, there were also more subtle and deviously envious attacks that didn't have the same quality of psychotic hate as the sequence described but still created an impasse. When this more knowing and treacherous attack was in evidence the anxiety was more depressive in its nature as there was fear of doing harm to someone.

Before interrupting her analysis to go abroad on holiday, she came to her sessions in a state of such anxiety she thought she would have to cancel the trip. Her previous partner was in hospital with a serious illness and she thought she was going to die if she went on her trip. The understanding that dissolved the intense depressive anxiety was the recognition that there was something opportunistic about her trip. She had, with an eye to the main chance, decided on the trip because it wouldn't cost her anything. "Something for nothing" was irresistible, her analysis could be put aside for a free trip. She was sceptical that her cynical opportunism could cause such a state of panic, but she could not argue that the panic had disappeared with its recognition.

Coniunctio

My patient's main defences were primitive ones of splitting and projection, somatization and schizoid withdrawal. As the splitting lessened during the analytic work, she became able to relate to the parts of herself that had been lost. After the long three-month absence from Monday sessions mentioned above she was present on a Monday but very remote and contemptuous. I had been interpreting the way she had dismissed everything I said in the session as if it was all rubbish or already known by her. She replied, "That's not true, if I didn't think much of you I wouldn't come". Then she burst out laughing as she realized what she had said. The laughter marked the healing of a split because it was a moment of real emotional contact between us.

A year later she took a holiday break during the analytic term. She had planned it shortly after the previous summer break and acknowledged that there was an element of retaliation in it. She wrote to me twice while she was on holiday and in the second letter she included the following dream:

I was walking home to my parents' last house when suddenly it became very dark. Vampyre bats were flying overhead and then suddenly landing and adopting human forms. I was very frightened—frozen to the spot. Then the vampyres turned into Nazis in black and red shirts and trousers. They were rounding people up to join a cult. I was scared and trying to get home to my family but I knew I would not be able to escape. I started walking with them as if I was going to a rally and then at the top of the hill just before the woods I tried to escape. As we were passing through the woods I threw myself into the river and hid under the water, breathing through a plastic tube. I think I continued to move under water until I got to the back of my parents' house.

The archaic spelling of "vampyre" was hers and I think is part of her recognition that primitive forms of destructiveness were lurking during her absence from analysis. My consulting room is at the back of the house.

The dream shows her trying to resist organizations (cults) which encourage mindlessness and parasitic forms of relationship. In this evocative dream the splitting processes in her mind are recognized and the struggle between allegiance to a cult and membership of a family can be clearly observed. But her sense of dependency on internal parental figures and on her analysis is revealed as stronger. She takes refuge in a womb-like container and is sustained by the umbilical cord of the plastic tube. At this stage in our work together she is able to sustain an observer position from which she can think about her emotional experience. The beauty of the dream's symbolism is a sign of a higher level of development and integration within the self and considerable changes in her relationship to internal parental figures. This dream marks a movement equivalent to the changes depicted through Figures 8, 9 and 10 of the coniunctio sequence: the healing dew; the return of the soul; the establishing of a new position.

The second dream which she had dreamed on the following night shows how hard these changes are to hold on to. In fact, the psychic change so clearly in evidence in the first dream actually seemed to have stirred up anxieties of an intensely persecutory nature. In the second dream she wrote:

I was leaving the building with a group of friends. We were about to go our separate ways but we talked about meeting up again. I did not have a permanent job. A friend of mine and myself started walking over a bridge. I'm not sure where, as I did not recognize the place, but I think we were near an airport. Suddenly a plane flew low overhead and dropped a bag of something on the runway. What appeared to be two large grenades jumped out and went over the bridge. Myself and the others walking on the bridge thought they were bombs and we ran for cover behind a wall waiting for the bridge to blow up. It didn't but overhead war planes lit up the sky and I realized the gulf war had started. Suddenly from behind the houses on the other side of the road tanks appeared and started firing their guns in the air. I became very frightened and started to run. I realized I had become separated from my friend. I was worried for her safety and was trying to find her. I also wanted to get home as I was anxious about what would happen to my family. I managed to meet with my friend but then became frightened about my circumstances. I realized that a war was going on, I had no permanent job and I had just bought a flat. I was very irritated that I had bought a flat with a war just about to begin. I feared it would be worthless and was concerned about how I would manage the bills in my position.

She was to move into a new flat on her return, which she had bought with some help from her parents. This was the first flat she had owned herself. This friendly state of mind, in which she is accompanied by a friend whose name could be either male or female, seems to be associated with the nurturing aspects of both mother and father. This is a very different state of mind from the gulf war state which is dominated by paranoid anxieties. The fear that the more securely established position of the bridge on which she is walking with a friend may be under attack, is clearly represented in the plane's ambiguous load. I was inclined to think that the delivery of the two grenades might refer to the dreaming of the two dreams as she was extremely fearful in her first letter to me that she "might get into her fears too much". She didn't want to experience any worries on what I came to think of as "the flight abroad". She would rather not know.

The two dreams show an oscillating movement between two very different states of mind; one characterized by hostile invaders and the other by more attachment and concern for herself and others. Perhaps she sent the two letters and the dreams to me so that these dangerous psychic messages could be defused and shared.

The dream seemed to contain several ambiguous elements and I thought she wanted to ward off my feared retaliation and at the same time to make reparation.

There was ambiguity, for example, over whether communication was a good or bad thing and whether investment in her future was worth it. But ambiguity may be the beginning of complexity, as I thought it was here, and not just a lack of clarity used in the service of trickery and avoidance. The dreams illustrate the richness of symbolic functioning that can hold many meanings together. The strange hermaphrodite figure in the coniunctio may be a paradigm for this.

Conclusion

In his work on hysteria Freud understood the powerful effect and the disastrous consequences of "not wanting to know". Psychic events became physical symptoms. In Jung's work the symbol conveys the archetypal image and creates links. This is variously described by Jung as the "transcendent function" or the soul as a "function of relationship" in the coniunctio. Bion underlines how the mind's development is intimately dependent on the internalized mind of a receptive external figure and that fragmentation occurs when this is not available.

In contemporary Jungian and psychoanalytic thinking the archetypal image of the coniunctio is being actively elaborated. Our most sophisticated mental activities reflect the linking functions of the primitive breast or penis. The damaged and damaging aspects of Nina had to be experienced and understood within the analytic relationship before the symbolizing function could be restored. It took many years of analytic work before she could experience a sense of "having her own mind". If the wish to understand and find meaning drives the development of the self, as Jung and Bion believed, then the recovery of linking capacities in my patient's mind were central to our work.

Nina's attack on meaning was relentless for long periods in the analysis and any understanding link forged with me seemed often to accelerate this. These moments were exhausting and terrifying for both of us as they seemed to enact a meaningless attack that happened like an automatic reflex. It was pointless activity but irresistible. It was only when she could see the link between these attacking states of mind and the onset of psychotic panic that she could begin to resist her cynicism, opportunism, lack of curiosity and expectation of easy answers.

Bion talks about the need to help our patients to *suffer* pain rather than to evade it so that emotional life, however painful, becomes real and nourishing (1970). Nina's pain related to a feeling that, in some very basic way she was unsure of her place in the world and primarily, unsure of her place in mother's mind. Perhaps she couldn't give up the security of her habitual destructiveness until she had somewhere else to be.

The "thoughtless" intercourse that had produced her echoed again and again in the difficulty of establishing a triangular space within which she could begin to develop. She existed but she wasn't meaningful. The most important factor in remedying this situation was first, to be able to bear it and then to be able to talk to her about how her mind worked. It was the development of this observer position in the midst of real passion and tumult that made a difference (Britton, 1989). The dreams from her holiday showed the establishing of a container that could generate dream thoughts and an observer that can experience and think about them. Nina was beginning to see herself as identified with the dreamer who dreams the dreams and no longer with an internal object characterized by its habitual and callous destruction of links.

References

Bick, E. (1968). The experience of the skin in early object relations. *International Journal of Psychoanalysis, 49*: 484–486.

Bion, W. R. (1959). Attacks on linking. *International Journal of Psychoanalysis, 40*.

Bion, W. R. (1962). *Learning from Experience*. London: Heinemann.

Bion, W. R. (1967). *Second Thoughts*. London: Heinemann.

Bion, W. R. (1970). *Attention and Interpretation*. London: Tavistock Publications.

Britton, R. (1989). The missing link: parental sexuality in the Oedipus complex. In: R. Britton, M. Feldman & E. O'Shaughnessy (Eds.), *The Oedipus Complex Today*. London: Karnac Books.

Britton, R. (1998). *Belief and Imagination—Explorations in Psychoanalysis.* London: Routledge.

Fabricius, J. (1971). The individuation process as reflected by "the rosary of the philosophers" (1550). *Journal of Analytical Psychology, 16*(1).

Fiumara, G. C. (1995). *The Metaphoric Process.* London: Routledge.

Fordham, M. (1957). *New Developments in Analytical Psychology.* London: Routledge.

Freud, S. (1895) (with Breuer, J.). *Studies on Hysteria. S.E.,* 2.

Freud, S. (1911). *Psychoanalytic Notes on an Autobiographical Account of a Case of Paranoia. S.E.,* 12.

Green, A. (1998). The primordial mind and the work of the negative. *International Journal of Psychoanalysis, 79*(4): 649–665.

Grubrich-Simitis, I. (1997). *Early Freud and Late Freud.* London: Routledge.

Jung, C. G. (1916). *The Transcendent Function, C.W.,* 8.

Jung, C. G. (1946). *The Psychology of the Transference, C.W.,* 16.

Jung, C. G. (1953). *Psychology and Alchemy.* London: Routledge.

Mitchell, J., & Bollas, C. (2000). *Mad Men and Medusas.* London: Allen Lane.

O'Shaughnessy, E. (1992). Psychosis: not thinking in a bizarre world. In: R. Anderson (Ed.), *Clinical Lectures on Klein and Bion.* London: Routledge.

Rupprecht-Schreyer, U. (1995). The concept of "early triangulation" as a key to a unified model of hysteria. *International Journal of Psychoanalysis, 76*(3): 457–473.

Schwartz-Salant, N. (1992). Anima and animus in Jung's alchemical mirror. In: N. Schwartz-Salant & M. Stein (Eds.), *Gender and Soul in Psychotherapy.* Illinois: Chiron Publications.

Yarom, N. (1997). A matrix of hysteria. *International Journal of Psychoanalysis, 78*(6): 1119–1134.

PART IV
REFLECTIONS: PERSPECTIVES ON
ANALYTIC PRACTICE

CHAPTER ELEVEN

Analytic dependency

Joan Reggiori

Introduction

We may anticipate that the analysand, during the course of the analysis will become analytically, and therefore therapeutically, dependent in one form or another, on the analyst, in the interests of the analysis. The definition of dependence in the English dictionary includes reliance, trust and confidence. The analyst aims to provide a psychologically safe enough environment in which the analysand can explore and share feelings and experiences which may include loving as well as hostile ones, conscious and unconscious, in an empathic environment. This necessarily entails a fundamental degree of trust and closeness before there can be an exposure of painful, sometimes unacceptable, and often hitherto unconscious, experiences. At the heart of this is a dependence on the analyst, and therefore a trust that he or she will be sensitively available to, respectful and not judgmental of, whatever emerges during the analytic journey. Being dependent, in some form or another, is part of the transference and implies a closeness in the relationship.

Loving dependency

A degree of dependence is present in every relationship throughout life. The young baby is dependent on his or her mother and enjoys the trust and intimacy at the centre of their interaction epitomized, for example, by the interactive stimulating nature of breast feeding. The mother and father respectively enjoy a variety of interactions with their baby, and the immense pleasure which its presence, including its touching dependence on them, brings to them. They each depend on the baby's response to their love and caring for an acknowledgement and affirmation of the relationship. There is a mutual and reinforcing dependence between them, albeit that these have different ingredients and needs. Attachment and affection are aspects of dependency in a relationship. Bowlby writes: "During the course of healthy development attachment behaviour leads into the development of affectional bonds or attachments, initially between child and parent and later between adult and adult" and are "active throughout the life cycle" (Bowlby, 1980, p. 39). Lovers depend on each other's presence and demonstrated love, to bring pleasure and an affirmation that they are loved, valued and are special to each other. The capacity to be dependent and to be able to allow others to depend on oneself, is a sign of emotional maturity.

The very wide spectrum of what constitutes being dependent has at one end a mutual dependency which arises from loving another person and evoking a situation of mutual trust which affirms and encourages a deepening of a loving relationship. In this state each person will be able to respond to the needs of the other, when the shifting demands of a relationship calls for this.

Hostile dependency

At the other end of the spectrum can be a hostile dependency when one person depends on another who can be constantly criticized and attacked but from whom they cannot separate. This may be seen in "unhappy" marriages where one partner needs the other to carry the projected part of themselves which they cannot acknowledge. The complexities in the spectrum of dependence in the analytic relationship are considerable. Attachment can be part of dependency but generally it is less exclusive of other relationships. There are degrees, as well as forms, of dependency within the analytic dyad.

For example, a young person may come to analysis suffering from depression and with a history of unsatisfactory relationships. Such an analysand may gradually develop a fairly positive transference as some of the inhibiting depression begins to be worked through. Later on, the dependence becomes hostile with even an aggressive quality, as the relationship with the mother and the father is projected on to the analyst in the course of the analysis. This can also be accompanied by an emerging intrapsychic conflict as the rejected part of the analysand also gets projected in the transference. I have experienced a degree of sadism in the aggressive verbal attacks which can arise in such hostile dependency, so much so that my body has responded with an increased heart rate and an inhibition in breathing that suggests a degree of very primitive communication.

Another example is that of a middle aged woman who had difficulty in becoming dependent on the analyst. Her mother's clinging emotional dependency on her had made her feel that any substantial growth of dependency in the analysis would eventually be resented by the analyst and felt to be intrusive. She was therefore somewhat inhibited from allowing a significant degree of closeness to develop in the analytic sessions. It took a long time before she was able to experience in the sessions that she was acceptable to the analyst as a whole person which included her potential analytic dependency needs, and not feel that she had to "protect" the analyst from them by being overly independent herself. This helped her towards feeling affirmed and able to make her appropriate needs known. It also helped her to sense that boundaries could be respected in close encounters. Closeness for her had meant being exposed and found wanting. There was also an anxiety about the pain of eventual separation with its central feature of loss, after becoming close to someone. Her mother's fear of loss had caused her to feel guilty for not protecting her mother from this pain when she had separated from her, which had felt like abandoning the child part of her mother. As Redfearn states, "non-differentiation or clinging by one makes it impossible for the other to be creatively separate" (Redfearn, 1972, p. 178).

Dependency in the elderly patient

Not infrequently, older persons who have been widowed or are expecting such a bereavement, even if unconsciously, may become dependent quite quickly. There is a longing for the companionship which they have lost, or an affirmation of one aspect of an identity which they once enjoyed. The latter may be for the status of being one of a couple, or an enjoyment of a position at their former work place. The need is for closeness which offers both an intimacy and a place in which that person can be seen and feel they exist. This brings up the question of what, at their time of life, is likely to alter so that eventually they can work through the transference and the dependency contained within it, and cathect someone else or a new interest. I shall be referring to resolving the analytic dependency later in this paper.

Zoja writes that "we should try to conceive of analysis for the old as an initiatory rather than a clinical process" (Zoja, 1983, p. 64). To my mind, this places greater emphasis on the movement towards death, a movement and exploration in which the analyst can accompany the analysand and be depended on to share their experiences as well as to analyse them. Many older patients say it is not the thought of death which frightens them but the, sometimes anticipated, loneliness of a drawn out period of dying. Hence the urgent need for someone on whom they can reliably depend. There may well be a re-enactment of their dependency in the early years but, in my opinion, it may also be the result of cultural attitudes towards them as a group. Martindale (1989) writes about the fear of becoming dependent in persons seeking psychotherapeutic help in later life and the fear in their younger therapists of the extent of their dependent demands. I shall refer to this subject again.

The archetypal nature of dependency

Guggenbuhl-Craig when writing about the archetype of the invalid states "I understand 'archetype' not so much as an image, but rather as an 'inborn pattern of behaviour in a classical, typically human situation'" (Guggenbuhl-Craig, 1980, p. 12). An archetype of itself is neither good nor bad. Dependency states in the invalid, as in others, can be very annoying or they can be very pleasant for the person depended upon. I do not want to argue the case here as to whether dependency is an archetype or not, but I find it very helpful to apply the concept of the positive and negative pole, as applied by Guggenbuhl-Craig in his discussion of invalidism, to other states of dependency.

All of us are dependent on someone. This dependency can be coloured by love and gratitude and a respect for the autonomy of the other person, to which the latter can respond with considerable pleasure. It can make them feel they are of value, as in the case of the response from a baby which is essentially enjoyable. At the other and negative end of the pole, the dependency can include a clinging, demanding need to make the other person submit to the dependent's wishes. This is similar to a baby in its autistic state and may well be a childlike part of that adult, but its actions have the power of an adult. If the demands are powerful and persistent enough the analyst can be made to feel frustrated and even threatened by a wearying intrusion of their boundaries. As Fordham writes, in his paper on countertransference, the analyst "can be pushed into masochistic acquiescence to become persecuted and guilty at not being able to help his patient, whom he may feel he is robbing, especially if the patient is relatively poor" (Fordham, 1995, p. 155).

Developmental changes in dependency

I have referred to the dependency needs of the baby. This will change through childhood and through the period of adolescence, when there will be considerable changes in the degree and the quality of the state of dependence. Becoming an adult includes coping with the variety of dependency demands made upon oneself. There are those who attach themselves to another person, sometimes as though they are an extension of themselves, and through whom they try to live their lives and consequently control. There are others whose dependency needs are met by, for example, alcohol abuse because, unlike people, the alcohol is always there and available, and makes no emotional demands on them.

Dependency in the analytic setting

Having referred to early dependency needs I want now to turn to other later dependency needs. As I have pointed out, the needs are not all the same. What is projected on to the analyst will be an indication of what it is necessary to explore. This can include a search for an identity, a religious attitude, a sexual experience, a loving relationship or a relief from depression. Jung suggests that it is vital to recognize the purpose of the dependence as well as its origins. In *C.W., 8* he writes:

> The patient clings by means of the transference to the person who seems to promise him a renewal of attitude: through it he seeks this change, which is vital to him, even though he may not be conscious of doing so. For the patient, therefore, the analyst has the character of an indispensable figure absolutely necessary for life. However infantile this dependency may appear to be, it expresses an extremely important demand which, if disappointed, often turns to bitter hatred of the analyst. It is therefore important to know what this demand conceals in the transference is really aiming at: there is a tendency to understand it in the reductive sense only, as an erotic infantile fantasy. But that would mean taking the fantasy, which is usually concerned with our parents, literally, as though the patient, or rather his unconscious, still has the expectations the child once had towards the parents ... but the child has become an adult, and what was normal for a child is improper in an adult. [Jung, *C.W., 8*, para. 146]

He continues later in the same paragraph:

> The one-sided, reductive explanation becomes in the end nonsensical ... The sense of boredom which then appears in the analysis is simply an expression of the monotony and poverty of ideas—not of the unconscious, as is sometimes supposed, but of the analyst who does not understand that these fantasies should not be taken merely in a concretistic reductive sense, but rather a constructive one. [*C.W., 8*, para. 146]

This attitude is expressed in Jung's teleological approach. This is an orientation which maintains that the symptoms of the neurosis are purposive and therefore contain the seeds of recovery, as well as the roots of the problem. An example of this is an adult patient suffering from agoraphobia who may well have the roots of his or her problem in difficulties in separating from the mother, as a result of the latter's inability to let go of the child. But the current purpose of the continuing symptoms may well include an unconscious wish or need to control other members of the family, by insisting on claiming their attention and closeness because of the distressing and incapacitating disabilities of agoraphobia.

When one refers to a patient as being dependent, it is diagnostically useful to ask "dependent for what or on whom?". Could it be dependent for love from the analyst, for being trustworthy, for intimacy, for companionship, for support, for insight, and so on. The use of the term "dependent" is sometimes used without discrimination, in a similar way to when patients are described as being "depressed", when they are reacting to loneliness. Loneliness can be a component of depression, but loneliness is not in itself a clinical depression. Similarly, being dependent is not necessarily pathological, at times it represents a lifeline, but it can be very demanding on others if it is intense or manipulative.

The nature of analyst's needs for dependency

The dependence of the patient is frequently referred to, but now I would like to address the dependence of the analyst on the analysand, on the analytic process and consequently the effect this has on himself or herself. This applies whether the relationship, at any given time, is mainly a positive or a negative one, or a combination of both. Some analysts may enjoy, more than others, the satisfaction of receiving transference affection and perhaps admiration, from the analysand because it fulfils one of their own emotional needs at the time. It is not unknown for analysts to remark, with satisfaction, that all their analysands are angry with them for taking a break, thus implying that they are indispensable. (This situation can be seen in other professionals as well.) However, others may like the challenge of negative, even hostile, dependency within the transference, as something to be worked through with interest. This may depend on where the analyst is in his or her inner world at the time. In a previous paper (Reggiori, 1999), I refer to the state of the inner world of the analysand and of the analyst, respectively, at the time of their meeting, and how this affects the progress of the ensuing analysis.

One cannot be an analyst without having an analysand with whom to interact. In this sense the analyst is dependent on the analysand's existence. One role or function defines the other. Solomon demonstrated this in relation to Jung's central concept of psychic transformation via the transcendent function, derived from Hegel's notion of dialectical change (Solomon, 1994, p. 98). Marshak addresses the same area when she writes that:

> it's not only the patient who projects into the analyst, but also the analyst into the patient. What constitutes the "third" is not that the separate entities or subjectivities of analyst and patient are combined, but that the "third" is a product of a dialectic, or what Fordham has called the "interactional dialogue" generated between separate subjects. [Marshak, 1998, p. 59]

Having an analysand, with whatever degree of dependence affirms the professional identity of the analyst. The fact that the analysand provides the analyst with a professional status and an income, neither of which are available to the analysand as a result of the analysis, is obvious and hardly needs stating. But the dynamic movement between the two participants is in another category. This is crucial to the healing process, to the effecting of change, and it affects the analyst as well as the analysand, as Jung maintained:

> the personalities of doctor and patient are often infinitively more important for the outcome of the treatment than what the doctor says and thinks (although what he says and thinks may be a disturbing or a healing factor not to be underestimated). For two personalities to meet is like mixing two different chemical substances: if there is any communication at all, both are transformed. In any effective psychological treatment the doctor is bound to influence the patient but this influence can only take place if the patient has a reciprocal influence on the doctor. You can exert no influence if you are not susceptible to influence. It is futile for the doctor to shield himself from the influence of the patient and to surround himself with a smoke screen of fatherly and professional authority. By so doing he only denies himself the use of a highly important organ of information. [Jung, C.W., 16, para. 163]

The interdependence and interactive nature of the analytic relationship is also explored by Redfearn (2000). He writes:

> Our patients, our professional colleagues, our place of work and our financial security are normally part of our self object structure. [p. 177]

He continues:

> However mature and individuated therapist and patient may be, "there will be an important component of boundariless at-one-ness in the interaction reflecting what I am calling a normal autistic position" (Ogden, 1992) on both sides. Healing might not occur otherwise. [Redfearn, 2000, pp. 177–178]

His view is that:

> Individuation is something that two people have to work towards together. The therapist is therefore emotionally and hence somatically affected according to the maturity of the patient, and the balance between the amounts of loving and hating in him/her. [*Ibid.*, p. 178]

For me this supports the view that there may be periods when the analyst needs to seek further analysis for himself or herself, if he is to be therapeutically available to the patient and so practise effectively.

It seems to me that to practise therapeutically one needs a sufficient number of patients during the week who leave one feeling "good enough". Without such occasional affirmation one can feel depleted. Interacting therapeutically is not only the result of making "correct" or "impressive" interpretations but of being emotionally available. As Zinkin observes, "after long analysis it is not the interpretations that the patient remembers but the relationship with the analyst" (Zinkin, 1998, p. 95). This is dependent on the analyst's emotional maturity. By this I mean the analyst's ability to meet the analysand's needs from the depth and range of his or her emotional experience, development and sensitivity. This may include remaining with the patient in silence. To be vulnerable, in its positive sense, whether this is to the attacks or the affection from the analysand, is an essential factor in the process of interactive change.

Shame and dependency

Some patients feel shame during the analytic process as a result of exposing their problems, their needs and especially their dependency needs. After all, in the analytic dyad the analyst does not disclose, consciously anyway, his problems and his dependency needs, whatever these might be. The patient may feel small, certainly vulnerable, and a trust that the analyst will not exploit this situation is essential. As Jacoby writes:

> A basic sense of being "unloved" severely damages one's sense of self-esteem and makes the self extremely vulnerable to shame. The analyst who is not sufficiently aware of how fragile the patient must feel when his or her innermost and intense longings are not recognized lessens himself or herself in that he misses the opportunity of that precious intimate interaction which can contribute to change and healing. Patients can withdraw or even try to end the analysis prematurely if the shame of intimacy in the dependent relationship is too intense. [Jacoby, 1993, p. 427]

Without the dependent factor, which is part of the closeness inherent in the analytic relationship, it is more difficult to enable change to take place. I am not promoting dependence for dependency's sake. It is an inherent part of the analytic process. A longing to be with the analyst can be assuaged by his or her presence. There is therefore a dependence on the physical presence, as well as the fantasy about the relationship which may be experienced between sessions. This can be a re-experiencing of the infant's longing for the presence of the mother. At the same time, it can be a longing to experience a unity with another human being and can be seen as an example of what Redfearn describes as a "self object" experience, to which I have referred earlier in this paper. To long for the presence of another and to know that the intensity is not reciprocated (by the analyst) is frustrating but there are times when it can feel humiliating. As Jacoby writes, "A huge factor in the agony of patients who have fallen into intense transference-love is due to the shame and humiliation it causes them. We have to consider that this suffering may be a very human and 'natural' reaction" (Jacoby, 1993, p. 419).

Dependence on the analytic frame

I have been discussing the interactive nature of the analytic process. This includes a dependence on the facilitating continuity of the familiar physical setting provided by the analyst. It involves part of the "temenos" which has been created by the physical presence and psychological availability of the analyst together with the similar qualities brought by the analysand. The consulting room becomes imbued with this. There are, however, circumstances when, for whatever reason, the physical place for meeting has to be changed.

Changing the consulting room can disturb or, in some cases, even disrupt, the analytic holding framework to which the analysand has become accustomed and depends for a familiar continuity and security and which is the container which he or she has cathected. There will be anger with the analyst for disturbing this security. The analyst will have to become part of a transitional object on whom the patient can depend when making the crossing to another place or site. The emergence of the effect of other losses of security will need to be explored if the analytic trust which has been built up is to continue. In a prevous paper (Reggiori, 1999). I pointed out that such a move is made at a time chosen by the analyst but not by the patient, who may feel that the analyst is destroying a part of the boundary of the alchemical vessel in which they are held. I am not suggesting that the analyst should feel prohibited from ever moving to another consulting room, but that the dependence on the containing environment for the patient should be borne in mind and worked with analytically.

Not infrequently, it is said that patients will not become dependent, and therefore likely to be accessible to change, if they attend sessions only once or twice weekly. Certainly it is easier for the analyst to establish a close relationship and to retain relevant information if the sessions are three, four or five times a week. However, in my experience patients can become dependent on a once or twice a week arrangement, depending on the circumstances that surround their seeking therapy. For example, someone who has had a long intensive analysis in the past may use once a week sessions and become therapeutically dependent because the nature of dependency has been dealt with previously. Another example is of an isolated person who, nevertheless, is capable of experiencing a degree of trust, and so is likely to become dependent in the analytic sense. On the other hand patients who are firmly held within a tightly knit family structure are less likely to easily cathect the analyst to any significant degree, because much of their psychological energy is invested in their dependence on the containing family. Similarly, someone who has fallen in love is also less likely to invest a great deal of libidinal energy in the analytic relationship even if they attend sessions quite frequently. In these circumstances, patients can be worked with analytically, but the analyst's technique may have to be adjusted to accommodate the emotional circumstances. There may be fewer references to transference feelings for the analyst but more for members of the patient's family. Consequently the analytic closeness is not so likely to be present consciously as it is in the previous circumstances. In fact the analyst can sometimes be made to feel somewhat more of an observer than a participant.

Resolving analytic dependency

Resolving of the analytic dependency at the end of an analysis is a vital part of the analytic process. Sometimes the analysand finds that, as a result of the process, other potential situations arise, other avenues open up, which can meet their dependent needs in another form. This can include forming a new close relationship, examining a new venture, enjoying freedom from previous restraints or finding an ability to accept what was previously unacceptable. Any of these can emanate from shifts in the unconscious which open up new perspectives. At this stage of separation, other separations in the past need to be explored, if they have not been made sufficiently conscious already. There will be a sadness over the loss of an intimate relationship with the analyst but hopefully there may be a sense of achievement at the same time.

I mentioned earlier in this paper the difficulty that some, often older, patients find in the prospect of moving on to a degree of independence. Martindale (1989) focuses on the position of younger therapists who, because of the needs of their own elderly parents at the time, find the long term dependency demands of their older patients rather daunting. Support for such therapists in these circumstances may be needed. Elderly patients may consciously want change, but faced with the demands which are attendant on change, they may find it difficult to relinquish the, albeit unsatisfactory but familiar, situations on which they have depended for a sense of identity and security. Analytic help for them in accepting this situation may be the best outcome.

Analysts may feel sadness and perhaps sometimes a sense of loss when long term analysands depart. In certain circumstances there may be a loss of a self object. The awareness of this has to be acknowledged if an appropriate separation is to be achieved for both participants. Redfearn writes that an ability to exist as a separate individual involves the ability to relinquish and is part of the process of individuation (Redfearn, 1972, p. 16). Those who have suffered an enforced separation, such as on the occasion of the death of a spouse, will know that, after a period of time, they begin to take on some of the qualities which they saw in the other person. By this, I do not mean an unhealthy identification, but a freedom to enjoy for themselves some of the qualities which they saw in the other person. Some of these were projections which they can now withdraw and claim for themselves. This is part of the growth in the process of individuation. The withdrawing of analytic dependence can be part of a similar process.

Conclusion

Dependency of some degree is present in, and essential to, every meaningful relationship. In this paper I have attempted to explore a few of the many forms, positive and negative, of analytic dependency present in the analytic relationship and the effect this has on the participants. In the closeness inherent in the interactive and interdependent movement within the analytic dyadic process, it would seem that not only is there a dependency in the analysand but also, albeit of a different quality, an analytic dependency in the analyst. Whilst the understanding of theory and technique is essential in analytic training, the emotional maturity of the analyst is a foremost and crucial factor in contributing to change and healing in the analysand.

References

Bowlby, J. (1980). *Attachment and Loss, Volume 3*. Hogarth Press and the Institute of Psycho-Analysis.

Fordham, M. (1995). Countertransference, Chapter 10. *Explorations into the Self. The Library of Analytical Psychology, Volume 7*. London: Academic Press.

Guggenbuhl-Craig, A. (1980). *The Archetype of the Invalid. Eros on Crutches*. Texas: Spring Publications.

Jacoby, M. (1993). Is the analytic situation shame producing? *Journal of Analytical Psychology*, 38(4). London: Routledge.

Marshak, M. (1998). The intersubjective nature of analysis. In: *Contemporary Jungian Analysis*. London: Routledge.

Martindale, B. (1989). Becoming dependent again: the fears of some elderly patients and their younger therapists. *Journal of Psychoanalytic Psychotherapy*, 4(1). Charlesworth Group UK.

Redfearn, J. (1972). *Parting, Clinging, Individuation*. Guild of Pastoral Psychology. No. 166. London: Greaves.

Redfearn, J. (2000). Possible psychosomatic hazards to the therapist: patients as self objects. *Journal of Analytical Psychology*, 45(2). Blackwell, UK.

Reggiori, J. (1999). Who am I? When am I myself? What's the time? *Journal of British Association of Psychotherapists*, 37. UK: Training Publications.

Solomon, H. (1994). The transcendent function and Hegel's dialectical vision. *Journal of Analytical Psychology*, 39(1). London: Routledge.

Zinkin, L. (1998). *The Klein Connection in the London School: the Search for Origins and Dialogue in the Analytic Setting*. London: Jessica Kingsley.

Zoja, L. (1983). *Working against Dorian Gray: the Analyst and the Old Journal of Analytical Psychology, Volume 28(1)*. London: Academic Press.

CHAPTER TWELVE

Between fear and blindness: the white therapist and the black patient[1]

Helen Morgan

Introduction

This paper is an attempt by a white psychotherapist to consider issues of racism and how they might impact on the work in the consulting room. There are two main features of this first statement that I want to emphasize by way of introduction. The first is that I intend to explore questions of difference in colour, and not issues of culture. This is not because I believe that matters of cultural differences in the consulting room are not interesting, or that culture and race are not often conflated, but rather that there is something so visible, so apparent, and yet so empty about colour, that to include a discussion of culture can muddle the debate and take us away from facing some difficult and painful issues. A black patient may come from a culture more similar to my own than a white patient, yet it is the fact of our colours that can provoke primitive internal responses that are hard to acknowledge and face.

Clearly there are many differences, such as culture, class, gender, sexuality, etc., that form divides within the wider society and where the power balance is asymmetrical. But those are the subjects of other papers. It is my experience that when the subject of race and psychotherapy arises among white therapists, we often quickly widen the question out to include other issues. It is as if we are trying to swallow up this difficult subject and lose it in a generality of difference. I am always struck by how very hard it is to think about racism for it is essentially such an irrational phenomenon and yet one that is so insidious and pervasive. Colour blindness, ignoring difference of this nature, is more comfortable, but I believe it to be a denial and a defence against a complex array of emotions that includes anxiety, fear, guilt, shame and envy. No wonder we do our best to avoid the subject.

The other point I wish to make is that this paper is written from the perspective of the white therapist. It is the only position I might have any authority from which to speak. There are worryingly few black people entering this profession but it seems that those who have are impelled by their experience in the consulting room with both black and white patients to consider matters of racism. Some have written of their subsequent thinking. On the other hand, there is a notable paucity of writing from white therapists on this subject. Paul Gordon (1993a) conducted a survey of psychoanalytic psychotherapy trainings and equal opportunity policies in 1993 and concluded;

> ... not only that few organizations had actually done anything meaningful in this respect, but that many simply did not regard it as a problem and some completely misunderstood the issues. [Gordon, 1996, p. 196]

Because this is an essentially white profession within a society where white holds power, the white therapist can go through life avoiding this matter altogether, assuming it to be a problem only for black colleagues. Pressures to think about it may be dismissed as mere fashion and political correctness. I will suggest that we as individuals, our work and the profession in general are the poorer for such avoidance.

A paper by Bob Young (1994) on how little the issue of racism is addressed within training organizations, is entitled "A loud silence". There is a silence generally within our profession concerning racism, but I believe also that a silence can too easily develop in the consulting room. It is a dangerous silence for the therapy because it contains too much background noise for it not to infect all the other work we try to do. A frequent response by the black patient is to stop and leave therapy, often silently. Another response is not to enter in the first place—which is the loudest silence of all.

Psychotherapy—"What's race got to do with it . . .?"

In its essence psychotherapy is a process of an individual therapist working with an individual patient. In that work a relationship develops which is specific to those two individuals. The focus is on the vicissitudes of the internal world of the patient and how it emerges transferentially within that relationship. The terms "black" and "white" are definitions of collective categories of so-called "race". Racism involves such collective definitions which carry a process of de-personalization, seeing only the characteristics ascribed to that category and not the individual. What, therefore, has such a topic to do with the business of psychotherapy?

Assuming racism to be a non-issue for psychotherapy is tempting. However, I believe that racism forms a backdrop which exists to any therapeutic encounter. It is a form of pathology and, therefore, should be open to the exploration of therapy. It is so for our white patients and needs, therefore, to be available to analysis where it appears. When a black patient enters therapy, because of the effects racism will have had on him or her, these experiences will be present in the room. Power differences, both real and perceived, between a white therapist and a black patient will exist, and we need a way of exploring them, especially when they occur as transference resistances.

Racism

In *The Good Society and the Inner World* Michael Rustin describes the concept of "race" as "an empty category":

> ... differences of biological race are largely lacking in substance. Racial differences go no further, in their essence, than superficial variations in bodily appearance and shape—modal tallness of different groups, colour of skin, facial shape, hair, etc. Given the variations that occur within these so-called groups, and give rise to

no general categorisations or clusterings . . ., it is hard to find any
significance in these differences except those that are arbitrarily
assigned to them (. . . even physical visibility has been lacking in
important cases of racism as a ground of distinction—the Nazis
compelled Jews to wear the Star of David because they were not
readily identifiable as Jews . . .). Racial differences depend on the
definition given to them by the other . . . and the most powerful
definitions of these kinds are those which are negative—definitions
that we can call racist. [Rustin, 1991, p. 58]

The emptiness of this category "race" emphasizes the irrational
foundation of racism. Any analysis of these foundations has to
include a political and economic perspective. Colonization and the
riches of power and wealth that were exploited by white
Europeans in the past, and the continuation of such exploitation
in the process of globalization, require moral and psychological
constructs as a justification for the exploiters. Exploration of the
psychology behind and within the process can be helpful if it goes
alongside other approaches. In his paper "Souls in armour" Paul
Gordon argues that:

Psychoanalysis cannot provide a theory of racism. although it can—
and should—be part of one. Racism is in the material world as well
as the psyche and our attempt to understand it—like our attempts
to understand all other phenomena—must be in two places at once.
[Gordon, 1993b, p. 73]

Those who have considered the subject of racism from a
psychoanalytic perspective focus on different possible aspects.
Rustin sees racism as akin to a psychotic state of mind. The
mechanism includes a paranoid splitting of objects into the loved,
and the hated and the racial other becomes the container for the
split-off, hated aspect which is then feared and attacked. Rustin
argues that it is the very meaninglessness of the racial distinction in
real terms that makes it such an ideal container, for no other
complications of reality can intrude. Splitting mechanisms include
idealization as well as denigration. The latter is mobilized and
expressed in political speeches which refer to excrement and the
terror of floods of immigrants taking over the country. The former
is evident in the idealization of African Caribbean youth culture
and the attribution of abilities in sport, music and dance. This

process of idealization carries with it the dynamics of envy.

Stephen Frosh (1989) argues that racism is a response to modernity and the fragmentation that is experienced. The move to a more pluralistic society together with the dismantling of much of the external forms of superego control carried by the established institutions, such as church and state, may mean greater freedom but places a considerable strain on the individual ego to manage that freedom and hold the depressive position. The fragile ego, fearful of fragmentation must find ways of defending itself. The need is to establish a boundary between self and other and to then define the other as inferior and thus the self as superior. Hated feelings can be projected into the other and feared, envied and attacked. Frosh predicts that the retreat to fundamentalism and the growth of racism will be the key problem for modern society.

From a Jungian perspective James Hillman in his paper "Notes on white supremacy" explores the meaning of the colours white and black:

> Our culture, by which I mean the imagination, beliefs, enactments and values collectively and unconsciously shared by Northern Europeans and Americans, is white supremacist. Inescapably white supremacist, in that superiority of whiteness is affirmed by our major texts and is fundamental to our linguistic roots, and thus our perceptual structures. We tend to see white as first, as best, as most embracing, and define it in superior terms. [Hillman, 1986, p. 29]

In his paper "The soul of underdevelopment" to the International Congress for Analytical Psychology in Zurich in 1995, Roberto Gambini quotes a statement of the Pope at the time of the conquest of South America; "There is no sin below the Equator". Gambini notes that:

> In sixteenth Century catholic Europe, the shadow was kept under relative control by ethical institutions and civil law ... The shadow stayed in the corner, pressed for a way out to be lived and projected. Thus, when a vast geographical area was opened under the rubic, "Here it is allowed", the shadow disembarks on the shore and runs free, proclaiming gladly: "I made it! This is home!". [Gambini, 1997, p. 142]

Hillman talks of the projection of the shadow onto the black population. The very nature of white and its equation with light, bright and innocent means it cannot include the dark within it. He suggests that "whiteness does not admit shadow, that its supremacy rejects distinctions and perceives any tincture as dullness, stain, dirt or obscurity" (Hillman, 1986, p. 40). White, therefore, casts its own white shadow and casts it into the black.

The concept of projection of the shadow into the other who is then feared, hated, envied, etc. allows a generality that leaves open the question of what that shadow aspect might consist of. Different so-called racial groups—the Jew, the African, the African Caribbean, the Asian, the Middle Eastern and others—all carry separate collective projections and evoke various primitive responses. The threat each category is perceived to contain, from a white racist perspective, is seen to be different in each case, as is what is perceived to be enviable. Each is seen to be available to carry an aspect of the white shadow. The effect of the process in each case is one of depersonalization and dehumanization.

Furthermore I am not saying that the process of shadow projection is the perogative of white people only. To do so would be to engage in a reverse form of splitting, assuming pathology to belong to white people and health to black people. This would be to deny the facts and to idealize the other. However, I do want to keep focused on white racism for two reasons. One is that the power balance between white and black in this society is not symmetrical and that needs to be owned as a reality. The second is that my concern in this paper is the white therapist and the implications of white racism for him or her.

The white liberal

The racist self is an ugly creature and one to which we wish to give no house room. This ugliness has expression in such groups as the BNP, the Klu Klux Klan, apartheid, etc. It does untold harm to the black "Other" who is the recipient of the evacuation of the hated parts of the racist self and who then is hated and attacked. Their existence is also a problem for the white liberal in that, in themselves, they provide a container into which we can project the racist self.

When we consider racism as a splitting or projective mechanism it is easiest to focus on the extreme forms of overt racist attack, genocide, slavery and exploitation. Of course this is important, but the danger can be that those of us who do not engage in such acts of hatred and who abhor such groups can retreat to a fairly comfortable position of disassociating ourselves from the whole process. Racism is a pervasive business and it gets into everything and everyone. I doubt whether there is any black person living in this country who hasn't been subject to it in some form or another in their life. But nor am I, as a white person, free of it. Like everyone else I grew up in a racist society, and it would be a supreme statement of omnipotence to say that it has not got into me too. When we attempt to disassociate ourselves from the phenomena I believe that this is denial and another sort of defence, a defence against something ugly we fear in ourselves.

Julian Lousada describes two traumatic aspects of racism in his paper "The hidden history of an idea. The difficulties of adopting anti-racism":

> There are, it seems to me, two primary traumas associated with racism. The first is the appalling inhumanity that is perpetrated in its name. The second is the recognition of the failure of the "natural" caring/humanitarian instincts and of thinking to be victorious over this evil. We should not underestimate the anxiety that attends the recognition of these traumas. In its extreme form this anxiety can produce an obsequious guilt which undertakes reparation (towards the oppressed object) regardless of the price. What this recognition of a profoundly negative force fundamentally challenges is the comfort of optimism, the back to basics idea that we are all inherently decent and that evil and hatred belong to others. Being able to tolerate the renunciation of this idea, and the capacity to live in the presence of our own positive and destructive thoughts and instincts is the only basis on which the commitment to change can survive without recourse to fundamentalism. [Lousada, 1997, p. 41]

This trauma of racism, therefore, is not in Lousada's view just the horror of the racist act but the problem for us all that it exists. The problem for the white liberal is not only the negative racist feelings we may have towards the black "other", but our need for denial of them out of guilt and shame.

On being white

When I first began to think about these issues, largely via my contact with black friends, colleagues and clients, I found that the previous basic assumptions about my own identity were challenged. Growing up as a white person in a white society, I had no cause to question either my culture or my colour. If asked to describe who I was, I would not have even considered defining myself as white.

Doubtless such primary assumptions exist for all human beings. However, I cannot imagine a black child growing up in this country who does not have to face, fairly early on, that he or she is black. The luxury of it never crossing my mind that I was white is not allowed the black person. I call it a "luxury" because of the sense of ease that being permitted to take an aspect of my identity for granted brings. But I wonder. Taking something for granted is a near relative of it being unconscious.

In his book *Partisans in an Uncertain World*, Paul Hoggett says:

> ... uncritical thought will not simply be passive but will actively cling to a belief in the appearance of certain things. It actively refuses, rejects as perverse or crazy, any view that may contradict it. To think critically one must therefore be able to use aggression to break through the limitations of one's own assumptions or to challenge the "squatting rights" of the colonizer within one's own internal world. [Hoggett, 1992, p. 29]

He goes on to suggest that if the movement of thought is to be sustained, the act of aggression must be followed up by the act of play. He quotes Winnicott:

> The creativity that we are studying belongs to the approach of the individual to external reality ... Contrasted with this is a relationship with external reality which is one of compliance, the world and its details being recognized but only as something to be fitted in with or demanding adaptation ... [Winnicott, 1974, p. 76]

Given the fact of global colonization by white western Christian culture, for us who are defined as belonging to such a culture, we can, if we choose, avoid external pressure to make that act of aggression that challenges the "squatting rights" of the internal colonizer. But not noticing this figure who inhabits at least a corner of our minds demanding compliance does not mean he does not exist. I suggest that we are the poorer if we do not attempt the act of aggression to break through our assumptions for they then remain an area of internal life that is unexamined. The tenacity of the uncritical thought that actively clings to a belief in the appearance of certain things in Hoggett's quote may give us a clue to the tenacity of the fact of racism despite legislation and attempts at training. For me to think differently about my place in the world and the privileges it has brought me requires an undoing of a well-laid system of assumptions about myself. The fact that those assumptions existed and continue to exist does not make me an inherently bad person, but to break through their limitations is hard work. For Hoggett to then suggest I am required to take it further into the area of play is asking a lot. This is a not an easy subject to "play" with. It raises feelings of guilt, shame, envy, denial and defiance, all of which are hard enough to face in the privacy of one's own life. To explore it publicly can bring up in me a fear of getting it wrong, of saying the unforgivable and of exposing a badness in me.

*   *   *

I wish now to consider work with two patients, one white and one black, to illustrate the issues as I perceive them in therapeutic work.

A white therapist and a white patient

J was a white woman in her late forties who at the time of the incident described below had been in therapy with me for several years. She arrived at one session disturbed and shocked. J was a social worker in an inner city area. She had been working with a client for some time and she had become emotionally close to this young woman of eighteen who she saw as vulnerable and abused. That day the client had told J that she had started going out with a black man she had met in Brixton. J's immediate reaction to this news had been one of fear and loathing, this was followed by real distress at her own "unthinking" reaction. J considered herself to be a rational liberal person who was used to having black colleagues and friends and thought she had "worked through" issues of racism.

J reported the news and her reaction at the start of the session but hastened to assure me that she had had a chance to think it through and things were OK now. She realized her reaction had been from a stereotype of a black man and she was ashamed of her initial response which she considered primitive and racist. Soon she was on to another subject and apparently the matter was over and done with. I was struggling to work out what might be going on here. The telling me of this event had the feel of the confessional, where J was telling her secret "sin" to me. It seemed that the telling of the secret was enough and, with a sigh of relief, we could both move on.

In this she seemed to be appealing to my "understanding" as another white woman on two levels. One was a recognition of the stereotypes conjured up by the words "black man" and "Brixton". The other was a liberalism that had no truck with such silly notions. Both expectations were accurate. The questions in my mind, then were: What was her immediate response about in terms of her internal world? What was she defending against in the shame and the wish to move on? What was being re-enacted in the transference?

Despite an uncomfortable feeling in the room I returned to the subject of the client's boyfriend and tried to explore her associations more explicitly. Brixton, it emerged, was like London's "Heart of Darkness". It was for J a vibrant, but fearful, place which both repelled and fascinated her. Locating this black man in Brixton embued him with both excitement and fear. J imagined this man to be sexually active and attractive and she feared what he might do to her client. She was able to acknowledge both her fear of him as threat, and her envy of the client having this exciting sexual object. She feared he might have AIDS, and had already imagined the man making the young woman pregnant then abandoning her. The fear of the aggressive, contaminating and feckless man was evident.

Clearly there are some complex processes occurring here that were specific to the internal world of my patient. For the purpose of this paper I want to emphasize a few main themes. Put simplistically one theme was how she had projected a primitive animal male sexuality onto the man, and an innocent pure femininity onto the client who had to be protected. But there was also the issue of her sense of "badness" and shame at having these feelings. After all the work she had done on herself in developing her awareness of her racism, she still was capable of such "bad" thoughts. These thoughts had intruded into her mind like an aggressive attack. In themselves they were shadow aspects which penetrated, left her with a shitty baby and then abandoned her. The client, perceived as the victim of the black man, was also "innocent" and "pure" of such nasty thoughts.

In seeing the black man through her initial lens which she defined as "racist", she employed a mechanism of projecting the aggressive, physical and sexual masculinity onto him and the innocent feminine victim onto the white female client. As such it was a projective defence. However, the more difficult issue to explore was how her denial of her racist feelings was also a defence against her own aggressive and penetrating thoughts. By telling me of the initial reaction and the subsequent process back to a more comfortable position she was inviting me to collude both with her initial disgust and with her subsequent shame. We were to be "in this together". Her "confession" followed by the response "its all right now" seemed to be an appeal for me to ally myself with the aggressive intruding thought, with the innocent female victim and the rescuer who protected my patient from this attack by denial.

What I want to emphasize for the purposes of this paper are the following:

1. "Bad" intolerable aspects of aggression and sexuality were projected onto the black man and onto Brixton. As with all projections, their acknowledgement allows the possibility of their withdrawal and these "bad" aspects integrated into the self;
2. The projection itself was experienced as a thought that was invasive and intolerable as it evoked shame, guilt and anxiety;
3. The patient tried to resolve a dilemma by "confessing" the initial reaction to me, and then making a speedy retreat from the subject. Shame and anxiety led her to avoid exploring the projective processes and their potential access into internal structures;
4. Because both the racist "bad" thought and the shame this produced echoed in me, the patient's invitation to collude with her avoidance was tempting. I was required to face and accept

my own responses in order that there was permission for the patient to explore some important material. Whilst these responses may have been used unconsciously by my patient to support her avoidance, they were not of themselves counter-transference responses. They were more general processes familiar to me as a white individual, living in a white racist society.

A white therapist and a black patient

D is a woman of African descent who was brought up abroad. In her mid fifties, when she first came to see me, she was the eldest of four having come from a religious family where a strict, sometimes harsh discipline was imposed on all the children. This discipline was often experienced as arbitrary and D responded by retreating into a fantasy world inside herself. It was only in her late teens that she discovered that she had been adopted when she was six months old and her "mother" was, in fact, her aunt who had just married at the time of D's birth. They had then had three children of their own. The birth mother left the area and all contact with her was lost since the adoption. The identity of the father was not known by the adoptive parents.

At our initial interview I raised the fact of the black/white differences between us. She assured me that this was not an issue, that she was used to living in a predominantly white culture and knew that she was unlikely to find a black therapist anyway. It made no difference to her. In my experience this is a common response. I know there is an argument that the therapist should wait for things to come up in the material and not refer to these matters unless the patient does. On the issue of difference in colour I disagree. I believe that, given power issues and possible anxiety the patient may be feeling about my response as a white person, it is a lot to expect that a black patient will risk raising the issue themselves. Stating that the difference is noticed and acknowledged by the therapist and that it can be talked about gives permission for the matter to emerge at a later date.

D was very polite and well-behaved in her sessions for some time and, whilst the work went on, there was a sense of a lack of

engagement. It was only after the first long break came that any
negativity surfaced when she began to miss occasional sessions. We
both understood this to be an expression of anger and a re-
enactment of her "disappearance" from the family as a child, but it
remained a theoretical understanding and was not felt in the room
by either of us. Gradually I became aware of a feeling in me in her
sessions of wanting her to leave. I would look at her on the couch
and the phrase that came into my mind was "cuckoo in the nest".
More to the point she was a "cuckoo in *my* nest" and I did not want
her there.

Usually, of course, when I have negative thoughts about patients
I am reasonably able to accept them, welcome them even, as a
countertransference feeling and therefore of an indication of what is
going on. This time I was also aware of an urge to push this feeling
away. I felt I "should not" feel this way towards her and an effort
was required to stay with the thought. Eventually I said something
about the wish for us not to be together. She seemed relieved and
said she had been feeling she did not belong, that being in therapy
was a betrayal of herself and maybe not right for her. There
followed a period where she verbally attacked therapy in a
contemptuous way, describing it as tyrannical and against people
thinking. Implicit in her attacks was her superiority to me. I had
been taken in by this tyranny whilst she remained free. At one point
she was saying how she feared that I would—and she meant to say
"brainwash" her—what she actually said was that I would
"whitewash" her.

She was initially shocked by the idea that she was relating to me
as a colonial, imperial power that could take her over with my
mind. She was well read and understood theoretical constructs
regarding transference and she began to "wonder" whether her fear
of brainwashing was about her fear of the therapist/mother. Her
invitation to me was to interpret in terms of her internal world only.
There were, indeed, thoughts about an engulfing adoptive mother
who disciplined harshly, of her struggle to fit in with what is
around her and only able to assert herself by leaving. I felt,
however, that we needed to take care. All that was in the
"brainwashing" scenario. Something more complex was expressed
in that of the "whitewash", something we both might be finding
difficult to face.

Staying with the subject of colour and the difference between us she began to express a disparagement of blackness. She said she had been relieved that I was white when she first met me because of a sense that a black therapist would be second rate and she wanted the best. She was deeply ashamed of these feelings as a woman who was politically aware and dismissive of the mimicry she saw in some black people. The self denigration in this was evident and illustrated how the black individual on the receiving end of white shadow projections can internalize this hostility and turn it into an attack on the self.

However, my job was to explore with her which aspects had been introjected by *her* and how this related to *her* internal world. From infancy D retained a sense of abandonment. She was the odd one out without understanding why. She had to be good to hold onto her mother's love but she still kept getting beaten for crimes she did not always understand. Her general feeling throughout was of not being good enough, and her sense of belonging was extremely tenuous. Her rage at this had had no expression as a child, except in fantasies of suicide. She could only cope with the situation by imagining there was something fundamentally wrong with her.

The fact of being black in a white society fitted this sense of not belonging. Her experiences of racism had provided an unconscious confirmation that she was 'bad' and deserving punishment. Despite political alignment with the black movement, her internal sense remained that of being an outsider, of being wrong and somehow dirty. White meant belonging and white meant what she was not, good, successful and of value. My whiteness meant she could get close to the source of what was good but she had to be careful that she did not antagonize me through any exposure of her "bad" rage.

As we explored the self-loathing inherent in her "secret" disparagement of "black", her comments switched from a denigration of the blackness of herself to a denigration of my whiteness. This was done largely through her accounts of the racism she had experienced. She seemed to be challenging me to take up a position. Was I allied with these white others or would I join with her in her attack, and become black like her? What was not to be allowed, it seemed, was our difference. I was to be for her or against her.

Which ever category was to be deemed superior to the other, the insistence that one *had* to be, served to perpetuate the perception of me as "Other". "Other" with a capital "O" as, this way, I was being safely removed behind a shield of categorization. Thus D could defend herself against the anxiety of her longing to become one with me and the terror of expulsion. If I rejected her it could be because she was black and bad, or because I was white and bad. The pain and frustration of me being different and separate from her could be avoided.

In his paper "Working with racism in the consulting room", Lennox Thomas describes a similar experience of a white therapist working with a black patient who was in supervision with him. Thomas says: "... it is difficult for the therapist to recognize that the unconscious does not distinguish between colour as far as the perpetrators of pain are concerned" (Thomas, 1992, p. 138).

In the same paper, Lennox Thomas cites the concept, put forward by Andrew Curry, distinguishing between the pre-transference and the personal transference. This, to my mind, is a useful distinction. The pre-transference is described as:

> ... the ideas, fantasies and values ascribed to the black psychothera-pist and his race which are held by the white patient long before the two meet for the first time in the consulting room. Brought up in the society which holds negative views about black people, the white patient will have to work through this before engaging properly in the transference. The white psychotherapist too will need to deal with this when working with black patients....This pre-transference is constituted of material from the past: fairy tales, images, myths and jokes. Current material, in the form of media images, may serve to top up this unconscious store of negative attributes. [Curry, 1964, quoted in Thomas, 1992, p. 137]

Dorothy Evans Holmes in her paper "Race and transference in psychoanalysis" considers the way that references to race can give access to transference reactions in the therapeutic situation. In the following extract she quotes from an earlier (1985) paper of hers:

> often it is said that patients' racist remarks in therapy constitute a defensive shift away from more important underlying conflict ... While it is the therapist's ultimate aim to help the patient understand the protective uses of defences, this aim can best be achieved *only after* the defences are elaborated. [Evans Holmes, 1992, p. 3]

For D the early loss of the mother, and the later felt tenuousness of the bond with the adoptive mother constituted the pain that lay at the centre of her self. It was this pain and her consequent rage that had to enter the therapy and be survived before transformation could occur. White and black as placed in opposition to each other served as a vehicle to keep us apart and away from an engagement with each other.

This opposition formed a dividing line, provided by the wider society, and we were perceived to be on opposite sides. The line *both* exists in reality *and* is an internal, defensive construct. We both needed, I believe, to acknowledge its external reality and its consequences for each of us. As the white therapist I was required to explore my pre-transference and where this colluded with the racist line. My shame and guilt had also to be owned internally. D needed to know I knew about the line and accepted its reality for her. A too hasty interpretation of her response, as only a recapitulation of the original pain and the original defence, would have been a defensive denial on my part of a real divide.

However, the analytic stance required an understanding that the divide was also being used as a defence and this had to be elaborated to give access to transference reactions. The generalities of race had to be interpreted and understood in terms of the specifics of *her* internal world and the transference. To do so we had to withstand an engagement that held the possibility of aggression and hate.

The wish to make everything all right and deny anger and hatred in the relationship was rooted in D in her original childhood scene where her anger was not allowable. She was, in many senses, the cuckoo in the nest, not a real part of the family and not conscious of why. She had had to defend against her angry destructive thoughts because she could be rejected altogether. Such a sense of not belonging was reinforced by her move to another country but also by her experience of being a black woman in a white world. In the transference, she had to take great care that she did not upset me for her aggressive impulses could be so destructive she could do me damage.

On my side, I did not actually fear her anger or aggression. More problematic was the possibility of shame at having any racist thought about her. It was the fear of shame that was potentially more debilitating and paralysing. It seems to me that, in order that we could work together, D and I had to hold two positions simultaneously, of "remembering" that she was black and I was white, and of "forgetting" it.

Conclusion

There are, it seems to me a variety of routes the white therapist can take in our attitude to work with a black patient.

The first is to ignore the issue. This is a form of colour blindness and, in my view, a denial. A denial of difference and a denial of uncomfortable feelings this difference may invoke in both and in the relationship. It has the appearance of good therapeutic practice for it seems to be seeing the individual and not the category. A consequence of this is that, should the patient bring material of racist experiences, the therapist will interpret it only in terms of the patient's internal world. A reality is not acknowledged and an abusive situation reinforced by the denial of the reality of the abuse.

The second is to acknowledge that there is an issue but it is one that exists for the black patient alone. It recognizes that the patient is likely to have experienced overt racism in his or her life and that needs to be acknowledged and understood. This, I believe, still removes the problem to outside of the consulting room and can be a defence on the part of the white therapist against his or her own racist responses and therefore against shame and guilt. The responsibility for the pre-transference is left on the shoulders of the black patient.

The third is to recognize that, if I acknowledge a racist backdrop to our society, then as a white person, I too cannot be free of the phenomena. I also have inherited a prejudicial veil which forms before my eyes when I see the blackness of the individual. Such a veil is likely to include an embroidery of guilt, shame and envy given that the relationship for the white liberal as opposed to the extreme racist is complicated by the hatred of the internal racist. Such shame is likely to prevent us from working through the reality of the external situation to an interpretation of the meaning of the situation for the individual.

Following on from this is a fourth position which also recognizes that racism will effect the relationship between us, and that there is a power differential inherent in that relationship over and above the power relationship which both exists and is perceived to exist between any therapist and any patient. Elaboration and exploration of the reality of this differential may provide an important means of access to the transference. My argument is that we have to manage this fourth position if we are to get to the place I think we need to be, that is, through to the point where the issue is not an issue.

Note

1. This paper was first published in the BAP Journal, No. 34, Vol. 3, Jan. 1998.

References

Evans Holmes, D. (1992). Race and transference in psychoanalysis and psychotherapy. *International Journal of Psychoanalysis*, 73(1): 1-11.

Frosh, S. (1989). Psychoanalysis and racism. In: B. Richards (Ed.), *Crisis of the Self: Further Essays on Psychoanalysis and Politics*. London: Free Association Books.

Gambini, R. (1997). The soul of underdevelopment: the case of Brazil. *Zurich '95 Proceedings of the Thirteenth International Congress for Analytical Psychology*. Switzerland: Daimon Verlag.

Gordon, P. (1993a). Keeping therapy white?: psychotherapy trainings and equal opportunities. *British Journal of Psychotherapy*, 10(1): 44–49.

Gordon, P. (1993b). Souls in armour: thoughts on psychoanalysis and racism. *British Journal of Psychotherapy*, 10(1): 62–76.

Gordon, P. (1996). A fear of difference? Some reservations about intercultural therapy and counselling. *Psychodynamic Counselling*, 2.2 May: 195–207.

Hillman, J. (1986). *Notes on White Supremacy. Essaying an archetypal account of historical events* (pp. 29–58). Switzerland: Spring Publications, 1986.

Hoggett, P. (1992). The art of the possible. *Partisans in an Uncertain World: The Psychoanalysis of Engagement*. London: Free Association Books.

Lousada, J. (1997). The hidden history of an idea: The difficulties of adopting anti-racism. In: E. Smith (Ed.), *Integrity and Change, Mental Health in the Market Place*. London: Routledge.

Rustin, M. (1991). Psychoanalysis, racism and anti-racism. *The Good Society and the Inner World*. London: Verso.

Thomas, L. (1992). Racism and psychotherapy: working with racism in the consulting room—an analytic view. In: J. Kareem & R. Littlewood (Eds.), *Intercultural Therapy*. Oxford: Blackwood Scientific Publications.

Winnicott, D. W. (1974). *Playing & Reality*. London: Harmondsworth Press.

Young, R. (1994). Psychoanalysis and racism: a loud silence. *Mental Space*. London: Process Press.

CHAPTER THIRTEEN

Reflections on retirement: questions raised

Susan Fisher

Introduction

I am seventy years old and I have recently retired from working full-time as a Jungian analyst in private practice, with a long commitment to and involvement in my professional association's training activities. I must admit that there is still a small panicky voice inside me yelling, "What have you done?" Retirement is not a topic frequently taken up in psychoanalytic literature. Much is written about the skills and techniques needed to begin practicing as a psychotherapist, but little is written about ending a career as a psychotherapist. The aim of this paper is to clarify and share my personal thoughts and to stimulate interest in my unanswered questions.

At the personal level, I feel fortunate to have had a fulfilling professional life, but I have come to the conclusion that, "I do not have to do it any longer". This may sound like a grandiose and arrogant statement, but the process of making this decision has been lengthy and difficult. Retirement involves complex issues and emotions. After struggling to evaluate the advantages and disadvantages of continuing to work, I have chosen to be unemployed.

Being free from the threat of poverty, I feel ready to "downshift" and make way for the next generation of psychotherapists. Perhaps beginning to understand how fragile and limited life is has made me understand how precious each day is and that I want to prioritize my time. It is time to do more of the things that give me pleasure and less of those that give me stress. I have decided to risk possible isolation, loneliness and emptiness to obtain flexibility and freedom from the restriction of regular commitments. I hope to establish a comfortable, new balance between modes of being active and passive. I realize that I am "letting go" of an important, valued part of my life and that at times the change of status may be disorientating and painful. My intention is to spend available free time and energy with my family and on interests and skills that I had neglected for my career. I feel a desire to reconnect with satisfying non-professional parts of my life—e.g. travel, nature and the arts. I ambivalently but enthusiastically look forward to the next phase of my life as a beginning as well as an ending, an opening up as well as a closing down, a rebirth as well as a death.

I started working in private practice as a Jungian analyst about twenty years ago and qualified as a Training Therapist and Supervisor for my professional association ten years ago. It has been challenging, rewarding work that I have enormously enjoyed, but at times the physical and emotional demands have also been burdensome and exhausting. The British Association of Psychotherapists has provided a stimulating, containing environment in which I could develop at my own pace. It has been an honor and a privilege to share in the emotional maturation of my patients. I have learned from each of them; they have enriched my life. So why have I stopped? In this paper I intend to examine the choice to retire in terms of the life cycle, addressing at the same time issues around narcissism and spirituality.

Life cycle

When I moan about the effects of ageing, a friend reminds me, "Old age is not for sissies". I realize that there are no other alternatives—either you die young or grow old. However, there seems to be a conspiracy of silence and denial about arriving at old age, Erikson's eighth and final stage of human development (Erikson, 1965). I am not aware of the ages of colleagues; it is not something that is openly discussed. When I proudly tell people my age their response is usually, "I do not believe it" or "You do not look it" (even though I never hid my white hair). This is flattering but it would be easier for me to face the reality of change if others could confirm it. We all need an accurate reflection of ourselves—to match inner with outer images. I need to be mirrored and accepted for who and what I am. I get a sense that others want to deny that I am old, to avoid the truth, possibly avoiding their own inevitable ageing.

Jung (C.W., 8, para. 796) observed people looking away and changing the subject when ageing was mentioned. Stereotypes of old age seem to stick and most people fear their own mortality. It is easy to depersonalize the elderly into old objects that are thrown away because they are too difficult to mend. Old people may diminish in value and become obsolete, be classified as unproductive and inferior. As a seventy-year-old, I have crossed over from Erikson's seventh stage of productive adulthood into the eighth, final stage of life. However, as Jung wrote, "A human being would certainly not grow to be seventy or eighty years old if this longevity had no meaning to the species" (Jung, C.W., 8, para. 787). I need to find a new equilibrium between creativity and destructiveness. I am curious, as well as apprehensive, as I approach unknown territory in the final stage of life.

Two painful realities underlie this paper: (1) everyone is going to die sometime; and (2) sooner or later every psychotherapist or analyst must stop working. Adult mortality rates increase with age. It is an illusion to believe that individuals can extend their working lives indefinitely. I agree with the Buddhist view that it is helpful to prepare for the ending, that it is naïve to think it will always work out all right. There needs to be financial and emotional preparation for old age. The difficulty, of course, is that nobody knows when the end is coming and we do not know our "sell-by" date. There is no doubt that individuals are living longer, healthier lives, but it is impossible to avoid the ageing process. A planned retirement offers a sense of gaining control at the anxious final stage of losing control in many areas.

Obviously, it is essential that individuals consider their unique personal family and financial situation before retirement. Everyone acquires and relinquishes skills and interests at their own pace. A wide range of circumstances and points of view need to be respected. In the UK, women are labeled Old Age Pensioners at sixty, men at sixty-five. From the age of seventy driving licenses are renewable for only three years. In the analytic world retirement is usually voluntary, not mandatory. There are no guidelines about assessing when it is time to stop working. Twenty years ago when I qualified, I anticipated working well into my eighties. There still seems to be an expectation that psychotherapists in private practice will continue to work as long as they can, until there is a noticeable decline in their physical or mental health, until they become critically ill or suddenly die. I have noticed that psychological health is rarely mentioned. Most therapists rely on continuous self-monitoring, since there are no assessment procedures. As memory, hearing, and energy begin to fail, competence and quickness may decrease. Nevertheless, elderly analysts usually retain a wealth of valuable professional experience from which younger practitioners and patients can benefit greatly. Some practitioners prefer to limit work with patients and emphasize work with supervisees. Continuing to share knowledge can be a way of achieving immortality.

The fairy tale of "Snow White" is deeply embedded in my psyche. I watched Walt Disney's film version of "Snow White and the Seven Dwarfs" throughout childhood. It was the first animated full-length movie and is now available on video so I can also watch it with my grandchildren. It is a well-known story that had been told for centuries in various forms and languages. I used the Snow White fairy tale in an earlier paper to illustrate narcissistic behaviour and mother–daughter (generation) rivalry (Fisher, 1990). The story portrays an ageing woman, faced with the truth of her fading beauty (value), who tries to kill off the younger woman who threatens to replace her. Snow White's ageing stepmother is portrayed as jealous of the girl's youth and attractiveness and the younger woman is jealous of the stepmother's material wealth and power. The older woman's death is necessary for the next generation to find love and happiness. The symbolism of death, reawakening and rebirth is used to represent a stage of higher maturity.

Now as I reflect on the meaning of the Snow White tale, pertaining to psychotherapists' retirement, different aspects of the story particularly impress me. My attention turns to Jung's theory of the tension between opposites with the purpose of widening consciousness. Jung (C.W., 14, para. 206) wrote, "The opposites are the ineradicable and indispensable pre-conditions of psychic life. Psychic energy comes from trying to resolve conflicts and attempting conciliation". He considered the polarized all-or-nothing, one-after-another phase to be a prelude to deeper understanding. In Snow White there are splits between irreconcilable polar opposites—e.g. evil against good, death against life, black and white, old against young, ugliness against beauty. There is no grayness, no compensatory factor, no transition from one state to another, no mutuality, no letting go or redistribution of power or beauty. Hopefully, during a planned retirement a balanced resolution can be negotiated, a third space which integrates the opposites of young and old, life and death.

My thoughts on retirement probably began to germinate when Peter Mudd (1990) read his paper, "The dark self: death as a transferential factor", at the 1986 Congress of the International Association of Analytical Psychology in Berlin. Mudd suggested that the fear of death or the self-preservation drive is the chief mover of relationships. He suggested that human relationships provide a space within which individuals can learn to die, thus facilitating a fuller life. His thesis, that death is the primary catalyst for individuation, makes sense to me. Mudd proposed that Jung's concept of the transcendent function, purposeful in essence, is built on the experience of living through the threat of physical death. Jung observed that, because we are so convinced that death is the end, it does not occur to us to describe death as a goal and fulfillment (Jung, C.W., 8, para. 797). "Life is an energy-process. Like every energy-process, it is in principle irreversible and is directed toward a goal. That goal is a state of rest" (Jung, C.W., 8, para. 798). I view retirement as a "small death". It is the killing off of something that can not easily be revived. It involves being able to face multiple losses, with rest as the goal, and a turning away from external gratification in order to strengthen inner resources.

Narcissism

In the process of negotiating a "retired" identity, both narcissistic injury and narcissistic gratification become relevant. Gordon (1993), discussing narcissism and the self, points out the difference between falling in love with oneself and falling in love with the reflection of one's image. My statement "I do not have to do it any longer", implies that I no longer need the narcissistic gratification that comes with being a psychotherapist. This is a powerful statement, which I may regret someday. I am giving myself permission to change directions. My role as "caretaker" was learned early and practiced well. It has been a lifelong pattern, so there is guilt about not continuing to fulfil that role.

A retired colleague recently pointed out the inevitable loss of a highly developed professional skill. Clinical experience sharpens and refines the art of psychotherapy. The ability to tune into the unconscious of another individual and make useful interpretations over long periods of time in an ongoing and reliable way is an unusual skill. It means sacrificing immediate gratification in the service of another. In intimate therapeutic relationships, patients seek and reward our skills. It is an exceptional bonus to be financially rewarded for work you enjoy, and to be needed, chosen, respected, listened to. Even when a patient manages to express hatred, envy, and rage toward the analyst or attacks the good therapeutic work done and progress made, it is often gratifying to recognize that the patient has become conscious of their negative feelings and behaviours. Outside of the consulting room, people rarely want to engage in conversations that include elements of their shadow or personal unconscious. The intimacy of intensive analysis is beyond the comprehension of those who have never experienced it.

Like many of my colleagues, I fit the role of the Wounded Healer and have used my work to help me repair early narcissistic injuries. It is dreadful to be abandoned, ignored, rejected, disregarded. However, narcissistic injuries are a part of therapeutic relationships. Most analytic patients struggle with their own early narcissistic injuries. They use primitive defenses such as denial, splitting, projection, introjection, and projective identification to protect them from the psychic pain these injuries can cause. Psychotherapists are expected to meet their patients' desire for unconditional attention and understanding, regardless of the patients' various demands on them. Holding negative (hate) and idealized (love) projections can be a distressing burden, which requires relentless self-examination, discipline, and provisions for recovery. If the burden of carrying disturbed patients' inner worlds becomes too heavy, physical or psychological health may be at risk. According to Jung (C.W., 9ii, para. 126), if an individual does not become conscious of his inner conflicts, he will act them out as fate. Weekends and regular holiday breaks may provide necessary time for the psychotherapist to reflect, relax, and replenish necessary physical or psychological resources. I strongly believe that therapists have an ethical responsibility to take care of themselves in appropriate ways. "Healthy" narcissism may be used to monitor physical and mental health and well being. Intense involvement in the therapeutic process means that both therapist and patient are affected, for better or worse.

As I grow older I seem to have more questions than answers. For example, at seventy who needs me? Will I be able to hold on to my identity in society without describing myself as a working psychotherapist? Do I need to hold on to a professional status to feel valued? If I am no longer in the spotlight, will I fade into the shadows? Is my self-esteem too firmly rooted in the stability and structure of external tasks?

Winding down my private practice has been difficult, stirring up painful feelings of guilt and anxiety. Ideally any decision to terminate an analysis would involve both therapist and patient, but of course we do not work in an ideal world. A decision to retire may mean that some patients' analyses will not have reached their natural conclusion. Except in cases of illness (and, of course death), the therapist who has decided to retire should fix a date well in advance. Reducing clinical hours and not accepting new referrals can be a way of beginning the long, painful process. Patients and therapists need sufficient time to work through the loss and make appropriate arrangements for the future. After recognizing what has and has not been achieved, additional therapy or alternative external circumstances may need to be considered.

Jung (C.W., 12, para. 3) lists nine reasons for reaching a temporary or definitive end of an analysis. Feelings of sadness, joy, dependency, envy, rage, love and hate need to be worked through and integrated during termination of an analysis. Projections need to be withdrawn, as participants can be perceived in more human and authentic ways. If the good aspects of the therapeutic process have been sufficiently integrated and identified with, a patient may be able to continue an internal self-analysis without assistance.

In thinking about these issues, it has been helpful to look at the correlation between therapeutic ambivalence and maternal ambivalence. I find it useful to compare retirement to the uncomfortable feelings when children leave home—the "empty nest syndrome". Mother/child relationships and therapist/patient relationships involve struggling to manage a sequence of separations from the beginning.

The important link between ambivalence and separation has been usefully discussed by Parker (1995). Parker argues that, paradoxically, maternal ambivalence is vital for separation. Although destruction and aggression are necessary, maternal ambivalence can make separation too dangerous to contemplate, entailing mixtures of love and hate, loss and release, fear and relief. Jung (C.W., 9i, para. 287) observed that the archetype of child "means something evolving toward independence. This it cannot do without detaching itself from its origins: abandonment is therefore a necessary condition, not just a concomitant symptom". The positive side of abandonment means freedom and spontaneity but the negative side means loss and betrayal. Children and parents, patients and therapists, need to deal with the anxiety and ambivalence involved in separation. While children and patients may have to struggle to get free of entrapping attachments, mothers and analysts must find ways to let go of similar attachments. A mother or an analyst, and/or a child or a patient may be unable to separate. One-sidedness or the inability of either side to let go creates tension and conflict. One or both of the pair may long for freedom but be afraid to let go of the nourishing and satisfying parts of the relationship. There are those who remain together as a protection from depression and/or anger. Gerrard, writing about psychotherapeutic relationships, explores Balint's term "ocnophilia", clinging to a firm protective object. The ocnophil denies the independence of the object by clinging to it (Gerrard, 2000). We can all think of examples of children, parents, patients, and psychotherapists that are unable to move on—those who remain in destructive, tangled, frustrating relationships.

I am interested in the possible risk of therapists becoming addicted to patients' neediness, praise and loving approval. In order to flourish, individuals need to be loved, valued and understood by various people for different aspects of themselves If there is an overwhelming attachment to a self-image of a "loving saviour", it could develop into an addiction. Like any addiction, it would be difficult to give up. A prolonged clinical practice could be seen as clinging to productive years of youth in an attempt to deny ageing. Psychotherapists may become overly dependent on patients' positive mirroring, just as insecure parents may become overly dependent upon their children to heal their own narcissistic wounds. Withdrawal of patients' positive gratification could lead to a sense of inferiority and depression. Retirement could revive badly resolved sorrow, and feelings of abandonment and uselessness. There could be a danger of acting out in an exhibitionist, grandiose, or hypochondriacal manner to compensate for low self-esteem.

How can these losses become bearable? What can be used to fill the empty internal and external spaces? While going through the process of retiring, it has been important for me to realize that after retirement I shall be the same person. I will continue to be curious, have dreams, aspirations and need intellectual challenges. I will still have choices and new things to explore and learn about.

Spirituality

In considering whether or not to retire, the most important aspect seems to be the acceptance of mortality while living life to the fullest. Confronted with the possibility of the outer and inner emptiness of ageing and retirement, questions arise about the purpose and meaning of life. What has been the purpose of my life? What residue will I leave with former patients and the next generation of psychotherapists? Can I give the fragile, uncertain final stage of life spiritual meaning? I find that I become inarticulate and childlike as I attempt to investigate spirituality. In exploring aspects of what they call "natural spirituality", Young-Eisendrath & Miller (2000) offered chapters by a number of authors with views that overlap and sometimes contradict each other. My own view is that spiritual development is about extending limits of ordinary consciousness and comprehension, more about being than doing. It is about bringing together opposing and different aspects of life and tolerating ambiguity. It is about respect and love for human life, and connectedness with nature and beauty. It combines reality, truth-fulness, responsibility, beauty and love. I am sympathetic with the description of natural spirituality in our time as acceptance of limitations, groundedness in the ordinary and willingness to be surprised (Young-Eisendrath & Miller, 2000). I also like the familiar saying, "Old age is being more and more grateful for less and less".

In ways which I find impossible to explain, I realize that I have changed internally as well as externally since beginning the journey toward retirement. The world looks different.—I see the bigger picture while I become smaller and less significant. I have embraced new interests and skills while also becoming more appreciative of silences and stillness. It is a relief to acknowledge that I am not as important or powerful as I once thought I was. It is a relief to acknowledge that my views and actions do not have the impact on society or individuals that I once believed they had. It is acceptable to acknowledge "mistakes" and gaps in knowledge.

Retirement has helped me recognize the things that give me pleasure and that I want more of. I enjoy and value spontaneity and flexibility, and the freedom from regular commitments. It is wonderful to ignore clocks! Slowing down has given me the time and internal space to appreciate more the beauty and wonders of nature and to more fully enjoy the arts, family and friends. Jung writes (C.W., 8, para. 785) that it is an ageing person's duty and a necessity to devote serious attention to himself. Can I justify continuously re-evaluating the usefulness of relationships and activities and my desire for freedom from the constraints of my working life? There seems to be a thin line between making the choice to "do nothing" and idleness, between "enlightened self-interest" and self-absorbed narcissistic behaviour. A new balance must be found between isolation and intimacy—a way to leave doors half closed and half-open. Remaining available within limits requires firmness and flexibility.

Sometimes I envy those who hold strong religious beliefs. Religious dogma and practice can offer comfort, security and structure during periods of uncertainty, loss or fear. Unfortunately, like many others, I cannot turn to the great religions for larger meaning or understanding. Struggling to find personal answers can be painful at times but it also offers rewards. All I know with confidence is that my "running down" process has begun, and that the future is uncontrollable. Working through the issues in this paper has been part of a process. I have recognized that fear of retirement is really fear of death and fear of being fully alive. "The negation of life's fulfilment is synonymous with the refusal to accept its ending. Both mean not wanting to live, and not wanting to live is identical with not wanting to die" (Jung, C.W., 8, para. 800).

Conclusion

I began and end with my statement, "I do not have to do it any longer". There is a part of me that wants to spread the joys of retirement in an evangelistic way. My view is narrow because I can only see retirement from my personal experience and perspective. Everyone starts from a different place, with different blind spots and wounds that can be accepted and even enjoyed. I am not confident enough to offer advice to colleagues about retirement, but I hope to stimulate thought about this important, badly neglected subject. I urge both young and old to begin thinking about retirement and accepting its inevitability. I can only say that, for me personally, the acceptance of this "small death" has already enriched my life.

References

Erikson, E. H. (1965). *Childhood and Society*. Harmondsworth: Penguin.

Fisher, S. (1990). Self-destructiveness in women: a female perversion. *Journal of the British Association of Psychotherapists, 21*: 20–31.

Gerrard, J. (2000). Ocnophilia and interpretation of transference. *British Journal of Psychotherapy, 16*(4): 400–411.

Gordon, R. (1993). *Bridges*. London: Karnac Books.

Mudd, P. (1990). The dark self: death as a transferential factor. *The Journal of Analytical Psychology, 35*(2): 125–142.

Parker, R. (1995). *Torn in Two*. London: Virago.

Young-Eisendrath, P., & Miller, M. E. (2000). *The Psychology Of Mature Spirituality*. London: Routledge.

CHAPTER FOURTEEN

Some thoughts on supervision

Jean Pearson

"What I suppose we shall go on calling 'supervision' is actually a shared fantasy. It is the resultant of the trainee trying to imagine what he and his patient have been doing together and the supervisor is trying to imagine too. It works best if both remain aware that what they are jointly imagining is not true. But both can profit enormously, both can enjoy the experience as well as suffer and there is teaching and learning to be found in this joint imaginative venture as there is in therapy itself"

Zinkin, 1988

This thought-provoking statement of Jungian analyst Louis Zinkin, although perhaps deliberately overstated, comes closest to expressing my own experience of supervision. The impossibility of achieving an objective perspective on human behaviour had begun to impinge on me during my undergraduate years as a psychology student, before my entry into the professional world of psychodynamic social casework and later on, psychotherapy. The observer's presence inevitably affects the interaction which is being observed. As John Urbano (1984) observes, the value system of the therapist will affect the therapeutic relationship with a client and, by implication, will also affect the reporting of his work in supervision. Likewise the value system of the supervisor in turn will affect both the therapist and the patient.

My present position on supervision is a distillation of all the different experiences of supervision which I have received over the years—first as a student social worker and then as a qualified social caseworker, and later becoming, first a trainee and then a qualified psychotherapist. Throughout this period as a supervisee, spanning over twenty years, I have had many supervisors, although all using a psychodynamic approach.

This rich experience has been particularly instructive in that, in a number of instances, I have had the opportunity of receiving supervision on the same patient from several different supervisors over a period of time. What has struck me most forcibly is that it has often felt that I have been presenting a very different person than the patient whom I had imagined I had been bringing to supervision with a previous supervisor. Over time I have come to the conclusion that there are as many different ways of seeing a patient as there are people attempting to reach an understanding of that patient and that no one way is the "right" way.

Working in the transitional space— *the* mundus imaginalis

In attempting to reconcile what could therefore have become a collection of different and perhaps disconnected "truths" about a particular patient I have found Winnicott's (1974) idea of the "third area"—the area of experience and the area of illusion—a useful way of understanding what I believe is always going on in the process of supervision. Two people—the supervisor and the supervisee—meet together in a shared endeavour—essentially playing with the clinical material in an attempt to imagine themselves into the patient's inner world—the better to understand the unconscious determinants of his dilemma. They cannot expect to arrive at the "truth" but they can aspire, through cross-fertilization of their ideas, to arrive at partial truths in a way that may have a transformative power when subsequently shared with the patient through interpretations.

In a sense one might think of this endeavour as involving a triangular relationship because the patient, as he is being imagined by the two workers, is also present in the "third area". It is in this area of "transitional space" that the two workers (and indirectly the patient) are essentially playing with different fantasies about the client's "reality".

What goes on within this transitional space, if it is to be helpful, is a non-rational process whereby projections pass to and fro between workers and some are transformed into a new insight about the patient. Thus, in this imaginative space a shared fantasy can develop between the supervisor and the supervisee which might then form the basis of an intervention which the therapist makes with the patient in a subsequent therapy session. Jungian analyst Andrew Samuels (1989) has likened this "mundus imaginalis" to the primary mutuality which is pre-existent between mother and infant. For me it is essentially a playful activity where neither the supervisor, nor the supervisee, can lay claim to having discovered a particular "truth" about a patient. What emerges, as they imaginatively play with the patient's material, is a shared fantasy which has come to life in the space between them.

Supervision is therefore not primarily about the didactic teaching of theory as applied to clinical material, although clearly there is a place for this, particularly with beginning therapists. Supervision, as I see it, is about facilitating the therapist's ability to enter the "mundus imaginalis", not only with the supervisor, but also, and more importantly, with the patient. Implicit in this approach is the centrality of working with the transference and the countertransference and the use of projective identification as rich sources of communication and shared fantasizing. It is essential to allow oneself to enter the patient's unconscious and be submerged in it sufficiently for a mutative process to develop between therapist and patient. In this process, not only is there potential for the patient to be changed, but also the therapist becomes open to change. This is the basis of Jung's statement that "You can exert no influence, if you are not susceptible to influence" (C.W., 16, para. 163).

The parallel process—uses and abuses

Alongside these transferential phenomena occurring between therapist and patient is a parallel process occurring between therapist and supervisor. This phenomenon, which he called the "reflection process", was first discussed by psychoanalyst Harold Searles. Searles stated that "the processes at work in the relationship between client and worker are often reflected in the relationship between worker and supervisor" (Searles, 1955).

Twenty years later, in London, Mattinson (1975) took up the concept of the reflection process in the social work literature on psychotherapeutic work with couples. Around this time the phenomenon was also re-named the "parallel process" by psychoanalytic writers such as Ekstein & Wallerstein (1972), Doehrman (1976) etc., a term which is now most commonly used. Recently there has been another resurgence of literature on the parallel process amongst Jungian analysts such as Kugler (1995), Gee (1996) and psychoanalysts like Grinberg (1997).

Doehrman remarks on how, if unacknowledged, this parallel process can have a "corrosive effect" upon the therapist's work by leading to interpersonal difficulties between the supervisor and supervisee. I myself have had experience of this as a trainee psychotherapist when the dominant personal myth of my training patient, in her case the "Cinderella" myth, began to be enacted between my supervisor and myself. It was sometime before "the wicked stepmother" in my supervisor and the "Cinderella" in me, which was being played out in the supervisory drama, became visible to us both. Unfortunately this insight came too late for the supervisory relationship to be rescued and a change of supervisor was needed.

Here we can see the enormous numinal power of the dominant themes of fairy tales in the dynamics within and between individuals. Jung believed that fairy stories are not just entertaining stories which have been passed down through the generations from pre-historic times. He claimed that they are vehicles for helping us deal with the dark forces within us, by making use of the accumulated wisdom of our forbears. Thus they are containers for archetypal behaviour, ways of teaching us how to recognize and deal with expressions of collective unconscious psychic processes.

Hence, Jungian analysts will directly make use of motifs occurring in clinical material to elucidate a patient's central myth, as described by von Franz (1996). In the case referred to above, the powerful forces of the negative mother archetype, enacted between my patient and her own mother, were paralleled by unconscious projections between my supervisor and myself. This suggests that the parallel negative transference operating between my patient and myself had not yet been sufficiently recognized and worked through.

When recognized, however, this parallel process can have, as several writers describe, a powerful transformative effect on the work. Through enabling a therapist to bring to supervision his own personal problems and emotional difficulties experienced in the work, not only with the patient, but also with the supervisor, parallel processes can be discovered. As Doehrman points out, it is when such things can be openly acknowledged between supervisee and supervisor that they can often be transformed from obstacles to learning into deeper understanding of the psychodynamic processes at work in the therapeutic relationship between therapist and client. Ultimately it is through these interpsychic processes between the three people involved—supervisor, supervisee and patient—that one can imagine the intra-psychic processes at work in the patient's inner world.

As I grapple in my own supervisory work with this more process-centered approach to supervision, I think back to the emphasis placed upon it in my psychotherapy training, during a fortnightly case discussion group. The group facilitator would sometimes call attention to group processes to make conscious those aspects of the case under discussion, which were being reflected in the group response to the clinical material being presented and to the trainee therapist presenting. The main emphasis of the training course, however, was on individual twice-weekly supervision, where, by reason of the exclusivity of the supervisory *claustrum*, the parallel process between supervisor and supervisee is not so easily open to scrutiny.

My own experience shows that there can sometimes be a tacit agreement not to look at this other aspect of the parallel process— the supervisee's feelings towards the supervisor and vice versa— ostensibly for fear of intruding into matters best left to the super-visee's training analyst. This, in effect, makes a major assumption that these difficulties are solely activated by the pathology of the therapist. Such an assumption therefore misses the valuable contribution which could be made in achieving a better understanding of the patient's inner world through what is being transferred into the relationship between the two workers in supervision.

This does, however, raise a valid point about the supervisor needing to respect the privacy of the inner world of the supervisee and to be circumspect about the use of the parallel process. Harold Searles (1955) raises this issue in his paper on the emotional experience of the supervisor. He recommends that supervisors focus on what the patient is doing to the therapist and use for informational purposes only what the supervisee and supervisor are doing to one another in the supervision. By this Searles suggests that the supervisor can avoid straining the professional relationship between the workers and reduce self-consciousness and defensiveness in the supervisee.

Similar concerns were also acknowledged by the Society of Analytical Psychology in London in a symposium on training, held in 1961. In this collection of papers Michael Fordham, writing on the role of the supervisor, warns against the supervisor inadvertently initiating an analysis with the trainee. Fordham states that the supervisor should:

> point out counter-transference manifestations but without analysing the candidate, only confronting him with them ... It is one of the unstated assumptions of candidates that supervisors will refrain from analysing them, and the supervisor, realising this, implicitly agrees. Unless both want consciously to alter the agreement it should be scrupulously kept. [Fordham, 1961]

This concurs with the original recommendation made by Harold Searles.

Case discussion

Here I would like to bring in some case material to illustrate my experience of recognizing and trying to work with the parallel process and the difficulties of coping with what the supervisee was doing to me without becoming retaliatory. Instead I tried to use my own painful feelings as information to understanding what was going on between supervisee and patient and to keep my interventions focused on this.

A woman therapist I was supervising had been working psychodynamically with a female patient with a congenital absence of uterus and vagina. The patient entered therapy fourteen months after this condition had first been diagnosed, seeking to come to terms with her loss. It had become powerfully evident to me within the supervisory relationship that the supervisee was suffering from an intense envy of me which had an inhibiting effect on my capacity to be creative within the supervisory task. This paralleled the patient's intense envy of the therapist, which seemed to have invaded the therapist in an alarming way, leading to her developing severe gynaecological symptoms with the threat of a hysterectomy.

As far back as 1935, Jung drew attention to this phenomenon of openness to projections as:

> a typical occupational hazard of the psychotherapist to become psychically infected and poisoned by the projections to which he is exposed. He has to be continually on his guard against inflation. But the poison does not only affect him psychologically; it may even disturb his sympathetic system. I have observed quite a number of the most extraordinary cases of physical illness amongst psychotherapists, illness which does not fit in with the known medical symptomatology, and which I ascribe to the effect of this continuous onslaught of projections from which the analyst does not discriminate his own psychology. The peculiar emotional condition of the patient does have a contagious effect. One could almost say it arouses similar vibrations in the nervous system of the analyst ... [1982, p. 172]

Jung's words were amazingly portentous and it has taken another sixty years before recent developments in psychoneurobiological findings have brought us closer to understanding the mechanisms through which these processes occur. An interesting discussion of how these findings can be applied to contemporary analytical theory and clinical treatment techniques can be found in a recent paper by Hester Solomon (Solomon, 2000a).

To return to the case under discussion, the unconscious processes whereby the patient's envy had actually invaded the therapist's body, seeking to destroy her organs of generativity, could be understood through the paradigm of psychosomatic illness, described by psychoanalyst Joyce McDougall. She shows how intense psychological stress can lead to a breakdown in the capacity for symbolic thinking, leading to regression to preverbal ways of coping. Language is bypassed and the distress is manifested in purely somatic symptoms (McDougall, 1989).

This, I think, is what had happened to the therapist. The intensity of the patient's envious attack had proved to be so unbearable that neither the patient, nor the therapist, could bear to think about it and express it in words, in a form where it could be psychologically worked through. This must have paralleled the patient's envy of her own mother's generativity. Melanie Klein has described how this is normally present in an archaic form in early life, but if all goes well, becomes sufficiently sublimated by a little girl's growing awareness of her own capacity to bear children (Klein, 1937). Usually the onset of the menarche and its external proof of her generativity are confirmation for the growing girl that she too can become a woman like her mother, thus lessening the envy towards her mother. In the patient's case menarche had not occurred because of a congenital absence of the uterus. Her worst fears had been confirmed and with it a re-intensification of her archaic envy of her mother.

I tried to look at these processes with the supervisee—focusing on the patient's intense envy of the therapist's creativity, i.e. her reproductive organs, and how the therapist was colluding with this destructive rage by coming close to assenting to the mutilation of her own sexual parts through a hysterectomy. Presumably the unconscious rationale was that, if what was envied was destroyed, then the patient's rage would be appeased, a terrible price for the supervisee to pay and one that would certainly not have helped the patient. It would only have confirmed to her the deadliness of her envy, which no one could contain. Helping the supervisee to recognize and make constructive use of these processes, rather than acting out the patient's destructive wishes, proved a difficult and demanding task. A hysterectomy was narrowly averted only to be followed by the threat of a colostomy for a bowel disorder.

Not all writers on the subject would agree with this approach, however. For instance Warren Wilner (1990) gives several supervisory vignettes where he openly confronts supervisees about their own pathology which is hindering the work with a patient. He describes several women therapists with a character-structure of obsessive–compulsiveness, used as a defence against the supervisees' own borderline state. He does not inform us of how the supervisees reacted to such comments. My reaction was to feel taken aback by his insensitivity, and I was left thinking that, in freely confronting the supervisee, the supervisor was caught in unconscious shadow projections in the relation between them.

The bi-modal approach to supervision

Nevertheless I find Wilner's "bi-modal approach to supervision" a useful way of integrating the imaginal method which I have been discussing above with the didactic. With beginning therapists especially, there is a clear need to provide some straightforward teaching about the apparent meaning of the patient's material and how this might then be reflected back to the client in a digestible form by means of an interpretation.

There is also the need for the supervisor to pass onto the supervisee the ethics, beliefs and values of the profession, together with the boundaries of behaviour, often by modelling these for the worker in the supervisory relationship and setting. In particular I think it is crucial for the supervisor to model for the therapist the fundamental importance of providing a safe container within which the work can be carried out. This necessitates being as conscientious about the boundary-setting functions of time, place and money with a supervisee as one would be with a patient.

All this is part of the first mode of supervision as outlined by Wilner. This he calls the mode of "interpretation and secondary process" and is essentially a didactic approach. The second mode he calls that of "primary experience" which he describes as under-scoring "the fact that supervisor and supervisee, therapist and patient, and the patient and the people in the patient's life are continually acting upon one another through words, gestures and deeds" (Wilner, 1990). Whilst functioning in the primary modes the supervisor is "an observing participant in addition to being a participant observer". Thus therapist and supervisor must let themselves get caught up in the patient's inner world as participants and later emerge in order to ascribe meaning as an observer.

The point that Wilner emphasizes is that an exclusively secondary process of a search for meaning and the making of interpretations, i.e. a didactic approach, is insufficient, just as an exclusively primary process based on the experiental would be. In fact an exclusive approach could well be a defence against the other mode. Only the supervisor can decide in the present moment within the supervision session where the emphasis should lie.

Process recordings in supervision

Lastly I want to emphasize that, in my experience of supervision, the most effective tool is the use of the process recording. Not only does this give a verbatim account of the session as it is recalled at the time of writing, but it also contains an account of the non-verbal behaviour of both parties and the counter-transference of the therapist. This provides a rich source of material, which is further amplified as supervisee and supervisor elaborate on it in the supervisory session. In the course of this supervisory "play" further material will be brought into consciousness, which has been temporarily repressed.

Here I am reminded of some case material from a recent supervisory session. The supervisee was presenting a process recording of her work with a woman patient. The patient had recently come into therapy, seeking help with the trauma of having been suddenly abandoned by her husband after many years of married life. She described herself as being in a state of shock and unable to find any explanation for the breakdown in the relationship. A phrase she kept repeating, and the supervisee kept repeating, was that it was "a complete mystery".

For a few moments I became aware of being overwhelmed by an almost physical sense of shock, so mind-numbing that my thought processes were as equally knocked out, as they evidently were in both the patient and the supervisee. Then the word "mystery" aroused in me an association to Sherlock Holmes and I voiced the opinion that there must be a clue somewhere in the clinical material. The supervisee continued to insist that there was not and continued with the process recording.

Almost as an aside the supervisee then mentioned that the patient had spoken of a recent shock she had experienced in her relationship with her manager at work. This man, whom she had fantasized was as mutually attracted to her as she was to him, had suddenly taken her on one side and told her that her work was unsatisfactory. When confronted by her mistakes she admitted that she had known about them, but had not bothered to rectify them because she believed them to be too trivial. Instead she could only dwell on her aggrieved feelings about the manager's "betrayal" of their relationship.

It was at this point that a half-forgotten piece of information provided a link in my mind to understanding the "mystery" of the husband's inexplicable abandonment. I suggested that the vignette of what was happening in the patient's work relationship suggested parallels with what had been going on in the marital relationship. Probably the husband had for many years been voicing complaints about difficulties in their relationship, but the patient had been unable hear them and realize that all was not well. As a last resort the husband had been driven to walk out. Even then the patient was unable to think about what had gone wrong. It would be the task of the therapeutic endeavour to uncover the defensiveness and resistances around this denial. Interestingly enough, the patient then began to describe how her relationship with her own father, previously described as cold and distant, had began to warm up since the husband had left her.

It is often the recall of repressed material such as this, during the delivery of a process recording, that carries the greatest informational value to the work of supervision. What starts off as an unconscious process occurring within and between supervisor and supervisee will, when brought into consciousness, yield the most useful information of all, leading to fresh insights and the development of a new "truth" about the client. Of course, these "truths" are at best only partial and will subsequently be superseded by fresh insights.

Summary

I have attempted to outline some thoughts on supervision as a shared imaginative task between supervisor and supervisee in which transferential phenomena occurring not only between patient and therapist, but also between supervisee and supervisor, can be used to enter and so better understand the patient's inner world.

In terms of methodology I have described a dual track approach of didactic teaching, particularly important with the beginning therapist, alongside an experiental approach, which is essentially a form of playing with shared fantasies between supervisee and supervisor. Both approaches are essential, but the degree of emphasis the supervisor gives to one mode or another would depend on the supervisee's degree of experience and creative ability.

References

Doehrman, M. (1976). The use of primary experience in the supervisory process. In: R. C. Lane (Ed.), *Psychoanalytic Approaches to Supervision*. New York: Brunner/Magel, 1990.

Ekstein, R., & Wallerstein, R. (1972). *The Teaching & Learning of Psychotherapy*. New York: International Universities Press, 1972.

Fordham, M. (1961). Suggestions towards a theory of supervision. *Journal of Analytical Psychology*, 6(2): 110—111.

Gee, H. (1996). Developing insight through supervision: relating then defining. *Journal of Analytical Psychology*, 41(4): 529–552.

Grinberg, L. (1997). On transference and countertransference and the technique of supervision. In: Martindale *et al.* (Ed.), *Supervision & Its Vicissitudes*. London: Karnac Books.

Jung, C. G. (1982). *Analytical Psychology: its Theory & Practice. The Tavistock Lectures*. London & Henley: Routledge & Kegan Paul.

Klein, M. (1937). *Love, Hate & Reparation*. London: The Hogarth Press & the Institute of Psycho-Analysis.

Kugler, P. (1995). *Jungian Perspectives on Clinical Supervision*. Switzerland: Daimon.

Mattinson, J. (1975). *The Reflection Process in Casework Supervision*. London: The Institute of Marital Studies, the Tavistock Institute of Human Relations.

McDougall, J. (1989). *Theatres of the Body. A Psychoanalytic Approach to Psychosomatic Illness*. London: Free Association Books.

Samuels, A. (1989). *The Plural Psyche*. London: Routledge.

Searles, H. (1955). The informational value of the supervisor's emotional experience. In: *Collected Papers on Schizophrenia*. London: Hogarth Press, 1965.

Solomon, H. (2000). Recent developments in the neurosciences. In: E. Christopher & H. Solomon (Eds.), *Jungian Thought in the Modern World*.

Urbano, J. (1984). Supervision of counsellors: ingredients for effectiveness. Paper presented at British Association for Counselling Conference, 1984.

Von Franz, M.-L. (1996). *The Interpretation of Fairy Tales*. Dallas, Texas: Spring Publications.

Wilner, W. (1990). The use of primary experience in the supervisory process. In: R. C. Lane (Ed.), *Psychoanalytic Approaches to Supervision*. New York: Brunner/Magel.

Winnicott, D. W. (1974). *Playing & Reality*. London: Harmondsworth Press.

Zinkin, L. (1988). Supervision: the impossible profession. Paper presented at British Association of Psychotherapists Conference on Supervision, 1988.

CHAPTER FIFTEEN

The ethics of supervision: developmental and archetypal perspectives

Hester McFarland Solomon

Introduction: *integrating the ethical attitude in analytic practice*

This chapter argues that the provision of ongoing supervision, peer supervision, or consultation helps to ensure, amongst other important functions, reliable access to ethical thinking in analytic practice. This does not in any way preclude the importance of, or suggest the lack of, an ongoing, active internal capacity for ethical thinking or an internal supervisory function that comes through the processes of internalization of the analytic attitude during the course of training and post-qualification professional development. I am, however, advocating the expectation that analytic practitioners be aware of the need for constant attention to the ethical dimensions of their clinical work, and that this may best be fostered by supervision as a present factor in clinical practice.

The struggle to keep ethical thinking integral to clinical work and the theory building that develops out of clinical experience requires sustained diligence and is particularly needed in those areas of our analytic and therapeutic practice where we are likely to be the most tested as clinicians. The function of the ethical attitude in clinical practice is not simply a matter of a set of rules that can be forgotten as long as they are not contravened in the clinical setting. I have argued in other contexts (Solomon, 2000b, in press) that the ethical attitude is integral to all our activities and relationships as human beings as well as clinicians, and especially to that most intimate, intense and demanding of relationships, the analytic relationship. Since the time of the Hippocratic Oath, professional Codes of Ethics and Codes of Practice state the practitioner's commitment to ethical practice and the principles that underpin it.

In this chapter I will explore the role of supervision in helping to maintain ethical thinking and practice in clinical work. I refer to the terms supervision (in which a younger practitioner, often a trainee, seeks regular, often weekly, supervision on one patient seen intensively, and where a fee is paid to the supervisor by the trainee), consultation (which usually refers to two colleagues, one senior and one junior, who discuss, regularly but not necessarily weekly, patients or clinical issues, and where the senior colleague receives payment from the junior one), or peer supervision (often in a small group of colleagues who are more or less at the same level of clinical experience and where payment is not involved, who meet regularly but not necessarily weekly). Unless there is a specific point of differentiation to be made between these modalities, for the purposes of this chapter I will use the term "supervision" to cover all three.

Crucial to my argument is the view that the analytic attitude is in essence an ethical attitude, and that the achievement of the ethical attitude is tantamount to the achievement of a developmental position. Here, "developmental position" is meant in much the same way that Klein or Bion had in mind when they referred to the paranoid–schizoid or the depressive positions as stages in the developmental process. Much of the argument of this chapter will revolve around the notion that the ethical attitude, like the paranoid–schizoid and depressive positions, is not a once-and-for-all achievement, but rather is part of an internal human dynamic that is experienced alongside and in relation to more primitive and sometimes more dangerous states of mind. Hence, just like the depressive position, the achievement of an ethical attitude can be considered in developmental terms which requires mental effort, in particular, conscious effort, to sustain. This perspective has much to offer when we think of the importance of an ongoing supervisory function in the practitioner's clinical work as offering a place where that conscious effort is shared and reinforced.

The view that I set out in this chapter incorporates the role of both developmental and archetypal perspectives in the understanding of the achievement of ethical thinking through the supervisory function. Alongside the triangular developmental perspective in which an ethical attitude may be fostered, in whatever way that may be accomplished (this chapter focuses on the role of supervision in this achievement), there lies the archetypal nature of the triangular relationship underpinning the achievement of the mental capacity for thinking, including ethical thinking.

Achieving an ethical attitude: a developmental model

It is a truism that it is not possible to be ethical in a vacuum. The ethical function is a relational function involving the assessment of subjective and intersubjective states. Jung pointed out (C.W., 10, paras. 371–399) that it is ubiquitous and hence has a collective dimension, while at the same time being experienced most vividly at the personal level. In thinking about the development of the young mind and how an ethical attitude might come into being, the Kleinian model shows that, because of the massive onslaught of internal and external stimuli on its limited mental capacities, the infant is at first suffused with psychotic states of mind that may cause profound anxieties, particularly if the holding environment is deficient and unable to process such states. These anxieties are primarily managed defensively through splitting and projection. Communicating, relating and using the other psychodynamically often take place through projective identification (Klein, 1946). Hence self and other are mixed up, and parts of each are allocated to different and separate psychic locations, either internally or externally, in the self or in the other. Klein called this the paranoid–schizoid position, where the perception and experience of the bad and good parts of the self and the other are not psychically found together, and where relating is at the level of part objects, because the young mind is not as yet capable of holding together opposite affective states. In a later development, called the depressive position (Klein, 1935), the infant or child is more able to experience the other as a whole object, separate from the self, and containing both good and bad aspects. Thus the child's feelings of love and hatred for the object, which had previously been split off and experienced as separate, are now capable, at times, of being held together in the infant's mind, giving rise to feelings of ambivalence towards the object, as well as feelings of guilt and the wish to repair the damage that the self might have wrecked on the object in the previous, part object mode of relating. In elaborating how this dynamic occurs, Britton (1998) has made a helpful contribution in offering a model which involves the circularity of the dynamic movement between the paranoid–schizoid and the depressive positions, such that each new cycle builds on the experience of the previous ones. Schematically, this has similarities with Fordham's model of deintegration and reintegration (Fordham, 1957).

In thinking in developmental terms about what are the conditions that foster an ethical capacity (Solomon, 2000a,b, and in press), I have suggested that it is through the combination of the infant or child's earliest experiences of devotion and reflection of the parental couple, who maintain an ethical attitude in relation to their infant or child, and that it is this combination that is eventually internalized by the child and is activated as the self and ego develop in dynamic relation, eventual internal parents in the psyche. The first stirrings of a nascent ethical capacity occurs as the infant experiences being the recipient of the non-talionic responses of the parental couple in face of his or her various states of distress, including rage and dread. Under the right conditions, the infant's experience of the parent's non-talionic responses is eventually internalized and identified with, and becomes the basis for gratitude. The idea of the ordinarily devoted parent, mother or father, represents a deeply ethical mode in their instinctual and unconditional devotedness to another, their infant, overcoming their narcissistic needs and frustrated rages, their shadow projections, and resisting by and large the impulse to skew their infant's development through requiring undue acquiescence.

Later they will leave this state of primary preoccupation and devotedness and will begin the processes of socialization which are so necessary a part of ethical development—the capacity to say, in different ways, "no", thereby establishing boundaries and expectations of self regulation, including those in relation to others. Thus, to the image of ordinary devotedness to a nascent self I am combining the notion of the discriminating and thinking function of the masculine principle, thus evoking a notion that appears in various guises in psychoanalytic and Jungian analytic literature, that of the creative potential of the third, whether a third person, a third position, or a third dimension. The activation of an archetypal potential for eventual ethical behaviour will be thus reinforced in ordinary good enough situations by caregivers capable of sharing acts of thoughtful devotedness and of empathic and devoted thinking about their infant. This has a clear parallel with what happens in the consulting room, where the analyst's willingness to go on sacrificing their own narcissistic needs through the sustained activity of thoughtful devotedness to the patient that we call the analytic attitude protects the patient so that they may develop and grow according to the needs of their self.

From dyad to triad:
the eventual achievement of triangulation

I am conjecturing that the internalization of and identification with the agapaic function of the parental figures in their empathic holding as well as their thinking and discriminating aspects can trigger or catalyse a nascent ethical capacity in a young mind, the first steps of which include those primitive acts of discriminating good and bad which constitute the foundations of splitting and projection. Early (as well as later) splitting and projecting may therefore be instances of primitive moral activity, what Samuels (1989) calls original morality—the expulsion from the self of what is unwanted and felt to be bad into the other, where it is identified as bad and eschewed. Even in situations where the good is split and projected, it is in the service of maintaining a discriminating, but highly defensive, psychic structure. This is a two dimensional internal world, in which primitive psychic acts discriminate good from bad experience, and split the bad from the psyche by projection into the care-givers—a first, primordial or prototypical moral discernment prior to the state where there is sufficient ego strength for anything resembling mature moral or ethical behaviour to arise. This constitutes the very preconditions for the creation of the personal shadow, which eventually will require a further ethical action of reintegration when the person has achieved an internal position of moral and ethical capacity.

As we posit, following Fordham (1969/1994), the self as a primary integrate, autonomous but very much in relation to another or others, so we are alone as moral beings while at the same time finding our moral nature in relation to others. To truly find another represents a transcendence of narcissistic ways of relating in which the other is appropriated for use in the internal world, denying the other's subjective reality. To live with the implications of this capacity to recognize and relate to the truth of the other is a step in the development of—and perhaps eventually beyond—the depressive position. The depressive position is usually considered to contain acts of reparation through guilt and fear that the object may have been damaged and therefore may be unable to go on caring for one's self (Hinshelwood, 1989). As such, acts of reparation remain contingent on preserving the other for the benefit of the self. The ethical attitude envisaged here goes beyond this contingency and suggests a noncontingent realm of ethical behaviour. This situation has direct implications for what transpires in the consulting room between the analytic couple (see previous discussions in Solomon, in press).

This represents a two-stage, dyad-to-triad process which reflects the two-stage developmental process in the infant (the neuro-physiological implications are also considered in Solomon, 2000a) in which the neural development of the infant's brain post partum must be matched by a parallel nurturing provision such that: (i) at first infant and mother are highly attuned (a "me/me" relationship); and (ii) where, later, there follows complementary and compensatory discriminations (a "self/other" relationship). The differentiation would then be between when to be "caring" and flexible and when to be "tough" and resilient, both of which have implications for the interactions in the consulting room. Just as the analyst can have a two-stage developmental relationship with their patient, so the intensive dyadic work would have a counterbalancing relationship created by the triangular space of supervision.

In this developmental framework, it is evident that there evolves a gradual demarcation between self and other, including an enquiry about how the self individuates from out of a projective and identificatory mix-up between self and other through to a fuller experience of the reality of the self's subjectivity in relation to the reality of the subjectivity of another. This is the beginning of the capacity for triangulation, that "theory of mind" (Fonagy, 1989) which the child has achieved when he or she is aware that their thoughts and those of the other are separate and not available directly to each other (as assumed in states of fusion or identification), but only through reference to a third perspective. As Cavell has described:

> ... the child needs not just one but two other persons, one of whom, at least in theory, might be only the child's idea of a third ... the child must move from interacting with his mother to grasping the idea that both his perspective on the world and hers are *perspectives*; that there is a possible third point of view, more inclusive than theirs, from which both his mother's and his own can be seen and from which the interaction between them can be understood. [Cavell, 1998, pp. 459–460]

Jungians would amplify this view by addressing the difficult but necessary work on the withdrawal of the projections of those negative aspects of the self, called shadow projections, through to a gradual capacity to view the self along with the other as separate but interrelated subjectivities with multivariate motivations, including shadow motivations that project the bad outside one's self. The withdrawal of shadow projections, predicated on the realization that the other is truly other and not assumed to be a function or aspect of the self, which otherwise might sully the gradual more mature experiences of intersubjectivity, underpins the ethical attitude. As such it is a developmental achievement that derives from an innate potential, activated at birth, and fostered by the continuous "good enough" experience of living in an ethical environment. It represents a constant struggle through acts and attitudes that are against the natural selfish inclinations of the self, acts which are *contra naturam*, foregoing insistence on the self's limited perspectives in order to encompass a wider view, including the recognition of that which is not ethical within the self. In Jungian terms, that recognition represents the integration of the shadow back into the self, steps toward incremental advances in the self's movement towards greater states of integration and wholeness. This is the individuation process, and it is predicated on a teleological view of the self in which the self's capacity for change, growth, and development are understood and experienced as being suffused with a sense of purpose and meaning.

Triangulation: the archetypal third

In 1916, a short time after the split between Freud and Jung, when he was suffering what might be described as a psychotic regression in the face of his loss of Freud who represented the centrally organizing psychic function of the father figure he had never had before, Jung wrote two landmark papers that can appear to be diametrically opposite in content and form: "VII Sermones ad mortuos" (1916) ("Seven sermons to the dead") and "The transcendent function". The former was published at the time, but not in a separate English edition until 1982, whereas the latter was not published until 1958, only a few years before Jung's death in 1961. Both reflect, in different ways, the immediacy of Jung's distressing and threatening psychic experiences that arose from his self analysis, undertaken, as Freud's self analysis, on his own. At the same time Jung continued to function as Clinical Director of the Burgholzli Hospital in Zurich and also fathered a growing family. If the tone of the "Seven sermons" was that of a chilling account of the horrifyingly vivid psychic experiences he endured at the time of his "confrontation with the unconscious" (Jung, 1963, p. 194), that of the "Transcendent function" was of a measured, scientific con-tribution to analytic theory building, which he compared to a "mathematical formula" (Jung, C.W., 8, para. 131), and which we could interpret as a dispassionate exteriorization of his highly emotive internal state at the time, a kind of self supervision. In this paper, Jung set out an archetypal, deep structural schema of triangulation in which he demonstrated that psychic change occurs through the emergence of a third position out of an original conflictual internal or external situation, the characteristics of which cannot be predicted alone by those of the original dyad. In relation to this idea, it is interesting to note that the philosopher and psychoanalyst, Marcia Cavell, who has recently put forward the idea of triangulation in a psychoanalytic context, refers to Polanyi's notion of "emergent properties" in much the same manner as that pertaining to the dialectical nature of the transcendent function, that is, as "properties that in a developmental process arise spontaneously from elements at the preceding levels and are not specifiable or predictable in terms of them" (Cavell, 1998, p. 461).

Whether or not he consciously drew on its philosophical origins, Jung's notion of the transcendent function is based on the idea of the dialectical and deep structural nature of all change in the living world expounded by the nineteenth century German philosopher, Hegel, in his great work, *The Phenomenology of the Spirit* (see Solomon, 1994). Hegel posited a tripartite schema as fundamental to all change, including psychic change, a situation in which an original oppositional pair, a dyad, which he called thesis and antithesis, struggle together until, under the right conditions, a third position, a synthesis, is achieved. This third position heralds the transformation of the oppositional elements of the dyad into a position with new properties which could not have been known about before their encounter—the *tertium quid non datur* in Jung's terms. Hegel called this ubiquitous struggle dialectical, because it demonstrated how transformations in the natural world happen through the resolution of an oppositional struggle and can be understood to have meaning and purposefulness. This was a deep structural patterning of dynamic change that was archetypal by nature and developmental as a dynamic movement in time.

This archetypal schema can also be thought of as the basis of the tripartite Oedipal situation, where transformation from out of a primordial pair, mother and child, can be achieved through the third position afforded by the paternal function, whether this be a real father, or a capacity of mind in the mother or in the child, or both, as Fonagy illustrates (Fonagy, 1989). It is in this sense that we might speak of the emergence of the mind of the child, the child's identity, as separate from his or her mother, through the provision of a third perspective. For Jung, this would be thought of as the emergence of the self, through successive states of transformation and individuation via the transcendent function. In the context of the function of supervision with which we are concerned in this chapter, we could say that it is through the provision of the supervisory third that both patient and analyst are helped to emerge from out of the *massa confusa* of the analytic dyad. Both change as a result as individuation progresses.

In psychoanalytic theory, the importance of the negotiation of the Oedipal threesome, that archetypal triad *par excellence*, constitutes much of the psychoanalytic understanding of developmental achievement. Freud first used the term "Oedipus complex" in 1910, following Jung's scientific researches on the complexes using the Word Association Test (WAT). At that time, the Oedipus complex was considered to be one of many organizing complexes of the psyche, but soon became the core psychoanalytic concept. Britton sums up concisely the Oedipal situation:

> ... we notice in the two different sexes the same elements: a parental couple ...; a death wish towards the parent of the same sex; and a wish-fulfilling dream or myth of taking the place of one parent and marrying the other. [Britton, 1998, p. 30]

Britton stresses the necessity of working through the Oedipus complex in order to resolve the depressive position and of working through the depressive position in order to resolve the Oedipus complex (Britton, *ibid.*, p. 29). He evokes the notion of internal triangulation, which requires the toleration of an internal version of the Oedipal situation in order to do this. He describes "triangular psychic space" as "a *third* position in mental space ... from which the *subjective self* can be observed having a relationship with an idea" (Britton, *ibid.*, p. 13). He concludes that "in all analyses the basic Oedipus situation exists whenever the analyst exercises his or her mind independently of the inter-subjective relationship of patient and analyst" (Britton, *ibid.*, p. 44).

In developing Britton's idea of the Oedipal triangle as present through the internal events and relationships that occur in the analyst's mind, as links to an internal object or to psychoanalytic theory, I wish to reiterate that the external manifestation and facilitation of this internal triangular state is quintessentially present in the supervisory or consultative relationship. Here, two people, the analyst and the supervisor, are linked in relation to a third, the patient.

Within psychoanalysis, the current debate about the implications of intersubjectivity—that the analyst and patient are acting together within a treatment relationship, in which the analyst's countertransference to the patient's transference as much as the reverse (for example, Atwood & Stolorow, 1993, p. 47) offer essential information—has been enhanced by Cavell's (1998) notion of "progressive triangulation". Rose summarizes her notion succinctly: "... in order to know our own minds, we require an interaction with another mind in relation to what would be termed objective reality" (Rose, 2000, p. 454). I hold that the provision of supervision, including the internal supervision that happens when the analyst thinks about aspects of the patient and the analytic relationship, is an important instance of "progressive triangulation", in that it allows for ongoing interaction with another mind in relation to a third, the patient, who can be thought about because differentiated from the dyadic relating of the patient—analyst couple.

Triangular space and supervision in analytic practice

The provision and function of supervision of analytic and psychotherapeutic work with individuals, children, couples, or families, creates a needed triangular space essential to the care and maintenance, the ongoing hygiene, of the dyadic relationships. I use the term "hygiene" in the sense that, through its provision, supervision keeps constantly activated the awareness of the analytic attitude, including its ethical component, in and through the presence of a third person (the supervisor), or a third position (the supervisory space), and that it acts as an aid in the restoration of the analytic and ethical attitudes when at times they might be lost in the maelstrom of clinical practice. Supervision is itself the representation of that attitude through the provision of a third area of reflection. The treatment, at profound levels, of the psyche in distress always involves a regressive and/or narcissistic pull back into part object relating, those primitive either/or, dichotomous states of mind that Jung and others have shown are dominated by the internal experience of the archetypal warring opposites at the basis of the defences of the self (Kalsched, 1996; Solomon, 1997).

Ensuring the provision of the sustained triangular space of the supervisory situation creates the necessary opportunity for analytic reflection, where two people work together to think about a third, whether the third is an individual, a couple, or a family, or an idea or aspect within the therapist or analyst, that is relevant to their clinical work. The provision of triangular space through internal or external supervision, or both, is essential to the maintenance of the analytic attitude in the face of the multitudinous forces and pressures at work within the analytic and therapeutic situation, arising from the conscious and unconscious dynamics within and between patient and analyst alike, and the consequently inevitable, often unconscious, intersubjective exchanges between them as a pair, that would seek, for defensive reasons, to undermine analytic achievements.

To the extent that this triangular space created by supervision is necessary to the hygiene of the analytic couple, (just as the paternal, reflective principle is essential to the hygiene of the mother–infant dyad, providing the space for psychological growth to occur), then supervision has an ethical as well as a clinical and didactic role to play in all analytic and therapeutic work, notwithstanding the years of experience of the practitioner. Whether supervision is provided in the same way as during training, with weekly meetings in a one-to-one situation with a senior practitioner, or in consultations with a senior practitioner at agreed intervals, or whether peer supervision in small groups is selected as the means of providing the triangular space, these are questions which are up to each clinician to decide upon, according to personal need and inclination.

In the case of the analysis and supervision of training candidates, where there are particular ongoing boundary issues and other pressures inherent in the training situation that do not usually pertain in work with non-training patients, such as the need to see a patient under regular supervision at a certain minimum intensity (three, four or five times per week), over a certain minimum amount of time (often for a minimum of either eighteen months or two years), supervision will help to identify and work under these constraints without foregoing the analytic attitude. This will in turn foster in the candidate their own ethical attitude, as they internalize the expectation that all analytic work, including the work of their own analysts and supervisors, is in turn supervised.

The trainee will then know from the very outset of his or her training that there is always a third space created in which he or she as a patient or as a supervisee will be thought about by another supervisor–practitioner pair.

Fostering the ethical–supervisory expectation is more likely to engender a generationally based commitment to the analytic attitude within a training institution, as the tradition of good clinical practice is passed down across the analytic and therapeutic training generations. Currently, there is an assumption that the aim and goals of training can often be summed up in almost the opposite way: that is, that the success of the candidate's progress through his or her training is assessed according to whether he or she is judged to be ready to "work independently". Of course, the assessment of the trainee's capacity for independent judgement and a sense of their own viable autonomy is an important, indeed crucial, factor in the process of assessing whether someone is ready to qualify to practice as an analyst or therapist. I am arguing here that, included in this assessment should be a judgment about the candidate's awareness of the need for and usefulness of the provision of a triangular space in which to discuss their clinical practice, in order best to ensure against the risks inherent in working in such intimate and depth psychological ways, including the dangers of mutual identificatory states or the abuse of power.

My contention is that, as well as its obvious advantages, the expectation that the practitioner will ensure that they have ongoing supervision or consultation on their clinical practice is a sign of maturation, both on the part of the practitioner as well as that of the training institution, as they assess their own and others' clinical competence. This is part of the assessment process which results in the authorization to practice as members of the training institution. There is the added dimension that some members go on to become eventual trainers, that is, training analysts, supervisors, and clinical and theoretical seminar leaders, entrusted with the responsibility for training future generations of analysts and therapists. The expectation in the trainee of ongoing supervisory and consultative provision is modelled by the trainers, fostering the candidate's respect for and understanding of the conditions that create and sustain the analytic and ethical attitude. This includes attention to boundary issues that can arise within and through the intensity of the intersubjective dynamics within the analytic and therapeutic relationship. (See Gabbard & Lester, 1995, for a detail discussion of boundary issues in analytic practice.) These intersubjective dynamics are inevitably released by the interpenetrative, projective, introjective and projective identificatory exchanges within the transference and countertransference.

The recommendation that: (i) members of analytic training institutions seek to establish an ongoing supervisory ethos to discuss their work, even if the provision is not systematically maintained; and that (ii) all training analysts and supervisors of the institutions have regular consultations regarding their training cases (including patients, supervisees, or training patients) represents a further development of those ubiquitous triads creating by the training situation: the trainee–training analyst–supervisor; the trainee–training patient–supervisor; and the trainee–supervisor–Training Committee. The expectation of providing a space for reflection with another would benefit all parties concerned and at the same time increase clinical awareness. Without this benefit, we run the risk of identifying with those narcissistic and other pathological processes and pressures, inevitable in analytic practice, as we are liable to treat those aspects in our patients that correspond and resonate with our own internal issues and personal histories. Hence the importance of clinical "hygiene", of creating the third space of supervision, that can help us to maintain our connection to genuine object relating and to staying alert to the pitfalls of intense dyadic relating.

Conclusion

I have explored some aspects of the supervisory function in analytic practice in relation to developmental and archetypal perspectives. The provision through supervision of a triangular space in which clinical work with patients can be thought about creates the necessary dimensionality for psychological transformation to occur and has resonance with developmental reality and archetypal truth. The ethical aspect of supervisory provision is predicated on the notion that genuine object relating arises out of such dimensionality, in which one mind is aware of the subjective reality of another and chooses to take ethical responsibility towards the other, as the parent in relation to the child, and the analyst or therapist in relation to the patient. This is fostered in the supervisory setting, where the triangular relationship of supervisor–analyst/therapist–patient makes manifest in concrete form a universal triangular and deep structural situation which is necessary if psychological development is to occur.

It may be that the emergence of an ethical capacity represents a development on from the depressive position, in that it seeks to provide for and protect a non contingent space or place for reflection about another, be it a person, a relationship or an idea. Such reflection may result in decisions taken with respect to another, and may be followed by actions, which include the content, form, timing and other characteristics of interpretations, as well as other, more subtle, modes of being in the presence of another, that will have a direct impact on the quality of their internal world. It is for this reason—because of the possibility of doing harm to the vulnerable interior reality of another—that the Hippocratic Oath was first established two thousand five hundred years ago with its main premise, *nolo nocere*, and why we, as practitioners, continue to seek to hone its ethos.

References

Atwood, G., & Stolorow, R. (1993). *Structures of Subjectivity*. Northvale, NJ: Analytic Press.

Britton, R. (1998). *Belief and Imagination*. London: Routledge.

Cavell, M. (1998). Triangulation, one's own mind and objectivity. *International Journal of Psychoanalysis*, 79(3): 449–468.

Fonagy, P. (1989). On tolerating mental states: theory of mind in borderline personality. *Bulln. Anna Freud Centre*, 12: 91–115.

Fordham, M. (1969, 1994). *Children as Individuals*. London: Free Association Books.

Fordham, M. (1957). *New Developments in Analytical Psychology*. London: Routledge & Kegan Paul.

Freud, S. (1910). Leonardo da Vinci and a memory of his childhood. *S.E.*, 9. London: Hogarth Press, 1950/1974.

Gabbard, G., & Lester, E. (1995). *Boundaries and Boundary Violations in Psychoanalysis*. New York: Basic Books.

Hinshelwood, R. (1989). *A Dictionary of Kleinian Thought*. London: Free Association Books.

Jung, C. G. (1916). *VII Sermones ad Mortuos*. London: Watkins, 1967.

Kalsched, D. E. (1996). *The Inner World of Trauma*. London: Routledge.

Klein, M. (1935). A contribution to the psychogenesis of manic-depressive states. In: R. Money-Kyrle, B. Joseph, E. O'Shaughnessy & H. Segal (Eds.), *The Writings of Melanie Klein, Volume 1*. London: Hogarth Press, 1975.

Klein, M. (1946). Notes on some schizoid mechanisms. In: R. Money-Kyrle, B. Joseph, E. O'Shaughnessy & H. Segal (Eds.), *The Writings of Melanie Klein, Volume 1*. London: Hogarth Press, 1975.

Rose, J. (2000). Symbols and their function in managing the anxiety of change: an intersubjective approach. *International Journal of Psychoanalysis, 81*(3): 453–470.

Samuels, A. (1989). *The Plural Psyche*. London: Routledge.

Solomon, H. M. (1994). The transcendent function and Hegel's dialectical vision. *Journal of Analytical Psychology, 39*(1). Also in: M. Mattoon (Ed.), *Collected Papers from the 1992 IAAP Congress, The Transcendent Function*. Chicago.

Solomon, H. M. (1997). The not-so-silent couple in the individual. *Journal of Analytical Psychology, 42*(3). Also in *Bulletin of the Society of Psychoanalytic Marital Psychotherapists*, 1994, Bulletin 1, Inaugural Issue.

Solomon, H. M. (2000a). Recent developments in the neurosciences. In: E. Christopher & H. M. Solomon (Eds.), *Jungian Thought in the Modern World*. London: Free Association Books.

Solomon, H. M. (2000b). The ethical self. In: E. Christopher & H. M. Solomon (Eds.), *Jungian Thought in the Modern World*. London: Free Association Books.

Solomon, H. M. (in press). The ethical attitude: a bridge between psychoanalysis and analytical psychology. In: H. M. Solomon & M. Twyman (Ed.), *The Ethical Attitude in Analytic Practice*. London: Free Association Books.

CHAPTER SIXTEEN

Reflections on the process of seeking to obtain permission to publish clinical material

Elphis Christopher

Introduction

T his chapter will examine issues to do with the use of clinical material, the process of seeking to obtain permission to publish clinical material and the current thinking about and exploration of ethical concerns and dilemmas in relation to this process. It will be illustrated by what happened to the analyst with a particular patient and how and why the decision was taken not to publish clinical material.

Historical overview of the use of clinical material

Freud thought that analytic work could best be advanced by the use of clinical material. This is no simple or easy issue as Freud was well aware. The Hippocratic oath states that "all that may come to my knowledge in the exercise of my profession which ought not to be spread abroad, I will keep secret and never reveal". "The analytic relationship depends on the trust of both partners towards each other. An aspect of this inherent trust is the privacy which the patient expects the analyst to uphold with regard to what he reveals of himself" (Wharton, 1998). For analysis to work the setting must be protected and boundaries preserved. Jung (C.W., 12, para. 219) used the alchemical metaphor of the *vas bene clausum* to express the idea of the privacy of the analytic container to prevent leakage from within and intrusion from without. Thus, the use of clinical material goes to the very heart of clinical work and challenges it on many different levels each requiring serious thought and profound ethical considerations. "From the beginning, psychoanalysts have been plagued by conflicting needs: to protect patients' rights to absolute confidentiality and to serve research and teaching requirements by substantiating ideas with clinical data" (Lipton, 1991). Freud (1905) realizing the importance of case material wrote in his preface to the Dora case that his "Studies in Hysteria" lacked the data that other investigators could test. Stating the problem, he acknowledged that "whereas before I was accused of giving no information about my patients, now I shall be accused of giving information ... which ought not to be given". Later on in the preface, he asserted that asking patients "for leave to publish their case would be quite unavailing". Nevertheless, "the physician has taken upon himself duties not only towards the individual patient, but towards science as well as his duties towards the many other patients who are suffering from the same disorder ... it becomes a disgraceful piece of cowardice on his part to neglect doing so as long as he can avoid *causing direct personal injury to the single patient concerned*" (my italics). Almost a century later, Goldberg (1997) takes to task those clinicians who never write or present any patient material out of concern for breaching a patients' privacy and confidentiality and yet utilize others' presentations of case histories without seeing this as a breach of their own ethical stance.

Freud gave his patients different names, disguised their histories and revealed few external details. He thereby hoped that his precautions would guarantee secrecy. That it did not, would suggest caution in the light of recommendations given in the latest editorial of the International Journal of Psychoanalysis (Tuckett, 2001). This will be expanded upon later. Freud took the further precaution of writing about Dora four years after her treatment ended. However, Dora eventually found out about the publication and was reported by her subsequent analyst to be proud of the fact

(Deutsch, 1957). In recent years, a body of literature has grown up that has identified Freud and Jung's patients and traced what happened to them post analysis (Appighanesi & Forrester, 1992; Carotenuto, 1984; Kerr, 1993; Mahony, 1986, 1996; Obholzer, 1982; Roazen, 1995).

While possibly exciting prurient interest bordering on the voyeuristic, it remains true that case histories of real people rather than fictionalized or composite patients are fascinating and informative. As Freud noted, the case histories he wrote read like short stories (Freud, 1895). For the professional person working in the field such material furthers and enriches training and forms the ground on which theory building can happen. It is also important as evidence of clinical competence.

Also enriching this body of literature has been the number of accounts written by patients themselves, not all of them compli- mentary (Bancroft, 1983; Cardinal, 1984; Dinnage, 1988; Hilda Doolittle, 1985; Knight, 1950; Wortis 1954). Yet other patients have described being abused emotionally and sexually by their therapists (Rutter, 1990). Some analysts, for example, Stoller (1988) have involved their patients in what is to be written about them and have found this not only ethically indicated, but also actually beneficial for their treatment. Patients have also written together with their analysts (Barnes & Berke, 1991; Herman, 1999). Analysts such as Fordham (1993), Guntrip (1975), Herman (1985) and Little (1990) have written about their own analyses.

Contemporary views on the use of clinical material

The ethical issues of whether or not to obtain consent to publish clinical material, how and at what stage this consent should be obtained (before, during or after therapy has ended), whether the consent should be verbal or written, whether, indeed, informed consent is ever really possible given unresolved transference/ countertransference concerns, whether or not the patient should be disguised and to what extent, and how far the patient should be involved in the process (e.g. reading the material, contributing to it) are all issues currently at the forefront of psychotherapeutic thinking. There are both professional and societal imperatives for this. There is a greater emphasis on openness and accountability. In an environment of proliferating therapeutic methods, there is a need to explain and justify publicly a treatment which is so expensive in terms of both time and money (Wharton, 1998). Patients' rights to privacy and confidentiality have to be considered together with the requirements of continuing professional development and proofs of clinical competence and effectiveness.

It is important to unpack and explore these issues separately, as this will serve to illustrate why the use of clinical material, however beneficial professionally, scientifically and for society, cannot be a straightforward matter. Firstly, regarding the question of whether or not to obtain consent: it could be argued that it might be less damaging to the patient and to the relationship with the therapist not to be asked for permission. However, this leaves the possibility that should the patient discover that he/she has been written about, the damage will be even greater. Wharton (1998) tells of a patient who had been written about unknowingly, and when she discovered this, how she felt that her material had been stolen from her and used in ways which she did not recognize as belonging to her. Stoller (1988) writes of one of his patients still in analysis with him chancing on a paragraph he published about her. He invited her to write about it years after ending analysis. It is salutary to quote something of what she says as these are probably not uncommon reactions.

> Here I was being written about without knowledge of the fact ... I was stunned ... My feelings ranged from horror to outrage, from narcissistic pleasure to indignation. I felt used. How could you know that by not informing, or warning me that you were transgressing that sacred boundary, the infinite trust I placed in you. Why did it matter so?

Stoller does not relate how he responded to this. Philip Roth (1974) in his semi-autobiographical novel, *My Life as a Man* describes the rage his hero felt with his analyst publishing material about him without asking his permission, even though his identity was completely disguised.

That this hurt and sense of betrayal can occur in professional analytic circles is given in an example by Wallerstein (1981), where a supervising analyst kept a record of his interviews without his supervisee's knowledge. The first the supervisee heard about this was when he received galleys describing the report. The issue of obtaining permission begs the question in whose interests consciously and unconsciously is the clinical material being used. Michels (2000) lists and amplifies the purposes of the case history: learning, certification, teaching, research and scientific rhetoric. He, like Goldberg (1997), disapproves of analysts who have no analytic interests other than the analysis of their analysands. "They are practitioners, but not professionals since they fail to contribute to their colleagues or to future patients".

However, there are also narcissistic rewards in publishing for both the therapist and the patient. The therapist understandably wishes for the approval of colleagues and the patient wants to be thought of as special. Wharton (1998) draws attention to the fact that this sense of specialness can be tempered by the discovery that they are not the only ones to be written about in the paper. Some patients who have not been written about may be envious towards the "favoured one". Thus, painful sibling rivalries can be evoked. What of the effect on the analyst's practise if he/she publishes case material? Prospective patients may be discouraged by the thought of exposure (Casement, 1985). Alternatively, prospective patients might be encouraged by the possibility of being thought about carefully and sensitively in the way that is demonstrated in a good clinical account (Wharton, 1998).

It is significant *how* a patient experiences the request for permission to publish their clinical material. The patient may experience the request as a demand from a parent that cannot be refused or that the therapist will be hurt or angry if they decline. Alternatively, the request may play into omnipotent feelings of the patient in that they are thereby given the power to give or withhold permission. Gabbard (2000) questions how one takes into account the patients ambivalence in such situations. He further asks whether it is not a basic premise of psychoanalytic work that the analyst must maintain a degree of scepticism about the face value of any communication from the patient? It is, he states, inherent in analytic work that we are always wondering about multiple meanings, unconscious conflicts and a defensive use of transference feelings. Gabbard also states that the analyst's unresolved aggression towards the patient might be a significant unconscious factor in his/her motivation to write about the patient. Wharton (1998) describes her experience of seeking the consent of patients for publication while they are still in analysis. She says that it certainly created a disturbance and initially aroused justifiable anger. For some patients, the interference had particularly troubling personal meanings, echoing past abusive relationships in which the good of the child had in some way been subordinated to that of the caretaker. But, she goes on to say the working through of such situations has invariably resulted in benefits to the patient in terms of greater insight, increased freedom of emotional expression, and an enrichment of the analytic relationship.

The timing of the request has important clinical implications. The view that once a patient always a patient makes a case for the potentially problematic result of asking permission at any time. Lipton (1991) explores this issue at length. From a legal point of view, permission is best granted *before* the analysis proper begins. However, this might affect the analysis in unpredictable ways because of disturbances in trust. The patient might tend to withhold significant material, at least, early in the analysis. A request *during* treatment puts a strain on the transference relationship and requires the analyst to exercise judgement about whether a patient can sustain it. The patient is wrenched out of his natural transference and is called upon to relate on more equal terms. While there may be considerable gain to the patient, it can also be experienced as a profound loss akin to the loss of infantile dependence or the loss of innocence (Wharton, 1998).

The effect on the analyst requesting permission during treatment needs consideration. His/her preoccupation with a particular theme may lead to the neglect of others. It may also lead the analyst to concentrate his/her attention on one patient and possibly thereby neglect others. Asking *after* the termination of treatment can affect the patient in ways requiring further analysis, but the opportunity for this may be limited. Indeed, the request may recreate a problem the patient always had and interrupt the post-analytic healing of the problem which may take years.

Informed consent is the gold standard in clinical publishing. However, is it ever possible, given the nature of the analytic relationship with the unresolved or resurrected transference/ countertransference issues and the power imbalance already referred to? Goldberg (1997) states that it is difficult to determine just what informed consent consists of, in as much as one can never fully determine the consequences of such a request. Wharton (1998) suggests formulating "informed consent" in the analytic context as consent issuing from a thorough discussion and analysis of the patients' feelings and fantasies in relation to both the request and to the proposed publication itself.

Should the patient be disguised and if so, how far? In Philip Roth's novel already alluded to there is an amusing (but also hurt) account of how the analyst disguised his patient. He was turned from a young, late twenties, Jewish–American writer into a late middle-aged Italian–American poet, leading the patient to say to his analyst "How can you, who have done me so much good, have it all so wrong?" (Roth, 1974). For Wharton (1998) disguising case material has several drawbacks. To disguise other than superficial details might distort relevant dynamic factors. In addition, if the intention were to disguise the patient from himself, the questions of whether that would be feasible and whether it would be ethically justifiable would have to be faced.

To what extent should the patient be involved in presenting or determining the clinical material? Should the patient be given the material to read? Should this be in draft form and worked on together with the analyst or only given when the account is complete?

Wharton (1998) gives the patient the opportunity of commenting on and *possibly* (my italics) amending the material—and amendments have sometimes been worked out in discussion and incorporated. Wharton (1998) stresses that she wants the patient to know that it is *their* story that is being told and not to feel that she has stolen from them in any external, non-transference sense. Stoller (1988), who also involves his patients in what is to be written and published, also states that if his version does not agree with his patient's, he does not think that the two of them must publish a communiqué on their deliberations. He claims the right to his opinion, but believes that psychoanalysis should develop a new rhetoric in which patients' positions are visible. This, he writes, would enable a more rigorous and more readable, less jargon-soaked argument.

Both Stoller (1988) and Wharton (1998) consider that publishing clinical material with the patient's consent can foster a feeling in the patient of helping future generations of patients. On the other hand, Wharton (1998) also refers to the shadow side of writing about patients with their knowledge, that is the risk of arousing the unconscious envy in the patient, which can undermine subsequent analytic work. This might be an envy of the analyst's ability to write and thereby, to demonstrate a better understanding of the patient than the patient has of himself. It might also be an envy of the joint enterprise itself and may then be seen as a manifestation of a particular malignant form of envy described as envy of one's self (Proner, 1986). To have one's analyst become one's biographer must acquire a significance difficult to define over the long term (Stein, 1986).

In the medical field, the International Committee of Medical Journal Editors (ICMJE) has recently (1995) issued a statement that makes two very definite points regarding the use of clinical material. First, the Editors declare that it is necessary that in all cases where patients' clinical records are disclosed in any way, there should be *no* attempt to disguise or misrepresent details. Second, they state that the patient's informed consent should be obtained prior to inclusion in any study or case report in which the patient could possibly be identified and this fact should be published. The ICMJE declared that patients have a right to privacy that should not be infringed without informed consent. "Informed consent … requires that the patient be shown the manuscript to be published, identifying details should be omitted if they are not essential, but patient data should never be altered or falsified in an attempt to attain anonymity". This statement has led to a lively correspondence in both medical and psychoanalytic journals. A strongly worded letter in the British Medical Journal from the Department of Psychiatry of the Free University of Berlin (Vollman & Helmchen, 1996) stated that while gaining informed consent is an integral part of good medical care, the writers believe that showing case material to psychiatric and psychotherapy patients can be a risk to the patient's mental health. Such patients may not be able to tolerate the information required for them to be able to give valid informed consent for publication and that this makes it unethical to confront them with a scientific manuscript about their case.

The International Journal of Psychoanalysis carried an editorial

(Tuckett, 2000) that explored the issues relating to confidentiality, disguise and consent relating to analytic patients and written clinical material. Concern was expressed that adopting the ICMJE's recommendations might cause "the already too limited willingness to publish clinical material to dry up completely" (Tuckett, 2000, p. 1067). Reference has been made in the introductory chapter of this volume to the opposing forces at work in publishing clinical material: the need for trust and for the patient to be assured that what he/she says will not be used in such a way as to cause embarrassment, give offence or in any way have consequences for him/her outside the session versus the need for a transparently accountable discipline to encourage peer review publication and establish best practise. Gabbard (2000) thoroughly tackles the analyst's dilemmas regarding writing and presenting clinical data and states that "the patient's right to privacy, the profession's requirement to publish advances and new knowledge in the field and the analyst's need for recognition *are inevitably in conflict*" (p. 1083).

Gabbard & Williams (2001), currently the new Joint Editors in Chief of the International Journal of Psychoanalysis, in their editorial "Preserving Confidentiality in the Writing of Case Reports" write that they have developed a more flexible strategy that they believe is more protective of the patient's privacy—a special concern in psychoanalytic writings that is ignored by the ICMJE statement. Authors may choose to disguise superficial details of the patients' external life, so that the patient is essentially unrecognizable to a reader. Some analysts may ask for written consent from the patient in addition to disguise. When analysts choose to use thick disguise or distortion in order to avoid asking for consent from the patient, they must thoughtfully consider the consequences to the field. If the patient's consent is sought (as an addition to disguise), the impact of asking the patient's consent must be rigorously analysed. In all cases of consent, the author should be prepared to revise portions of the manuscript to which the patient objects (though nowhere in the editorial is it suggested that the manuscript is actually to be given to the patient to read and comment upon). They also state that written consent is preferred to verbal agreement. Thus, there does seem to be developing a view that there is and has to be a difference in seeking consent and writing about clinical material from a psychological as opposed to a medical perspective.

Other psychotherapeutic journals, such as the Journal of the British Association of Psychotherapists and The Journal of Analytical Psychology require their authors to ensure that publication does not involve any breach of confidentiality or professional ethics in a written statement.

Seeking permission to publish clinical material

It was bearing much of the above in mind that I sought permission from a patient to write about our clinical work together. I did this *before* I began writing. I also told the patient that I would share what I had written and would change anything that was found to be unacceptable. Times were arranged for discussions. No fees were charged for those sessions. The patient was also invited to contribute to the account.

Why did I attempt to seek permission at this time from this particular patient? Michels (2000) comments in his paper that he finds it more enlightening to have analysts tell as best they can *why* they want to tell us anything at all and then to weave an account of those intentions into their account of an analysis. After the publication of a largely theoretical book on Jung (Christopher & McFarland Solomon, 2000), we considered following it with an edited book on largely clinical work. My conscious choice of this particular patient was partly because the therapy had ended and a severe unconsciously-caused crisis that could have endangered life had been survived that we had worked on psychologically together. There was a feeling of pride in what had been achieved. Therapy had lasted many years and there was a wish to convey that deep psychological change can take that length of time and why that is so. I also wanted to convey something of the year on year work with long term intensive three-times-a-week therapy with the revisiting of unconscious conflicts and dilemmas from slightly different perspectives. This would hopefully demonstrate the spiralling upward process of therapy rather than its linear progression, although in actual clinical work it could be experienced as a static state with a repetition of situations that appeared to undo any progress.

As I went through the patient's notes and wrote the account of the therapy, I was unprepared for the powerful feelings that were stirred up in me. It was as if I was back with the patient again experiencing the pain and confusion we both felt at times. Through these experiences, the patient unconsciously let me know about the turmoil raging within. Inevitably, this re-experiencing coloured my writing which made the account too raw and immediate. Perhaps, unwisely with hindsight, I gave the patient this first draft to read. Not surprisingly, the impact was profound stirring up a mixture of feelings: pride in being special, dismay in learning what I had been through, and anger. The account was demolished almost line by line. I had got everything wrong.

It was difficult to hold onto any of the positive aspects of the work done, the suffering that we had both gone through together and separately. I felt in despair. I had to face the possibility that I had, indeed, wanted somehow to punish the patient for what I had been through. I had a dream around that time, the most terrifying that I have ever had, I dreamt that I had lost my mind and did not know who I was. I think that the patient and I were caught in a kind of madness. I thought deeply about the dream. My counter-transference must reflect the deeply disturbed state of the patient's mind. I wrote expressing my concern that it might appear that I did not appreciate how distressing it was reading the account. Although, there were aspects that were difficult and painful, there was also the deep suffering that we had worked on together to reach an understanding on what was going on inside to prevent life being happier and more fulfilled. I said that I would be disappointed if nothing came of it. (In retrospect, this might have been experienced by the patient as putting on pressure to publish.) I went on to say that perhaps we could try to salvage something and that sections could be omitted. The patient phoned in response saying that there was nothing wrong in the theoretical considerations of the account. We agreed to continue to work on the account. I wrote two further drafts, modified at the patient's request. The third draft focusing on the patient's dreams was found to be acceptable.

Nevertheless, I began to doubt my own motives. Was I writing for my own aggrandisement with a wish to impress colleagues and obtain reflected self-glory at the expense of my patient? In deciding to give a lengthy account of the actual therapy rather than focusing primarily on theoretical concerns or vignettes, I was taking a risk of it being rejected. I was also taking a risk in showing the whole of it to the patient with the possible consequence of the patient being retraumatized (which is what happened) and with the patient having to cope, not only with the therapist's version of what went on in the therapy, but also, learning what the therapist had experienced in the therapy.

I was often reminded, while we were working on the drafts of Freud's case histories especially that of Dora described by Appighanesi & Forrester (1992) as "an exemplary failure". Dora despite being pleased that she had been written about, could well have had her own version of what had happened between her and Freud, and how Freud (mis)understood what was going on between Dora, her parents and the "K" couple. Aware that there is the patient's version of therapy as well as the therapist's, I had very much wanted a contribution from the patient and for that reason, I had made the suggestion to the patient. Stoller (1998) draws attention to the fact that there can be no one version of the analysis, whether that of the patient or the analyst. What is the "truth" of what happens in analytic work? Ricoeur (1977) describes the nature of truth as it can appropriately be applied to the analytic experience, as a "saying true" which is to do with "reorganising the facts of the person's life into a meaningful whole, which constitutes a single and continuous history". Facts in psychoanalysis are in no way facts of observable behaviour, they are "reports". Even a dream recounted by a patient is a report of a dream not the dream itself. Thus, the historical truth of a person's life cannot be established through analysis. But in so far as the story created by the patient and analyst is "persuasive and compelling" to those who have made it, it has the characteristics of "narrative truth" (Spence, 1982). The purpose of analytic work is to endeavour to understand and enable the patient to understand his/her psychic reality, that is their inner world. This can free the patient to realize their potential and live more fulfilling and meaningful lives. To undertake this successfully requires close attention to the transference and countertransference thoughts and feelings. It was Freud's genius in the "Dora" case to discover the importance and significance of the "transference" that is the "transferring" onto the person of the analyst aspects of other emotionally important people from the patient's past or present.

However, to focus only onto the transference in creating a case history risks "positioning the therapist as hero or heroine ... overcoming obstacles on the way to a preordained resolution of the story" (Spence, 1997). Although Freud had described counter-transference, that is the analyst's response to the patient's material, he thought it was an impediment to analytic work that required further analysis for the therapist. It was Jung (*C.W., 16*, paras. 364–367) who saw its significance for understanding the patient's inner world. Furthermore, Jung (*C.W., 16*, para. 163) maintained that "the doctor could have no influence unless he was influenced". Hence, the intersubjectivity of the analytic process—the therapist is in the analytic work as much as the patient. This certainly happened with my patient and me both during the therapy and again during the lengthy process of writing, visiting, rewriting and revisiting the clinical material.

In the event, it was decided not to publish the account of the therapy. The patient was extremely relieved when told about this. It became increasingly evident over the year that we have talked about the drafts and discussed the therapy that the patient has experienced deep conflictual feelings about publication. I have had to accept and respect this. It has been painful to do this, requiring much hard psychological work to deal with my conflict between the wish to publish and the need to protect my patient. Jung (*C.W., 16*, para. 364) writes that "the doctor by voluntarily and consciously taking over the psychic sufferings of the patient exposes himself to the overpowering contents of the unconscious and hence, to their inductive action". Further, "each new case that requires thorough treatment is pioneer work and every trace of routine then proves to be a blind alley".

Initially, when I sought permission from the patient, I thought that since the material I had wanted to use had been well worked over that this would be relatively straightforward. However, it proved otherwise requiring further analytic work with the patient and psychological work on myself. The old work was revisited, but new work, new psychic suffering had to be undertaken. It was also pioneer work. During this process, I had doubts about the truth of the analysis, and the clinical account. Did I slant it so that I appeared in a better light? Was there a "narrative smoothing" to make an acceptable story? (Spence, 1997). I had to relinquish the accounts and the labour I had undertaken and respect the vulnerability and privacy of my patient or risk the destruction of what had been achieved, shattering the relationship between the patient and myself. Two further dreams seemed to warn me of the consequences to both the patient and myself if I did pursue the wish to publish the clinical account.

> I am going to a psychological meeting. I park my car in my usual parking place in a nearby road. When I return to my car. I am dismayed to discover all the cars including mine have been severely vandalized. No one has seen anything.

> In the second dream, I am driving my car. It is raining, I drive round a corner and there is a family crossing the road. I hit a member of it. It is accidental, but I will be held accountable.

I believe that if the account was published despite the patient's acceptance, it would prove very damaging. It might be questioned whether asking the patient's permission to publish in the light of what has been written in this chapter was worth the struggle and pain involved.

Paradoxically, perhaps, I think that for this patient the answer is an affirmative one. It provided a unique and privileged opportunity to reflect on our relationship (the patient's and mine) and to examine the therapy subjectively and objectively together. That we differed at times in our views on what happened in the therapy and why, and our understanding of it, and that it generated a re-enactment of the complex relationship between us was perhaps inevitable. Inevitable also was the awareness of what was not achieved and understood in the therapy and my limitations as a therapist.

What lessons can be learnt from this experience?

I think that it is important to seek the patient's permission and also to show the patient what has been written. It is after all the patient's story. We need to ask ourselves as therapists, how we would feel if our analysts wrote about us. There may have to develop new ways of obtaining this permission. Wharton (2002) suggests that a means is sought of developing a culture is which the publication of analytical material will, with due safeguards, be accepted as part of the analytic frame.

There are several risks that have to be faced. There is the risk that the patient might refuse or be compliant and agree to publication for the wrong reasons (to please the therapist, fear of making the therapist angry). Care needs to be taken with the timing of the request, assessing and working with how the request is received, Michels (2000) comments that the "low incidence of refusals to the analysts who seek permission to write case histories gives one pause. The best evidence for true autonomy would be that sometimes our patients refuse consent". The therapist has to be prepared to cope with the patient's anger and to continue with the analytic process. It cannot be assumed that the work on publication can be dispassionate or objectified. There is too much at stake for the patient. There is always the risk that the request will reactivate past conflicts, dilemmas and struggles and may have future consequences. Each patient's response will be in accordance with that patient's psychology. Lipton (1991) describes what happened when he asked a patient's permission to publish. His patient was accustomed to keeping his rage out of sight. He had a mother who would beat him when he displayed anger and he held onto a lifelong fantasy that his father loved him deeply and would one day rescue him from his mother. As a result of reading Lipton's account, he became covertly angry, criticizing Lipton as a poor writer and the ensuing months were marked by very frequent requests and demands for special considerations. The request of seeking permission, Lipton observed, had the unexpected effect of recreating the problem he always had with his parents. Lipton with admirable honesty acknowledges that his wish to present a paper was greater than he realized and that his own needs interfered with the neutral analytic stance he thought he was maintaining. I think that this happened between me and my patient.

There is a real danger that the therapeutic progress could be halted or destroyed. The therapist has to face their own limitations and mistakes and also cope with their own narcissistic injury if the patient refuses consent and to take care not to exercise talion law, but maintain an agapaic attitude (Lambert, 1981).

Britton (1995) states that securing consent does not relieve the author of a sense of guilt and being left with a feeling of betraying an affiliation.

The positive aspects can be that (although this was not the intention in this case), the analytic work is tested by this process of revisiting. With my patient, it showed its solidity and worth despite the enmeshment and re-enacting of past difficult situations. Indeed, it provided rich opportunities to re-work on past material and gain fresh insights and consolidate the therapy.

This experience also illustrates how important and how difficult it is to maintain an ethical stance in an analytic one, and the danger that both can be lost if the patient's needs are not seen as paramount and overriding. I needed to return to what Wiener (2001) has described as "the sanctum, that inner private place of feelings, of intuitions and of thoughts—the centre of the self—to search for subjective knowledge to foster an ethical space for reflection that facilitates ethical behaviour". Lipton (1991) reflected that in scanning the (analytic) literature, he found numerous references to the subject of confidentiality, but nothing on the vicissitudes of asking patients for permission to publish or otherwise use data having their source in the patient's clinical material. Hopefully, this account will make a contribution and stimulate further thinking in this area.

Finally, clinical writing is not just about narcissistic gratification of the author seeing themselves in print applauded by colleagues. There is real need if the profession is to develop and deepen, for clinicians to risk the travail of writing about their work with their patients if the profession is to remain alive. Indeed, if there is an ethical responsibility towards patients in seeking permission to publish their clinical material, there is an equal ethical responsibility towards the profession to ensure the ongoing examination of analytic work and theory building through writing and publication.

References

Appighanesi, L., & Forrester, J. (1992). *Freud's Women*. London: Weidenfeld & Nicolson Ltd.

Bancroft, M. (1983). *Autobiography of a Spy*. New York: William Morrow & Coln.

Barnes, M., & Berke, J. (1991). *Mary Barnes Two Accounts of a Journey Through Madness*. London: Free Association Books.

Britton, R. (1995). Making the private public. In: I. Ward (Ed.), *The Prevention of Case Material in Clinical Discourse*. London: Freud Museum.

Cardinal, M. (1984). *The Words to Say It*. London: Picador.

Carotenuto, A. (1984). *A Secret Symmetry*. London: Routledge and Kegan Paul.

Casement, P. (1985). *On Learning from the Patient*. London: Tavistock Publications.

Christopher, E., & McFarland Solomon, H. (2000). *Jungian Thought in The Modern World*. London: Free Association Press.

Deutsch, F. (1957). A footnote to Freud's "Fragment of an analysis of a case of hysteria". *Psychoanalytic Quarterly, 26*: 159–167.

Dinnage, R. (1988). *One to One: Experiences of Psychotherapy*. London: Viking.

Fordham, M. (1993). *The Making of an Analyst*. London: Free Association Books.

Freud, S. (1905). *A Fragment of the Analysis of a Case of Hysteria. S.E., 7*.

Freud, S. (1895). *Studies on Hysteria. S.E., 2*.

Gabbard, G. (2000). Disguise or consent. *The International Journal of Psychoanalysis, 81*: 1071–1085.

Gabbard, G., & Williams, P. (2001). Preserving confidentiality in the writing of case reports [Editorial]. *The International Journal of Psychoanalysis, 82*: 1067–1068.

Goldberg, A. (1997). Writing case histories. *The International Journal of Psychoanalysis, 78*: 435–438.

Guntrip, H. (1975). My experience of analysis with Fairburn and Winnicott. *International Review of Psycho-Analysis, 2*: 145–156.

Herman, N. (1985). *My Kleinian Home*. London: Quartet Books.

Herman, N. (1999). *Sister Mary: A Story of a Healing Relationship*. London: Whurr Publishers Ltd.

Hilda Doolittle (1985). *Tribute to Freud*. London: Carcanet.

International Committee of Medical Journal Editors. (1995). *British Medical Journal, 311*: 1272.

Kerr, J. (1993). *A Most Dangerous Method: The Story of Jung, Freud and Sabina Spielrein*. New York: Alfred A. Knopf.

Knight, J. (1950). *The Story of My Psychoanalysis*. New York: McGraw Hill.

Lambert, K. (1981). *Analysis, Repair and Individuation*. London: Academic Press.

Lipton, E. L. (1991). The analyst's use of clinical data and other issues of confidentiality. *Journal of American Psychoanalytical Association, 39*: 967–985.

Little, M. (1990). *Psychotic Anxieties and Containment: A Personal Record of an Analysis with Winnicott*. North Vale, New Jersey: Jason Aronson.

Mahony, P. J. (1986). *Freud and the Rat Man*. New Haven Connecticut: Yale University Press.

Mahony, P. J. (1996). *Freud's Dora: A Psychoanalytic, Historical and Textual Study*. New Haven Connecticut: Yale University Press.

Michels, R. (2000). The case history. *Journal of the American Psychoanalytic Association, 48*, 355–375.

Obholzer, K. (1982). *The Wolf-Man Sixty Years Later*. New York: Continuum.

Proner, B. (1986). Defences of the self and envy of oneself. *Journal of Analytical Psychology, 31*(3): 143–160.

Ricoeur, P. (1977). The question of proof in Freud's psychoanalytic writings. *Journal of the American Psychoanalytic Association, 25*: 835–871.

Roazen, J. (1995). *How Freud Worked: First Hand Accounts of Patients*. Northvale New Jersey: Jason Aronson.

Roth, P. (1974). *My Life as a Man*. New York: Holt, Rinehart & Winston.

Rutter, P. (1990). *Sex in the Forbidden Zone*. London: Unwin Hyman Paperbacks.

Spence, D. (1982). Narrative truth and theoretical truth. *Psychoanalytic Quarterly, 51*: 43–69.

Spence, D. (1997). Case reports and the reality they represent: the many faces of nachträglichkeit. In: I. Ward (Ed.), *The Presentation of Case Material in Clinical Discourse*. London: Freud Museum.

Stein, M. H. (1986). Writing about psychoanalysis. *Journal of American Psychoanalytic Association, 36*(1): 105–124.

Stoller, R. J. (1988). Patients' responses to their own case reports. *Journal of the American Psychoanalytic Association, 36*: 371–391.

Tuckett, D. (2000). Reporting clinical events in the Journal [Editorial]. *The International Journal of Psychoanalysis, 81*: 1065–1069.

Vollman, J., & Helmchen, H. (1996). Obtaining consent to publication may be unethical [Correspondence]. *British Medical Journal, 312*: 578.

Wallerstein, R. S. (Ed.) (1981). *Becoming a Psychoanalyst* New York: International University Press.

Wharton, B. (1998). What comes out of the consulting room. *The Journal of Analytical Psychology, 43*: 205–223.

Wiener, J. (2001). Confidentiality and paradox: The location of ethical space. *The Journal of Analytical Psychology*, *46*: 431–442.

Wortis, J. (1954). *Fragments of an Analysis with Freud*. New York: Simon & Schuster.

CHAPTER SEVENTEEN

Clinical paradigm as analytic third. Reflections on a century of analysis and an emergent paradigm for the millennium

Birgit Heuer

Introduction

I n a recent informal poll I asked a number of psychotherapist and analyst colleagues for their spontaneous answer to the question: In your work, what do you believe it is that heals? The answers ranged from "I do not know" to "God", "Love", the "Numinous" or the "Self". But, in addition, the reply often was: How can you ask me such a question! Yet I believe the questions we do or do not ask seriously limit the answers we shall get and ultimately the scope and effectiveness of psychotherapy. In this chapter, I shall bring questions to the analytical paradigm, argue for the desirability of a conscious paradigm rather than a host of unconscious assumptions and suggest the need for paradigmatic change.

According to Kuhn's (1962) seminal book, *The Structure of Scientific Revolutions*, every scientific approach is embedded in a paradigm. A paradigm structures and contains the thinking, the type of logic used and the way this logic generates and links ideas. Thus a Freudian, Kleinian or a Jungian paradigm each envisage quite a different patient. Other disciplines have undergone enormous paradigmatic shifts, most notably those brought about by research in quantum physics. But why should any of this be of interest to the clinician, and particularly the Jungian clinician? The most practical answer is: *In order to open up to a greater possibility for change.* This can be illustrated by an example of a historical shift in paradigm: If we still believed the world to be flat, we could never consciously be travelling around it. Thus a different clinical paradigm may enable a different therapeutic journey. In addition, reflecting on the paradigm that underlies clinical practice, might have a distinctive emancipatory function: Like the father *vis-à-vis* the mother–baby dyad, paradigmatic self-reflection represents the excluded third element. When this can be included, the dyad inevitably changes but also becomes enriched, just as clinical practice, in my view, has been enriched by gradually becoming able to value external realities and socio–political concerns (see Samuels, 1993). Paradigmatic self-reflection, when regarded as integral to clinical practice, could fulfil the symbolic father's emancipatory role and fertilize the world of clinical fact.

Another area that is only beginning to make its influence felt clinically is spirituality, although a term like spiritual intelligence is not usually part of clinical discourse, nor is spiritual experience necessarily a clinical value. Here again, clinical paradigmatic reflection might bring substantial changes. This leads us directly to Jung and the paradigmatic implications of his key concepts, such as the Self, which imply a belief in the human capacity to heal. Why, then, should we shy away from such implications clinically, as my informal poll seems to indicate. In another, even more informal poll, several colleagues talked to me in a somewhat confessional tone about the fact that they either pray for their patients generally or pray silently in sessions. The question then arises as to why we should operate within a paradigm that seemingly frowns on this option, even though research shows that prayer may speed up physical healing (Stannard, 1999). To answer such questions, I think we need to understand more about the underlying assumptions and values of clinical practice.

My intentions for this chapter then are: I shall introduce the term paradigm and explain my use of it, I will then try to trace the main areas of change in the clinical paradigm during the past century. The heart of this paper centres on Jung and the clinical implications of his ideas. I will try to show how following Jung through to the clinical level might bring about a paradigmatic shift in the clinical attitude towards change and healing and result in a paradigm which resonates with the changes that might be required of us in the new millennium.

On paradigm

When we sit with a patient, we might attempt an open mind and evenly suspended attention. Yet the clinical situation is, I believe, already governed and structured by the assumptions and values we hold about psychotherapy, its aims and its limitations. These could be tied together in the term clinical paradigm. Paradigm is a term borrowed from epistemology, the "theory of science" and is to do with scientific self-reflection in terms of the basic approach of a discipline. From this follow questions about the type of research-methodology used and the type of logic applied. Used as a critical term, paradigm implies the idea that what is *accepted as factual* and *felt as real* within a scientific discipline is always dependent on assumptions and on value-judgements of a personal, political or social nature. A paradigm thus provides the underlying structure of a scientific discipline and informs the scientific model used, but also determines what is felt to be real and what is thinkable within the approach. To make this conscious, from a philosophical point of view, each science needs to work out its own epistemological base. In analysis, the clinical situation is often implicitly regarded as given directly by experience. This bypasses the epistemological question and may result in limiting clinical scope and efficiency. Clinical practice in this regard stands on feet of clay that need examining and strengthening. Asking the right, i.e. appropriate, questions might provide the key to unlocking and opening up the paradigmatic dimension of the clinical enterprise. One of these questions concerns the historical context: In the past one hundred years, how has analysis changed clinically? Is there a way in which basic assumptions and values have changed? In addressing these questions, I shall look at the contents as well as the structure of the clinical paradigm as it developed and changed during the last century within psychoanalysis.

A century of analysis

The prototypical turn-of-the-century psychoanalyst had no proper training, as we know it. Although often from a medical background, he had no training analysis, no ethics specific to analysis. He saw patients for a relatively short time span and drew no clear boundaries around his family and his private life. Symptomatically, his patients were often hysterics or suffered from dementia. Analysis struggled to be accepted socially and epistemologically attempted to fit into a scientific Newtonian frame. The clinical paradigm employed bivalent, Aristotelian logic, and the idea of progress was linear, i.e. from hysteric to ordinary neurotic. In addition, the clinical paradigm was unilateral, in that it demanded a mirror-like stance of the analyst while positioning the illness within the patient. It was a gendered, male paradigm informed by an underlying belief in authority and Victorian values, even though it was revolutionary in content through its preoccupation with sexuality and the drives. But, most importantly, due to its limiting logic, linearity and unilaterality, the turn of the century paradigm could not provide its clinician with a horizon on health or healing. Eros and Thanathos remained in opposition with Thanathos potentially outweighing Eros. This is illustrated by such ideas as repetition compulsion or the perceived destructive nature of the id. The underlying belief guiding this clinical paradigm is in the ultimate power of human destructiveness. This belief is expressed by clinical ideas, which are linear, non-dialectical and unilateral in structure.

With Klein, the idea of human development changed from the context of instinct and the drives to the mother–infant relationship. Clinically this implies a change in thinking that is akin to the difference between a one-way street and a cluster of avenues on a map. It also indicated a shift from a medical–scientific paradigm, to which instinct theory was allied, to the hermeneutic concerns of interpreting unconscious infantile phantasy. In hermeneutics, context is created through meaning rather than cause-and-effect. A hermeneutic approach thus cannot be contained within a Newtonian universe. Although hermeneutic in her overall approach, clinically speaking, Klein used linear cause-and-effect thinking with infantile destructive phantasy being given the logical status of a primary cause. When Klein's followers began to view countertransference as a clinical tool, this opened the possibility of loosening the unilaterality of the clinical paradigm. Yet the belief in the primacy of human destructiveness still prevailed, now located clinically in the destructive primitive phantasy of the patient. Structurally, the idea of clinical change, i.e. from the paranoid–schizoid to the depressive position, is still linear although the Neo-Kleinian idea of moving back and forth between these positions is more dialectic.

With regard to clinical epistemology, many of the ideas advanced by Jung were of a different and more complex order. With Jung came bilaterality, a multivalent type of logic, and the inherent possibility of quantum change. The fact that Jung is sometimes regarded as a lesser clinician might be largely due to the complex implications of his ideas for the clinical paradigm. I shall explore the clinical Jung in more depth later.

What, then, are the main trends of the clinical paradigm structurally and content-wise during the past century? Heuristically, there is a shift from a medical–scientific to a hermeneutic frame, from the id and the drives to unconscious phantasy. In terms of the therapeutic relationship, the analyst-as-mirror becomes the countertransferentially-related analyst thus moving the paradigm from a unilateral to a bilateral idea. The idea of human development also turns relational. As the clinical paradigm changes in content, so the underlying structure of clinical concepts moves from being relatively static towards being more flexible and complex.

One specific aspect though seems comparatively stable in content and structure: Clinical ideas on the nature and possibilities of change appear to be mostly unaltered throughout the century. Contentwise, this rests on the powerful underlying belief in the primacy and unalterable fixity of human destructiveness and what might be called the clinical "culture of blame" (see Covington, 2001) engendered by it. This clinical belief could also be said to express a deep cultural pessimism. Given that it arose in a century that saw two world wars, this is quite understandable. Yet it might be asked whether we need to stay with the remnants of these wars as they subtly inform the depth-beliefs of our clinical paradigm. Once we are aware of such influences, might we then be inspired to extend the range of what has been thinkable clinically? In the new millennium might we endeavour to balance clinical pessimism with clinical optimism or hope? Posing this question does not imply that, as individual analysts, we are unable to feel hopeful for our patients or feel their hope for them when they are married to despair. Rather, it addresses, in a more generalized fashion, a lack of clinical concepts, clinical values, and clinical language, which specifically express ideas of hope and change. The intention here is to indicate a trend rather than making an exclusive statement.

In his inaugural speech, Nelson Mandela said that it is not our darkness we fear most but our light. Clinically, we have had a century of facing up to darkness but also believing in its ultimate power. I wonder what a clinical paradigm might be like that, symbolically speaking, moved from darkness into light, without losing awareness of darkness. Might this be a paradigm that valued spiritual experience and learning, as we presently value emotional–relational learning in the consulting room? Would health, healing, prayer then become more thinkable? In order to travel around the world, we need to conceive of it as three-dimensional or be inspired by our travels to come to a similar conclusion. In order to create a clinical perspective on change and healing, we need to re-examine depth-beliefs regarding human nature, and come up with clinical concepts, that are four- or five-dimensional in structure. Our heuristic frame may have to shift again. As mentioned above, the clinical implications of Jung's ideas are epistemologically of a different order and require a more complex clinical paradigm. In other words, the clinical paradigm of the last century, even with the shifts which occurred, could not adequately contain the clinical implications of Jung's thinking, as they do not fit into a Newtonian universe nor can their mystical aspect be fully contained by hermeneutics. This is pertinent for the split clinical identity many of us feel we grew up with in our training. On the one hand we were raised on Jungian thought, yet clinically we had to "borrow" from Freud and Klein. While this has fostered a clinical pluralism and the capacity to integrate, I think it is also due to a paradigm more firmly informed by the zeitgeist of the first half of the last century than is generally acknowledged. It might then be extremely timely, to explore the clinical Jung. Followed through on a clinical level, his thinking might prove instrumental in bringing our paradigm more fully into the millennium.

The clinical Jung

Jung met Einstein and kept in regular contact with the physicist Wolfgang Pauli with whom he discussed the new physics and exchanged many letters (see Meier, 2001). In quantum physics Jung eventually found the epistemological foundation for most of his ideas. The concept of synchronicity is directly acknowledged to have been sparked off by Einstein's relativity theory, while other, and earlier ideas simply found a home, as their rationality is congruent with the tenets of quantum physics. In fact, all of Jung's thinking seems much more compatible heuristically with quantum physics than with any of the other major analytical approaches of the last century. In considering Jung a clinician manqué, have we simply not yet translated the implication of his thinking clinically because, culturally, we have not yet made real a quantum universe? I shall therefore select a few of Jung's key concepts and follow them through to the level of clinical paradigm and its implications.

Jung's psychology is teleological, as Jung assumes an unconscious inbuilt motivation towards an equally unconscious goal. Clinically speaking, this implies an "orientation towards ends and purposes rather then causes" (Samuels *et al.*, 1986, p. 148). It also implies a belief in the *inevitability of change*. But is this just a blind optimism that Jung took a fancy to, or a more substantial matter? As we have seen, clinical ideas of change in Freud or Klein are oriented towards causes and range from being two- to three-dimensional. The current clinical idea of change represented by a spiral, i.e. visiting and revisiting suffering from a different, increasingly evolved vantage point, is equally three-dimensional. With quantum theory, physics gained a fourth dimension and the possibility of more so-called hyperdimensions. Psychologically, the idea of a fourth dimension is very clearly expressed by Jung's concept of synchronicity. What is possible in the fourth dimension? Materiality becomes energy, in that particles behave like waves, non-locality exists, the part contains the whole, antimatter exists, parts remain connected behaviorally no matter where they are, and logic becomes non-binary, that is acausal and non-linear. In the fourth dimension, the Buddha's logic, creating a reality that is simultaneously full and empty, real and unreal, applies. In addition, change that happens in the fourth dimension is not directly measurable in the other three but has to be inferred.

Clinically speaking, if linearity and causality no longer determine the "four-dimensional" patient's development, then the idea of compulsion does not hold in the usual way. Compulsion, as we know it, depends on the notion of linearity and causality, because it is not thinkable otherwise. Concepts that are clinically linked to compulsion, such as repetition compulsion, the return of the repressed, perversion, encapsulated narcissistic states or Meltzer's claustrum, are then no longer clinical absoluta. They do not exist in the same way outside a three-dimensional clinical world. In a four-dimensional paradigm, their perceived clinical intractability becomes something much more relative and fluid and thus becomes accessible to change. Jung's teleological view comes into its own in the quantum dimension because, where linearity and causality are transcended clinically, fluidity and change come into view more clearly. What kind of change, though? Cure, the hoped for outcome, is a linear concept, taking the patient from a to b. Healing, on the other hand, is non-linear and acausal. Jung expressed this with the alchemical "deo concedente" or "God willing". Cure is aligned to quantifyable, comparative change, while healing is aligned to change in quality and patterned by meaning. This kind of clinical change is connected to Jung's concept of the Self. The Self is a transpersonal concept that supersedes the ego. The Self is not as directly visible clinically as the ego, so that its presence has to be inferred. As a concept, it is timeless and acausal. All this makes the Self a four-dimensional quantum concept, or from a Newtonian point of view, a mystical concept.

In her paper "Opening the heart—analytical psychology and mysticism", Julienne Mclean (2001) makes the point that mystical experience is quite common, in that it happens to people and patients as part of their ordinary lives. A three-dimensional clinical paradigm will gravitate towards the ego while a four-dimensional paradigm allows the mystical dimension to become real and useful clinically. In theory, the Self is able to motivate substantial clinical change instantly, because it is "quantum-powered" in the way I have described. Neurophysiological research has discovered changes in the brain's synapses occurring during sessions which may connect to this capacity for change (Tresan, 1996). For Jung, the Self relates to the ego like the mover to the moved and Edinger (1973) uses the term ego-Self axis to express this vital dynamic. In quantum physics, two particles, once connected, will always communicate in a complimentary fashion wherever they are. When this principle is applied to the ego and the Self, the ego-Self axis gains a four-dimensional quantum-powered potentiality. What can this mean clinically? *When the clinical hour seems suffused with the patient's most powerfully compulsive defenses, this is precisely where the Self is engaged in an equally powerful way, but its presence—like the quantum particle's movement—has to be inferred.* The Self's capacity—it's four-dimensional potential—is simultaneously *activated* by the patient's pathology and—seemingly—*limited* by it. Here the "four-dimensional" clinician will hold in mind the patient's Self as containing *unlimited* capacity for change and healing. This does not mean letting go of the third dimension's clinical scope and its capacity to view clearly the patients pathology, past and present. Rather, it might mean holding two diametrically opposite views or experiences of the patient at one and the same time: *The patient in his or her pathology and the patient in his or her perfection.* I use the word perfection here in the mystical sense as the four-dimensional equivalent of wholeness. By bringing together pathology and perfection clinically, the solidifying effect of engaging with the patient's defences from a three-dimensional point of view is much softened. To enable such binary vision, the analyst's fourth dimension must be constellated, in that their Self needs to be engaged, for this radical view is only possible, symbolically speaking, through the Self's eyes. When fourth-dimensional phenomena are perceived in the third, they are commonly called miracles. It is possible, that the clinical equivalent of miracles sometimes remains hidden because we do not look for them and thus might not notice them. Through binary vision the miraculous aspect of change, shift and healing becomes more visible and available for mediating by the analyst either silently holding this awareness or using it more actively. The patient's capacity to tolerate and incorporate their authentic goodness, creativity and vitality might then become pivotal to the work.

Binary vision also links with the analyst's capacity for agape which Hester Solomon (2001) views as essential for the analyst's continued ethical attitude. To my mind, agape transcends the talion law just as quantum reality transcends cause and effect. Yet it might evoke in the patient their capacity beyond pathology, their capacity to tolerate their goodness, as well as their badness, while not negating either. I believe this to be the essence of Jung's transcendent function, "the function which mediates opposites" (Samuels *et al.*, 1986, p. 150). When the analyst uses binary vision as part of the analytic attitude, mystical, agapic vision joins with ordinary perception. I suspect that this subtle process plays a vital part when analytic work is going well.

Jung's four-dimensional paradigm thus entails a complex view of both patient and analyst in the clinical hour. Three-dimensional clinical concepts are extremely helpful and necessary to underpin the fourth dimension, yet their outline shifts in a quantum context. A major clinical implication of Jung's four-dimensionality is the patient's capacity for change and healing which is more fully conceivable—or perhaps even inevitable—in this way. Mystical and spiritual experience also have their place in a four-dimensional clinical universe and may enhance the work. Here, I have made reference only to some of Jung's central concepts to tease out their paradigmatic clinical implications. Most of his other concepts, in my view, function similarly and together they form a clinical universe that is four-dimensional yet complementary to and compatible with all the achievements possible within three.

Conclusion

In this paper, I have argued for clinical paradigmatic self-reflection as an emancipatory activity that transcends a dyadic view of the clinical situation. The latter view reduces the clinical situation to patient and analyst, excluding various possibilities of a third element, of which the clinical paradigm represents only one. I have traced Jung's teleological approach, his central concept of the Self and the transformative power of the transcendent function in terms of their clinical paradigmatic structure. I have found that they are four-dimensional, in that their structure resonates with the fourth dimension postulated by quantum physics, which gives rise to a more fluid view of materiality, causality and change. I have used Jung's central concept of the Self to illustrate how four-dimensionality enables full-on duality to be borne and held in the analyst's heart as well as his or her thinking. *This balances the patient's perceived darkness with their light in a profound way.* Clinical four-dimensionality also opens up the possibilities of change and healing by superceding the fixity of causality. The clinical paradigm implicit in Jung's thinking is, in my view, essentially the paradigm needed in the millennium as it contains a view of the world that is increasingly going to become reality for us collectively through the advances of physics and other sciences. Mysticism, spirituality and healing then become part of ordinary reality and perhaps a more consciously acknowledged part of the clinical hour. In the fourth dimension, we posses the logic to let two opposing views co-exist and we do not need to exclude the clinical beliefs and views of the third.

We can then make use of Freudian and Kleinian clinical perspectives and—at the same time—more fully make real our clinical inheritance as Jungians.

References

Covington, C. (2001). The future of analysis. *Journal of Analytical Psychology, 15*: 325–334.

Edinger, E. F. (1973). *Ego and Archetype.* Harmondsworth: Penguin Books.

Kuhn, T. S. (1962). *The Structure of Scientific Revolutions.* Chicago: The University of Chicago Press.

Mclean, J. (2001). Opening the heart—analytical psychology and mysticism. Unpublished manuscript.

Meier, C. A. (Ed.) (2001). *Atom and Archetype. The Pauli/Jung Letters 1932–1958.* London: Routledge.

Samuels, S. (1993). *The Political Psyche.* London: Routledge.

Samuels, S., Shorter, B., & Plaut, F. (1986). *A Critical Dictionary of Jungian Analysis.* London: Routledge.

Solomon, H. (2001). Origins of the ethical attitude. *Journal of Analytical Psychology, 46*: 443–454.

Stannard, R. (1999). *The God Experiment.* London: Faber & Faber.

Tresan, D. (1996). Jungian metapsychology and neurobiological theory. *Journal of Analytical Psychology, 41*: 339–436.

CITED WORKS OF JUNG

Jung, C. G. (1957–1979). *Collected Works (C.W.)*. London: Routledge, and New Jersey: Princeton University Press.

Volume 1, "Psychiatric studies", 1957; 2nd edn. 1970.

Volume 2, "Experimental researches", 1973.

Volume 3, "The psychogenesis of mental disease", 1960.

Volume 4, "Freud and psychoanalysis", 1961.

Volume 5, "Symbols of transformation", 1956; 2nd edn. 1966.

Volume 6, "Psychological types", 1971.

Volume 7, "Two essays on analytical psychology", 1953; 2nd edn. 1966.

Volume 8, "The structure and dynamics of the psyche", 1960; 2nd edn. 1966.

Volume 9i, "The archetypes and the collective unconscious", 1959; 2nd edn. 1968.

Volume 9ii, "Aion", 1959; 2nd edn. 1968.

Volume 10, "Civilization in transition", 1964.

Volume 11, "Psychology and religion: East and West", 1958; 2nd edn. 1969.

Volume 12, "Psychology and alchemy", 1953; 2nd edn. 1968.

Volume 13, "Alchemical studies", 1967.

Volume 14, "Mysterium coniunctionis", 1963; 2nd edn. 1970.

Volume 15, "The spirit in man, art and literature", 1966.

Volume 16, "The practice of psychotherapy", 1954; 2nd edn. 1966.
Volume 17, "The development of personality", 1954.
Volume 18, "The symbolic life", 1976.
Volume 19, "General bibliography", 1979; 2nd edn. 1992.
Volume 20, "General index", 1979.

INDEX